Planning Strategies That Work

The
Executive
Bookshelf

Sloan
Management
Review

Arnoldo C. Hax (Editor), *Planning Strategies That Work*

Stuart E. Madnick (Editor), *The Strategic Use of Information Technology* (in press)

Edward B. Roberts (Editor), *Generating Technological Innovation* (in press)

Edgar H. Schein (Editor), *The Art of Managing Human Resources*

Planning Strategies That Work

Edited by

Arnoldo C. Hax

New York   Oxford
OXFORD UNIVERSITY PRESS
1987

Oxford University Press

Oxford New York Toronto
Delhi Bombay Calcutta Madras Karachi
Petaling Jaya Singapore Hong Kong Tokyo
Nairobi Dar es Salaam Cape Town
Melbourne Auckland

and associated companies in
Beirut Berlin Ibadan Nicosia

Library of Congress Cataloging-in-Publication Data
Planning strategies that work.
Bibliography: p.   Includes index.
1. Strategic planning. I. Hax, Arnoldo C.
HD30.28.P555   1987   658.4'012   86-31117
ISBN 0-19-504883-0

9 8 7 6 5 4 3 2 1

Printed in the United States of America
on acid-free paper

Foreword

The Executive Bookshelf reflects the mission of the *Sloan Management Review,* which is to bridge the gap between the practicing manager and the management scholar. Based on real-world business concerns, *SMR* articles provide the practicing manager with state-of-the-art information on management theory and practice. These articles are of particular benefit to the executive who wants to stay abreast of some of the best research and analysis coming from top business schools.

This series draws together *SMR* articles that make significant contributions to the management fields they cover. Each book is edited by one of the Sloan School of Management's most respected professors in the field, and begins with the editor's introduction, which guides and broadens the reader's understanding of the subject at hand.

The great value of these collections lies in how the articles complement one another. The authors do not always agree, but each has something important to say. Consequently, when read in its entirety, each book will challenge the reader to think more carefully about specific management issues. The editors' selection of, and introduction to, the articles will help readers interpret the various perspectives that are presented.

The usefulness of this series is enhanced by the *Sloan Management Review*'s rigorous editorial standards. Articles must not only have a practical focus, but they must also be accessible to the reader. Before an article is accepted for publication, it must be reviewed and accepted by an independent referee. The combination of applicability, academic seriousness, and solid writing assures that the series is readable and authoritative. The language is nontechnical, with minimum discussion of research and methodology, and the authors are influential leaders in the field of management.

The qualities that make these books useful to managers also make them invaluable as assigned readings in academic executive development programs and in private sector management training. In addition, they are helpful to students needing practical information to complement the theoretical materials in standard textbooks.

On a broader scale, this series is an extension of the Alfred P. Sloan School of Management. As one of the leading business schools in the country, the Sloan School complements its educational programs with research intended to produce new and better solutions to management problems. The *Sloan Management Review* in general, and this series in particular, reflects this combined research and training orientation.

The *Review* has a tradition of facilitating communication between executives and academics, and this series is an exciting addition to that tradition. We hope that you share our enthusiasm and that these books help you to become increasingly challenged, informed, and successful.

Cambridge, Mass.   Abraham J. Siegel
March 1987   Dean, Alfred P. Sloan School
                                              of Management
                                         Massachusetts Institute of Technology

Preface

Planning Strategies That Work brings together for the first time some of the best and most influential articles that have appeared in the *Sloan Management Review*. The book is intended to provide practicing managers with a systematic range of ideas and applications in the ever-important area of planning for the future in organizations. Designed for easy reading and reference, the book should be equally valuable to line managers and staff planners alike.

There is no aspect of a firm's activities that is not concerned with strategic planning. The diversity of the topics covered in this book and the approaches discussed in its various articles reflect the breadth of strategic management as a practical and theoretical field. To organize the book, I have provided an integrative perspective of strategic management, covering the most important issues and managerial disciplines relevant to the field. Fortunately for me, the *Sloan Management Review* has published many excellent articles in the field over the years. In making the difficult choices among these riches I confess to a bias toward articles that would be of the greatest immediate use to practicing managers.

Cambridge, Mass.   A.C.H.
October 1986

Contents

Contributors

Charles A. Berry is Marketing Director of Barr and Stroud, Ltd., a wholly owned subsidiary of Pilkington Brothers, plc. His professional interests focus on corporate development and diversification, including acquisition, corporate ventures, corporate venture capital, and corporate strategic planning.

Mary Anne Devanna is Research Coordinator for the Management Institute at Columbia University, Graduate School of Business. She serves as Editor-in-Chief of the *Columbia Journal of World Business.*

Yves L. Doz is affiliated with INSEAD, the European Institute of Business Administration, in Fontainebleau, France. He is the author of *Government Control and Multinational Strategic Management* and *Multinational Strategic Management: Economic and Political Imperatives.*

Charles J. Fombrun is Associate Professor of Management at New York University, the Graduate School of Business Administration.

David A. Garvin is Associate Professor of Business Administration at the Graduate School of Business Administration, Harvard University. His primary research interests are in the areas of production and operations management and of industrial economics.

Arnoldo C. Hax is Alfred P. Sloan Professor of Management and Head of the Corporate Strategy and Policy Group at the Sloan School of Management, MIT. He has published extensively in the fields of strategic planning, management control, operations management, and operations research. His wide consulting experience has included assisting several companies in the development of formal strategic planning processes. His most recent book is *Strategic Management: An Integrative Perspective,* coauthored with Nicolas Majluf.

Robert H. Hayes is Professor of Business Administration at the Graduate School of Business Administration, Harvard University. He has consulted widely on issues of manufacturing strategy.

Modesto A. Maidique is Professor of Management at the University of Miami, Florida, and Director of the Innovation and Entrepreneurship Institute. Dr. Maidique has published widely on the subjects of innovation and technology.

Gregory L. Parsons is Assistant Professor of Business Administration at the School of Business, Economics and Management, the University of Southern Maine. He consults on information systems technology and its impact on competition and business strategy.

C. K. Prahalad is Associate Professor of Policy and Control at the University of Michigan, Graduate School of Business Administration. His teaching, research, and consulting interests lie in the area of strategic management and control in large, complex organizations. He is the coauthor of *Financial Management of Health Institutions* and *The Management of Health Care*.

James Brian Quinn is the William and Josephine Buchanan Professor of Management at the Amos Tuck School of Business Administration, Dartmouth College. He is a well-known lecturer and consultant to major U.S. and foreign corporations, the U.S. Congress, the State Department, and foreign nations. Dr. Quinn has written widely on corporate and national policy questions, particularly in the technological realm.

Edward B. Roberts is the David Sarnoff Professor of Management of Technology and Director of the Management of Technology Program at the Sloan School of Management, MIT. He is also President of Pugh-Roberts Associates, Inc., and a General Partner at Zero Stage Capital Co. He is a consultant to numerous industrial corporations in the fields of strategic planning, organization design, and the management of technical innovation.

Edgar H. Schein is the Sloan Fellows Professor of Management at the Sloan School of Management, MIT. He has extensive consulting experience in human resource planning and development, corporate culture, organization development, top management team building, and related fields. His most recent book is *Organizational Culture and Leadership*.

Noel M. Tichy is Professor of Organizational Behavior and Industrial Relations at the University of Michigan, Graduate School of Business Administration. He is Editor of the journal *Human Resource Management*.

David O. Ulrich is Assistant Professor of Organizational and Industrial Relations at the University of Michigan. His research interests include strategy implementation, organizational theory, U.S. and Japanese electronic industries, and managing upward.

Planning Strategies That Work

Introduction:
Ten Central Issues
in Strategic Management

Arnoldo C. Hax

The essence of strategy is for a firm to achieve a long-term sustainable advantage over its competitors in every business in which it participates. A firm's strategic management has, as its ultimate objective, the development of its corporate values, managerial capabilities, organizational responsibilities, and administrative systems in a way that links strategic and operational decision making, at all hierarchical levels, and across all business and functional lines of authority. An institution that reaches this stage of evolution will have eliminated the conflicts between long-term development and short-term profitability. Its strategic and operational concerns will not be driving it in opposite directions, but will be intent on defining the central managerial tasks of the organization. In short, the strategic thinking of such a firm will have been deeply anchored in its managerial style, beliefs, values, ethics, and accepted patterns of behavior—i.e., in the organizational culture.[1]

As a field of study, therefore, strategic management deals with an extraordinarily rich array of disciplines and interests. There is hardly any facet of management, either analytical or behavioral, that is not relevant to achieving a better understanding of strategic issues. Thus, strategic management represents both an *integrative area of knowledge*—because of the need to reconcile divergent points of view and coordinate a wide variety of disciplines from a strategic perspective—and a *pragmatic endeavor*—because it is necessary to go beyond conceptual paradigms to provide guidelines to practicing managers on how to run their businesses more effectively.

It is hard to do justice to such a broad subject, especially since the *Sloan Management Review* has been blessed throughout the years with first-rate collaborators in this field. Perhaps my most difficult task was to select only a dozen out of the many valuable and insightful articles available.

My criteria for inclusion were, first, the extent to which a particular article would contribute to the education of a practicing manager and, second, how at the same time it would help in describing the breadth of the field. The first criterion simply implies that the book has a bias toward action-oriented lessons, instead of an academic tone. To fulfill the second criterion, I reflected on all the topics I felt were central to strategic management and identified ten for coverage in this volume:

Managing Strategic Change—The Role of Formal-Analytical Processes Versus Power-Behavioral Approaches

Two schools of management have provided opposite points of view regarding the decision-making process.[2] One, founded on management science, economics, and statistical decision theory, conceives of the manager as a "rational person"—Homo economicus—who explicitly identifies objectives (based on quantitative utilities or preferences), formulates a comprehensive set of alternatives or action programs, and selects from among them an "optimum" program that leads toward the best possible outcome. Those favoring this school of management, although recognizing its inherent limitations, tend to advocate the use of formal planning systems, management control, and consistent reward mechanisms to increase the strategic quality of decision making.[3]

A second school of management, which rests on the behavioral theory of the firm, supports a power-behavioral approach to strategy formulation and implementation. This school focuses on such issues as the multiple-goal structures of organizations, the politics of strategic decisions, executive bargaining and negotiation processes, satisficing (as opposed to maximizing) in decision making, the role of coalitions in strategic management, and the practice of "muddling through."[4]

Recognizing the contributions and limitations of both approaches, James Brian Quinn undertook extensive field research on the actual strategic-change process as it took place in ten major corporations. His work was documented in three publications in the *Sloan Management Review,* the third of which, "Managing Strategic Change," has been chosen as the first article in this volume.[5]

Quinn concluded that neither the "power-behavioral" nor the "formal systems planning" paradigms adequately characterizes the way successful strategic processes operate. Rather, Quinn asserts, "Effective executives artfully blend formal analysis, behavioral techniques, and power politics to bring cohesive, set-by-step movement toward ends that initially are broadly conceived, but that are then constantly refined and reshaped as new information appears." Quinn calls this integrative methodology "logical incrementalism."

From his research, Quinn uncovers the following dominant patterns for successful management of strategic change in large organizations:

- *Creating awareness and commitment incrementally.* This includes developing informal networks to get information throughout the organization in order to sense possible needs for change, and to seek wide organizational support before initiating actions. Committees, task forces, and retreats tend to be favored mechanisms for accomplishing broad political support.
- *Solidifying progress incrementally.* Most managers are careful not to state new goals in concrete terms until they have built a consensus among key players. They search for "pockets of commitment," formed by small groups of executives working on the most successful programs. As events move forward, managers achieve a better understanding of the specific directions toward which the organization should and can move.
- *Integration of processes and interests.* The analytical-political consensus process central to strategy formulation and implementation, although highly incremental, is not piecemeal. It requires continual attempts by top managers to integrate their actions into an understandable, cohesive whole.

These are simple but powerful ideas. Logical incrementalism represents, in my opinion, a significant contribution to strategic management.

What Constitutes Good Strategic Management? Lessons from Well-Managed Companies

As is evident from our discussion of Quinn's work, empirical research—observing what practicing managers are doing, interpreting their actions, and attempting to draw general useful conclusions—is a fruitful approach to strategic management.[6]

The second article I've selected for this volume follows in this tradition. "The Art of High-Technology Management," by Modesto Maidique and Robert Hayes,[7] summarizes the research the authors conducted over two decades with a wide cross-section of high-technology firms in the biotechnology, semiconductor, computer, pharmaceutical, and aerospace industries. The basic question guiding their research was: What are the strategies, policies, practices, and decisions that result in successful management? They found, first, that no company has a monopoly on excellence; and, second, that the driving force behind the success of many companies is strong leadership. Accepting strong leadership as a given, Maidique and Hayes proceeded to try to understand what strategies and management practices can reinforce strong leadership. They observed six basic themes that contribute to success. Although no one firm in their study exhibited excellence in every one of these six categories, outstanding firms tend to score high in most of them. The six themes are:

1. *Business focus.* Successful companies tend to have closely related products, focused R&D, and consistent priorities.
2. *Adaptability.* A well-defined business focus is balanced with the ability and will to undertake major and rapid changes if necessary. This requires a great deal of organizational flexibility.
3. *Organizational cohesion.* A critical success factor is the integrative capability of the firm. This is enhanced by good communications, job rotation, the practice of integrating roles (such as multidisciplinary project teams, special venture groups, and matrixlike organizational structures), long-term employment, and intensive training.
4. *Entrepreneurial culture.* Successful firms nurture entrepreneurial characteristics that promote the development of internal agents of change. They tend to have small divisions, employ a variety of funding channels, have very high tolerances for failure, and provide ample opportunities to pursue speculative projects.
5. *Sense of integrity.* Successful firms tend to exhibit a commitment to long-term relationships, for their objective is to maintain stable associations with all of their stakeholders (e.g., employees, stockholders, customers, suppliers, local communities, etc.).
6. *"Hands-on" top management.* Senior executives are deeply involved in the management process.

When Maidique and Hayes arranged their findings according to these six themes, an apparent paradox emerged: characteristics (1), (3), and (5) imply stability and conservatism; while (2), (4), and (6) assume rapid, sometimes precipitous change. The successful high-technology firm must, then, they concluded, be managed ambivalently, for it must succeed in managing two conflicting trends: continuity and rapid change. There are two ways of resolving this dilemma: One is to manage different parts of the organization differently; the other is to manage differently at different times in the evolution of the life cycle of the firm. In the second case, the firm alternates periods of consolidation and continuity with periods of sharp reorientations that can lead to dramatic changes in its strategies.

I find this message tremendously valuable and insightful. Although it was developed by working with high-technology firms, it seems to me its applicability is much wider, particularly given the turbulent environment that most organizations are forced to face.

Leadership—Is There a Need for Change?

The driving force of any successful organization is leadership. But what are the attributes of that elusive quality? How are we supposed to identify and develop leadership qualifications? What are the different leadership characteristics that are required to manage businesses in different stages of their life cycles, or firms in different stages of evolution, or industries confronted with different competitive challenges?[8]

The third article in this volume, "The Leadership Challenge—A Call for the Transformational Leader," by Noel Tichy and David Ulrich,[9] argues that large American organizations must change their corporate lifestyles if they want to remain competitive. To revitalize these institutions a new brand of leadership is needed, which is provided by the *transformational leader* as exemplified by Lee Iacocca. The transformational leader must be able to help the organization develop a vision of what it can be, mobilize it to accept and work toward achieving the new vision, and institutionalize the changes that must last over time.

Two elements are central to the organizational dynamics of change. First, organizations do not change unless a trigger event indicates a change is needed. Second, strong forces of a technical, political, and cultural nature will resist change. Therefore, a felt need for change usually unleashes a set of mixed feelings. Transformational leadership is required to address properly the need to change. Defensive, transactional managers in search of quick fixes are destined to lead the organization to irrevocable decline.

Finally, organizational dynamics of change should be supported by a process of individual change: first comes the *ending* (a time to recognize when a job has been terminated), then a *neutral zone* (a time of transition from the old job to new patterns of behavior), and finally a *new beginning* (when individuals are able to work with new enthusiasm and commitment in the new assignments). The concept of transformational leadership is of great importance in addressing the strategic-management challenges of this generation.

The Significance of Corporate Culture

Ever since we started losing ground to the Japanese in our competitive capabilities, the issue of culture has been evoked to explain competitive advantage. Are we at a competitive disadvantage because the Far East nations adhere to ethical work values superior to ours? How do we define culture? Once defined, can we manage it? Can we change it? What is the link between strategy and culture? These probing questions have occupied many researchers in the past years.[10] Certainly among the best of them is Edgar Schein, a colleague at MIT, a frequent contributor to the *Sloan Management Review,* and author of the article I have selected to address the issue of culture and strategy, "Does Japanese Management Style Have a Message for American Managers?"[11]

A commentary on Ouchi's *Theory Z* and Pascale and Athos' *The Art of Japanese Management,* the article provides insightful views on the way in which human relations and participation have changed during the last two decades in America.[12] Schein uses a framework to study corporate culture that is based on three interconnecting levels: artifacts and creations, values and ideologies, and basic assumptions and premises.

According to this framework, the culture of a group is made visible in the *artifacts and creations* it produces—i.e., its language, technology, art, stratification and status systems, and its rules regarding sex and family. A high level of awareness exists on these issues, which correspond to things that can be seen, used, or clearly perceived. These artifacts and creations reflect in turn a more primary and underlying set of *values and ideologies,* which are defined in terms of ideals and goals and the means to achieve them. The deepest representation of the culture of a group is constructed on a few *basic assumptions and premises* regarding the relationships between the group and the environment, relationships among members of the group, the group's orientation to time, and the group's orientation to the use of space. A cultural analysis of a firm, therefore, should have as its ultimate objective the unveiling of the basic assumptions of that firm's cultural values, and study should be structured around the question of how the organization relates to its environment, how it manages time, how it deals with space, and what can be observed about the relationships of people within it to each other.

In a recent article in the *Sloan Management Review,* Schein defines organizational culture as the "pattern of basic assumptions that a given group has invented, discovered, or developed in learning to cope with its problems of external adaptation and internal integration, and that have worked well enough to be considered valid, and, therefore, to be taught to new members as the correct way to perceive, think, and feel in relation to these problems."[13]

Several elements of this definition are worth discussing. First, culture is expressed as a way of responding to external environmental pressures through the process of adaptation, by designing rules, perspectives and ways of thinking, which are internalized as norms of behavior for the group. Not surprisingly, these are the same central dimensions of strategic planning: *adaptation* toward the external environment, and *integration* in terms of internal commitments. Next, if properly executed, these norms of conduct represent explicit or implicit ways of affecting communication within the group, which develops a sort of character or personality for an institution. Finally, there is the element of permanence of accepted solutions, which are passed from one generation to the next. This means that there is some degree of molding of values and ethics which are recognized and become acceptable patterns of conduct in a given organization.

Strategic Management at the Corporate Level—The Issue of Diversification

Top executives are responsible for creating and institutionalizing the vision of the firm, offering the necessary leadership to guide the organization toward the pursuit of that vision, and contributing to shape the corporate culture of the firm.[14] There are also critical additional tasks of top executives that are central to strategic management:

- Defining the domains in which the firm will compete, and how to compete effectively in each domain. This leads to issues of business segmentation, definition of strategic business units, and strategies for diversifying into new businesses and exiting from old ones.
- Developing horizontal strategies to exploit synergistic opportunities among businesses. A horizontal strategy is a coordinated set of goals and policies across distinct but interrelated business units.[15] It allows group, sector, and corporate levels of a diversified firm to add value to what otherwise are independent business strategies.
- Managing the resulting business portfolio of the firm, assigning resources with a sense of strategies priorities.

An extensive coverage of each subject is obviously outside the scope of this volume. Thus, I have selected the issue of diversification into new businesses for inclusion, both because of its central importance to corporate strategy and because of the quality of the article, "Entering New Businesses: Selecting Strategies for Success," by Edward Roberts and Charles Berry.[16]

Roberts and Berry provide a powerful framework, particularly relevant to high-technology firms, to address two basic strategic questions related to diversification: (1) Which product markets should a corporation enter? and (2) How should the company enter these product markets to avoid failure and maximize gain?

To help in answering the first question, the potential new businesses are classified as belonging to the *base,* or as being *new familiar,* or *new unfamiliar,* both with regard to market factors and technological factors. A three-by-three matrix, the *familiarity matrix* shown in Figure I.1, is thus developed portraying the businesses in their corresponding market and technological dimensions.

In order to address the second question, the authors overlap on each cell in this matrix the optimum entry strategies they would recommend. These strategies are selected from among the following business development mechanisms: ① internal development, ② acquisition, ③ licensing, ④ internal ventures, ⑤ joint ventures or alliances, ⑥venture capital and nurturing, and ⑦educational acquisitions. The article is rich with useful conceptual guidelines to assist in developing effective strategies for diversification and

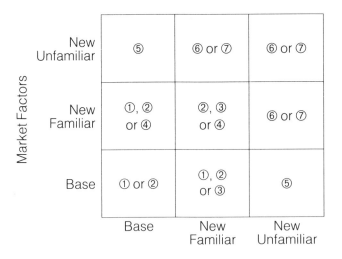

Figure I.1   The Familiarity Matrix

the familiarity matrix itself represents an exciting tool in the literature of portfolio management.[17]

Human Resource Strategy—A New Awareness

The central priority of most top managers is the proper identification, development, promotion, and reward of their people. In the words of General Electric chairman Jack Welch, if you define the right tasks, put the appropriate persons in charge of them, and back them up with the right kind of reward system, you don't need to be a good manager to obtain excellent results.

The undeniable importance of human resources for every organization has been intensified in U.S. firms by the development of a number of forces requiring a broad strategic-management oriented treatment of human resources. Beer, Spector, Lawrence, Mills, and Walton summarize these recent pressures as follows:[18]

- Increasing international competition, particularly from the Far East.
- Increasing complexity and size of organizations.
- Slower growth or declining markets in a great many industries.
- Greater government involvement in human resources practices.
- Increasing education of the work force.
- Changing values of the work force.
- Growing concern with career and life satisfaction.
- Changes in work force demographics.

These concerns have drawn attention to the problem of managing human resources in a strategic manner—that is, in a way that allows firms to establish and sustain a long-term advantage over their competitors.[19] However, in spite of growing interest, the strategic management of human resources is far from a reality in most American enterprises. The formulation of corporate and business strategies is becoming commonplace, but the issue of human resources is not being addressed with an appropriate sense of priority. Rather, the personnel requirements of those strategies are identified after the fact and passed along to personnel managers for them to supply the necessary workers at the various skill levels demanded by the strategic plans.

This practice not only diminishes the strategic role of human resources, but also fails to recognize that the effective use of human resources involves *every* line manager in the organization. It is not a staff activity to be relegated exclusively to the personnel function.

I selected two articles to address this important subject. In the first, "Strategic Human Resource Management," by Noel Tichy, Charles Fombrun, and Mary Anne Devanna, the authors provide a practical framework to link strategy, structure, and human resource management.[20] Furthermore, they identify four generic processes or functions inherent to human resource management in all organizations: (1) selection, promotion, and placement process; (2) reward process; (3) management development process; and (4) appraisal process. The authors distinguish three levels of managerial work—strategic, managerial, and operational—and illustrate how the four human resource management processes are handled at each managerial level. Finally, a step-by-step set of directions is provided to make the human resource function more strategic, and to assure better linkage between it and the line organization.

The second article is a genuine classic in the field: Edgar Schein's "Increasing Organizational Effectiveness Through Better Human Resource Planning and Development."[21] Schein provides a clear account of why human resource planning has become increasingly important as a determinant of organizational effectiveness, and gives a lucid description of the major components of human resource planning and career development systems.

What I find most significant about Schein's contribution is the way in which he matches the human resource organizational needs with those of the individual in the evolution of the individual's career in a given firm. This matching process provides the basis for his human resource planning model and forms the basis for his work on career dynamics.[22]

Manufacturing Strategy—Regaining Industrial Power in America

After many years of serious neglect, manufacturing is receiving central attention from most American managers. If we want to regain or maintain our industrial power, it is imperative that we view manufacturing as an essential competitive weapon. It is not surprising, therefore, to find most firms seriously engaged in a wide variety of activities aimed at enhancing their manufacturing capabilities. Attempts are being made to offer better products at lower costs with increased emphasis on quality and shorter deliveries. Plans are being refocused, with a better sense of the competitive objectives they are supposed to serve. Productivity programs and "quality circles" abound. New technologies such as computer-aided design, computer-aided manufacturing, flexible manufacturing systems, and robots are helping to structure the "factory of the future." Similar developments are changing our management systems in the same way that just-in-time, zero-inventories, and zero-reject programs are revolutionizing our more conventional ways of administering the manufacturing process.

Not surprisingly, a surge of articles and books has been published in the recent past reexamining the manufacturing function and analyzing its strategic significance.[23] Out of all the issues relevant to the pursuit of an effective manufacturing strategy, none is more central than quality management, the topic addressed by David Garvin's article, "What Does 'Product Quality' Really Mean?"[24]

Garvin starts by reviewing five different approaches to defining quality—transcendental, product-based, user-based, manufacturing-based, and value-based—and suggests that the existence of these multiple definitions helps to explain the often conflicting views of quality held by members of the marketing and manufacturing departments. To resolve this problem, Garvin proposes eight dimensions of quality that can be identified as a framework for thinking about its basic elements: performance, features, reliability, conformance, durability, serviceability, aesthetics, and perceived quality. Recognizing these eight dimensions is important for strategic purposes, since a firm that chooses to compete on the basis of quality can do so in several ways, but it need not pursue all eight dimensions at once. Instead, a segmentation strategy can be followed, with a few dimensions singled out for special attention, as many examples cited by Garvin in the article illustrate.

Finally, in order to study the marketing and financial implications of product quality, Garvin explores the relationships between quality and price, advertising, market share, cost, and profitability. Valuable managerial insights are uncovered in this discussion.

The Strategic Importance of Management of Technology and Innovation

Technology, and particularly technological change, is of great significance to strategy for a number of reasons. First, in many industries the proper management of technology is the key factor in achieving sustainable competitive advantage. Second, technological innovations can contribute to changing the industry structure or can create new industries. Most of the leading corporations in America succeeded by exploiting unique technological advantages that allowed them to reshape an old industry or create a new one. Finally, technology is a most pervasive activity. Innovation and technological change are not only strategically relevant in dealing with the technologies associated with the products, but they affect all managerial activities and functions. From this perspective, there is no such thing as a "low-technology" industry, and it becomes imperative to position the competitive role of technology in every step of the value chain.[25]

In Modesto Maidique's "Entrepreneurs, Champions, and Technological Innovation,"[26] the author presents an excellent survey of the literature dealing with entrepreneurship and corporate development, then proceeds to describe the three stages of development of a firm: small (entrepreneurial), integrated, and diversified. He elaborates on the following hypothesis: although successful innovation requires a special combination of entrepreneurial, managerial, and technological roles within the firm, those roles need to change as the firm evolves from a small to a large, diversified entity. An interesting framework is proposed that shows how the key roles of entrepreneur, technologist, product champion, and executive champion tend to relate as the firm evolves.[27]

Information Technology Is Changing the Ways To Compete

The previous issue addressed the significance of technology and innovation in the development of corporate and business strategies. Perhaps none of the existing technologies can match the potential impact that information technology has in reshaping industry structure and in transforming the nature of businesses and firms. We are living in the information revolution, where computer and communications technologies are affecting every facet of our society. That is why I believe the relationships between information technology and strategy should be investigated even further as a topic unto itself.

Information technology can offer endless opportunities for a firm to achieve competitive advantage. A company can use information technology to build barriers to entry, to build in switching costs, to completely change the basis of competition, to change the balance of power in supplier relationships, or to generate new products.[28]

Rockart and Scott Morton have asserted that we are now in the midst of the "third wave" of computer applications: providing information to middle and top managers.[29] As a result of powerful trends in hardware, software, and communications technology, as well as data availability, managers today have increasingly cost-effective hardware, user-friendly software systems, enhanced communication capabilities, and access to data that allows them to be better informed than ever before. A host of applications has been made possible by these technological changes, including robotics in the factory, decision-support systems for middle managers, data bases and executive data bases, electronic-mail systems, and many-to-many communications nets within corporations.[30]

To facilitate the full understanding of how to use information technology from a strategic perspective, managers need a comprehensive analytical framework. One such framework is Porter's famous industry and competitive analysis.[31] I have chosen G.L. Parsons's article, "Information Technology: A New Competitive Weapon," for inclusion in this volume, because it gives an exceedingly lucid illustration of Porter's analysis for assessing the competitive impact of information technology on a firm and provides a guide for integrating information systems with a firm's strategy.[32]

Parsons presents a three-level framework to help senior managers in assessing the current and potential impact of information technology at the *industry level* (products and services, markets, production economics), at the *firm level* (buyers, suppliers, substitution, new entrants, competitors' rivalry), and at the *strategy level* (cost leadership, differentiation, or focus).

Global Strategic Management—An Emerging Thrust for American Firms

In a recent meeting at MIT with the Sloan School Visiting Committee (composed of distinguished top executives of American firms), John Opel, chairman of IBM, indicated that his most important strategic concern was to make IBM into a truly global company. He quickly added that this objective could become a reality only if all the key IBM executives were to reach a deep understanding of world issues. Opel proceeded to say that IBM would not promote individuals above a certain critical level unless they had a substantial international component in their professional career backgrounds. To no one's surprise, Opel's comments were echoed by every other executive in the room.

Global management is today a critically relevant strategic challenge for most American firms. There is hardly an industry untouched by the trend toward globalization. Revolutions in technology and communications have led to a dramatic increase in international trade and the emergence of global competitors, buyers, and suppliers. Technology allows global companies to reap enormous benefits from economies of scale of standardized products in every major activity in the value chain (procurement, technology, production, logistics, marketing, service, and management). This creates what Ted Levitt refers to as the vindication of the Model T: "If a company forces costs and prices down and pushes quality and reliability up—while maintaining reasonable concern for suitability—customers will prefer its world-standardized products."[33] Worldwide communications have contributed greatly to the realization of a converging commonality in world consumer needs and desires, and have provided unprecedented opportunities to coordinate worldwide operations and to gather, process, and distribute global information.

An important aspect of global management is to recognize that the pattern of international competition varies greatly according to industry characteristics.[34] At one extreme is the *multidomestic industry,* where competition in one country is essentially independent of the competitive position in other countries. Multinational companies operating in multidomestic industries manage their various country activities as if they were a portfolio of loosely related businesses. At the opposite end of the spectrum is the *global industry,* where a firm's competitive position in one country is strongly influenced by its competitive position in other countries. A firm competing in that industry must coordinate very carefully its strategies across all the countries in which it participates.

The first article dealing with global management in this volume is "Strategic Management in Multinational Companies" by Yves Doz.[35] Doz sees multinational companies (MNCs) as responding to two central forces: the *economic imperative* (which imposes requirements for economic survival and success) and the *political imperative* (which determines the adjustments to be made to satisfy the demands of host governments). MNCs can respond with different strategies to resolve this conflict. Companies following a *worldwide integration strategy*—or a "global strategy" in the current terminology—choose to respond to the economic imperative. Companies that forgo the potential benefits of integration and provide much independence to their subsidiaries choose the *national responsive strategy*—or multidomestic strategy, as it is commonly called. Finally, according to Doz, companies can choose to live with the conflict and look for structural and administrative adjustments, rather than strategic solutions. These companies are identified as pursuing the *administrative coordination strategy.* Doz's article provides insightful comparisons of these three ways to compete in the international setting.

Having decided on the type of strategy it will adopt, a firm, depending upon the nature of global competition in its corresponding industry, must address the substance of its strategy itself. There are two key dimensions to an international strategy.[36] One is *configuring* the value chain, which resolves where and how each of the firm's activities is going to be executed. The other is *coordinating* the firm's various activities in different countries.

The coordination issue is effectively discussed in the final article, "An Approach to Strategic Control in MNCs," by C.K. Prahalad and Yves Doz.

Strategic control is defined as the extent of influence that a head office (HO) has over a subsidiary concerning decisions that affect subsidiary strategy. As resources such as capital, technology, and management become vested in the subsidiaries, HOs cannot continue to rely on control over those resources. Creating an *organizational context*—a blending of organizational structure, information systems, measurements and rewards systems, career planning, and a fostering of a common organizational culture—can compensate for the erosion of an HO's capacity to control its subsidiaries. The task of creating an appropriate organizational context for strategic control is built upon two sets of concepts: The first is the notion that an organization is an aggregation of four orientations—cognitive, strategic, power, and administrative. The second is that there are three major organizational mechanisms to manipulate these four orientations: data management, managers' management, and conflict-resolution mechanisms.

The authors outline a conceptual framework that helps in identifying the proper strategic control posture to use. Four categories of MNCs result from this framework: fragmental, dependent, autonomous, and integrated.

1

Managing Strategic Change

James Brian Quinn

In two articles published previously in the *SMR,* the author described the process of "logical incrementalism" for strategic planning and how it is used effectively in several large corporations. This third and final article in the series analyzes this approach to management—a sort of purposeful "muddling"—in greater detail, delineating the steps that successful managers generally follow in inaugurating and executing strategic change. *SMR.*

"Just as bad money has always driven out good, so the talented general manager—the person who makes a company go—is being overwhelmed by a flood of so-called *professionals,* textbook executives more interested in the form of management than the content, more concerned about defining and categorizing and quantifying the job, than in getting it done. . . . They have created false expectations and wasted untold man-hours by making a religion of formal long-range planning."[1]

In two previous articles, I have tried to demonstrate why executives managing strategic change in large organizations should not—and do not—follow highly formalized textbook approaches in long-range planning, goal generation, and strategy formulation.[2] Instead, they artfully blend formal analysis, behavioral techniques, and power politics to bring about cohesive, step-by-step movement toward ends that initially are broadly conceived, but that are then constantly refined and reshaped as new information appears.[3] Their integrating methodology can best be described as "logical incrementalism."

But is this truly a process in itself, capable of being managed? Or does it simply amount to applied intuition? Are there some conceptual structures, principles, or paradigms that are generally useful? Wrapp, Normann, Braybrooke, Lindblom, and Bennis have provided some macrostructures incorporating many important elements they have observed in strategic-change

From *Sloan Management Review,* Summer 1980, Vol. 21, No. 4. Reprinted with permission.

situations.[4] These studies and other contributions cited in this article offer important insights into the management of change in large organizations. But my data suggest that top managers in such enterprises develop their major strategies through processes that neither these studies nor more formal approaches to planning adequately explain. Managers consciously and proactively move forward incrementally:

- To improve the quality of information utilized in corporate strategic decisions.
- To cope with the varying lead times, pacing parameters, and sequencing needs of the "subsystems" through which such decisions tend to be made.
- To deal with the personal resistance and political pressures any important strategic change encounters.
- To build the organizational awareness, understanding, and psychological commitment needed for effective implementation.
- To decrease the uncertainty surrounding such decisions by allowing for interactive learning between the enterprise and its various impinging environments.
- To improve the quality of the strategic decisions themselves by (1) systematically involving those with most specific knowledge, (2) obtaining the participation of those who must carry out the decisions, and (3) avoiding premature closure that could lead the decision in undesirable directions.

How does one manage the complex incremental processes that can achieve these goals? My earlier two articles structured certain key elements not to be repeated here.[5] The following is perhaps the most articulate short statement on how executives proactively manage incrementalism in the development of corporate strategies:

Typically you start with general concerns, vaguely felt. Next you roll an issue around in your mind till you think you have a conclusion that makes sense for the company. You then go out and sort of post the idea without being too wedded to its details. You then start hearing the arguments pro and con, and some very good refinements of the idea usually emerge. Then you pull the idea in and put some resources together to study it so it cn be put forward as more of a formal presentation. You wait for "stimuli occurrences" or "crises," and launch pieces of the idea to help in these situations. But they lead toward your ultimate aim. You know where you want to get. You'd like to get there in six months. But it may take three years, or you may not get there. And when you do get there, you don't know whether it was originally your own idea—or somebody else had reached the same conclusion before you and just got you on board for it. You never know. The president would follow the same basic process, but he could drive it much faster than an executive lower in the organization.[6]

Because of differences in organizational form, management style, or the content of individual decisions, no single paradigm can hold for all strategic decisions.[7] However, very complex strategic decisions in my sample of large organizations tended to evoke certain kinds of broad process steps. These are briefly outlined below. While these process steps occur generally in the order presented, stages are by no means orderly or discrete. Executives do consciously manage individual steps proactively, but it is doubtful that any one person guides a major strategic change sequentially through all the steps. Developing most strategies requires numerous loops back to earlier stages as unexpected issues or new data dictate. Or decision times can become compressed and require short-circuiting leaps forward as crises occur.[8] Nevertheless, certain patterns are clearly dominant in the successful management of strategic change in large organizations.

Creating Awareness and Commitment—Incrementally

Although many of the sample companies had elaborate formal environmental scanning procedures, most major strategic issues first emerged in vague or undefined terms, such as "organizational overlap," "product proliferation," "excessive exposure in one market," or "lack of focus and motivation."[9] Some appeared as "inconsistencies" in internal action patterns or "anomalies" between the enterprise's current posture and some perception of its future environment.[10] Early signals may come from anywhere and may be difficult to distinguish from the background "noise" of ordinary communications. Crises, of course, announce themselves with strident urgency in operations control systems. But if organizations wait until signals reach amplitudes high enough to be sensed by formal measurement systems, smooth, efficient transitions may be impossible.[11]

Need Sensing: Leading the Formal Information System

To help them in sensing possible needs for change, effective change managers actively develop informal networks to get objective information from other staff and line executives, workers, customers, board members, suppliers, politicians, technologists, educators, outside professionals, government groups, and so on. They purposely use these networks to short-circuit all the careful screens their organizations build up to "tell the top only what it wants to hear."[12] For example:

◇ Peter McColough, chairman and CEO of Xerox, was active in many high-level political and charitable activities—from treasurer of the Democratic National Committee to chairman of the Urban League. In addition, he tried to decentralize decision making. "If something bothers me," he said, "I don't rely on reports or what other executives may want to tell me. I'll go down very deep into the organization, to certain issues and people, so I'll have a feeling for what they think." He refused to let his life be run by letters and memos. "Because I came up by that route, I know what a salesman can say. I also know that before I see [memos] they go through fifteen hands, and I know what that can do to them."[13]

To avoid undercutting intermediate managers, bypassing them has to be limited to information gathering. Properly handled, this practice actually improves formal communications and motivational systems. Line managers are less tempted to screen information, and lower levels are flattered to be able "to talk to the very top." Since people sift signals about threats and opportunities through perceptual screens defined by their own values, careful executives make sure their sensing networks include people who look at the world differently from those in the enterprise's dominating culture. Effective executives consciously seek options and threat signals beyond the status quo. "If I'm not two to three years ahead of my organization, I'm not doing my job" was a common comment of such executives in the sample.

Amplifying Understanding and Awareness

In some cases executives quickly perceive the broad dimensions of needed change. But they still may seek amplifying data, wider executive understanding of issues, or greater organizational support before initiating action. Far from accepting the first satisfactory (satisficing) solution—as some have suggested they do—successful managers seem to consider a broad array of alternatives.[14] Why? They want to stimulate and choose from the most creative solutions offered by the best minds in their organizations. They wish to have colleagues knowledgeable enough about issues to help them think through all the ramifications. They seek data and arguments sufficiently strong to dislodge preconceived ideas and past practices that were blindly followed. They do not want to be the prime supporters of losing ideas or to have their organizations slavishly adopt the "boss's solution." Nor do they want—by announcing decisions early—to prematurely threaten existing power centers and thus inadvertently kill any changes aborning.

Even when executives do not have in mind specific solutions to emerging problems, they can still proactively guide actions in intuitively desired directions by defining what issues staffs should investigate, by selecting principal investigators, and by controlling reporting processes. They can selectively "tap the collective wit" of their organizations, generating more awareness of critical issues and forcing initial thinking down to lower levels to achieve greater involvement. Yet they can also avoid irreconcilable opposition, emotional overcommitment,[15] or organizational momenta beyond their control by regarding all proposals as "strictly advisory" at this early stage.

As issues are clarified and options are narrowed, executives may systematically alert ever wider audiences. They may first "shop" key ideas among trusted colleagues to test responses. Then they may commission a few studies to illustrate emerging alternatives, contingencies, or opportunities. But key players might still not be ready to change their past action patterns or even be able to investigate options creatively. Only when persuasive data are in hand and enough people are alerted and "on board" to make a particular solution work might key executives finally commit themselves to it. Building awareness, concern, and interest to attention-getting levels is often a vital—and slowly achieved—step in the process of managing basic changes. For example:

◇ In the early 1970s there was a glut in world oil supplies. Nevertheless, analysts in the General Motors Chief Economist's Office began to project a developing U.S. dependency on foreign oil and the likelihood of higher future oil prices. These concerns led the board in 1972 to create an ad hoc energy task force headed by David C. Collier, then treasurer, later head of GM of Canada and then of the Buick Division. Collier's group included people from manufacturing, research, design, finance, industry-government relations, and the economics staff. After six months of research, in May 1973 the task force went to the board with three conclusions: (1) there was a developing energy problem, (2) the government had no particular plan to deal with it, (3) energy costs would have a profound effect on GM's business. Collier's report created a good deal of discussion around the company in the ensuing months. "We were trying to get other people to think about the issue," said Richard C. Gerstenberg, then chairman of GM.[16]

Changing Symbols: Building Credibility

As awareness of the need for change grows, managers often want to signal the organization that certain types of change are coming, even if specific solutions are not in hand. Knowing they cannot communicate directly with the thousands who would carry out the strategy, some executives purposely undertake highly visible actions to convey wordless but complex messages that could never be communicated as well—or as credibly—in verbal terms.[17] Some use symbolic moves to preview or verify intended changes in direction. At other times, such moves confirm the intention of top management to back a thrust already partially begun: Peter McColough's relocation of Xerox headquarters to Connecticut (away from the company's Rochester reprographics base) underscored that company's developing commitment to product diversification, organizational decentralization, and international operations. Organizations often need such symbolic moves—or decisions they regard as symbolic—to build credibility behind a new strategy. Without such actions even forceful verbiage might be interpreted as mere rhetoric. For example:

◇ In GM's downsizing move, engineers said that one of top management's early decisions affected the credibility of the whole weight-reduction program. "Initially, we proposed using a lot of aluminum and substitute materials to meet the new 'mass' targets. But this would have meant a very high cost, and would have strained the suppliers' aluminum capacity. However, when we presented this program to management, they said, 'Okay, if necessary, we'll do it.' They didn't back down. We began to understand then that they were dead serious. Feeling that the company would spend the money was critical to the success of the entire mass reduction effort."[18]

Legitimizing New Viewpoints

Often before reaching specific strategic decisions, it is necessary to legitimize new options that have been acknowledged as possibilities, but that still entail an undue aura of uncertainty or concern. Because of their familiarity, older options are usually perceived as having lower risks (or potential costs) than newer alternatives. Therefore, top managers seeking change often consciously create forums and allow slack time for their organizations to talk through threatening issues, work out the implications of new solutions, or gain an improved information base that will permit new options to be evaluated objectively in comparison with more familiar alternatives.[19] In many cases, strategic concepts that are at first strongly resisted gain acceptance and support simply by the passage of time, if executives do not exacerbate hostility by pushing them too fast from the top. For example:

◇ When Joe Wilson thought Haloid Corporation should change its name to include Xerox, he first submitted a memorandum asking colleagues what they thought of the idea. They rejected it. Wilson then explained his concerns more fully, but his executives rejected the idea again. Finally Wilson formed a committee headed by Sol Linowitz, who had thought a separate Xerox subsidiary might be the best solution. As this committee deliberated, negotiations were under way with the Rank Organization, and as the term Rank-Xerox began to be commonly heard, Haloid-Xerox no longer seemed so strange. "And so," according to John Dessauer, "a six-month delay having diluted most opposition, we of the committee agreed that the change to Haloid-Xerox might in the long run produce sound advantages."[20]

Many top executives consciously plan for such "gestation periods" and often find that the strategic concept itself is made more effective by the resulting feedback.

Tactical Shifts and Partial Solutions

At this stage in the process guiding executives might share a fairly clear vision of the general directions for movement. But rarely does a total new corporate posture emerge full grown—like Minerva from the brow of Jupiter—from any one source. Instead, early resolutions are likely to be partial, tentative, or experimental.[21] Beginning moves often appear as mere tactical adjustments in the enterprise's existing posture. As such, they encounter little opposition, yet each partial solution adds momentum in new directions. Guiding executives try carefully to maintain the enterprise's ongoing strengths, while shifting its total posture incrementally at the margin, toward new needs. Such executives themselves might not yet perceive the full nature of the strategic shifts they have begun. They can still experiment with partial new approaches and learn without risking the viability of the total enterprise. Their broad early steps can still legitimately lead to a variety of different success scenarios. Yet logic might dictate that they wait before committing themselves to a total new strategy.[22] As events unfurl, solutions to several interrelated problems might well flow together in a not-yet-perceived synthesis. For example:

◇ In the early 1970s at General Motors there was a distinct awareness of a developing fuel-economy ethic. General Motors executives said, "Our conclusions were really at the conversational level—that the big car trend was at an end. But we were not at all sure sufficient numbers of large car buyers were ready to move to dramatically lighter cars."

Nevertheless, GM did start concept studies that resulted in the Cadillac Seville.

When the oil crisis hit in Fall 1973, the company responded in further increments, at first merely increasing production of its existing small-car lines. Then as the crisis deepened, it added another partial solution, the subcompact "T car"—the Chevette—and accelerated the Seville's development cycle. Next, as fuel economy appeared more salable, executives set an initial target of removing 400 pounds from B-C bodies by 1977. As fuel-economy pressures persisted and engineering feasibilities offered greater confidence, this target was increased to 800–1000 pounds (three mpg). No one step shifted the company's total strategic posture until the full downsizing of all lines was announced. But each partial solution built confidence and commitment toward a new direction.

Broadening Political Support

Often these broad emerging strategic thrusts need expanded political support and understanding to achieve sufficient momentum to survive.[23] Committees, task forces, and retreats tend to be favored mechanisms for accomplishing this. If carefully managed, these do not become the "garbage cans" of emerging ideas, as some observers have suggested.[24] Rather, by selecting the committee's chairman, membership, timing, and agenda, guiding executives can largely influence and predict a desired outcome and can force other executives toward a consensus. Such groups can be balanced to evaluate, educate, neutralize, or overwhelm opponents. They can be used to legitimize new options or to generate broad cohesion among diverse thrusts, or they can be narrowly focused to build momentum. Guiding executives can constantly maintain complete control over these "advisory processes" through their various influences and veto potentials. For example:

◇ IBM's Chairman Watson and Executive Vice-President Learson had become concerned about third-generation computer technology, the proliferation of designs from various divisions, increasing costs of developing software, internal competition among their lines, and the needed breadth of line for the new computer applications they began to foresee. Step by step, they oversaw the killing of the company's huge Stretch computer line (uneconomic), a proposed 8000 series of computers (incompatible software), and the prototype English Scamp Computer (duplicative). They then initiated a series of "strategic dialogues" with divisional executives to define a new strategy. But none came into place because of the parochial nature of divisional viewpoints.

Learson, therefore, set up the SPREAD Committee, representing every major segment of the company. Its twelve members included the most likely opponent of an integrated line (Haanstra), the people who had earlier suggested the 8000 and Scamp designs, and Learson's handpicked lieutenant (Evans). When progress became "hellishly slow," Haanstra was removed as chairman, and Evans took over. Eventually the committee came forth with an integrating proposal for a single, compatible line of computers to blanket and open up the market for both scientific and business applications, with "standard interface" for peripheral equipment. At an all-day meeting of the fifty top executives of the company, the report was not received with enthusiasm, but there were no compelling objections. So Learson blessed the silence as consensus saying, "OK, we'll do it"—i.e., go ahead with a major development program.[25]

In addition to facilitating smooth implementation, many managers reported that interactive consensus-building processes also improve the quality of the strategic decisions themselves and help achieve positive and innovative assistance when things otherwise could go wrong.

Overcoming Opposition: "Zones of Indifference" and "No Lose" Situations

Executives of basically healthy companies in the sample realized that any attempt to introduce a new strategy would have to deal with the support its predecessor had. Barring a major crisis, a frontal attack on an old strategy could be regarded as an attack on those who espoused it and who brought the enterprise to its present levels of success. There are often a variety of legitimate views on what could and should be done in the new circumstances a company faces, and wise executives do not want to alienate people who would otherwise be supporters. Consequently, they try to get key people behind their concepts whenever possible, to co-opt or neutralize serious opposition if necessary, or to find "zones of indifference" where the proposition will not be disastrously opposed.[26] Most of all they seek "no lose" situations that will motivate all the important players toward a common goal. For example:

◇ When James McFarland took over at General Mills from his power base in the Grocery Products Division, a serious contender for the top spot had been Louis B. "Bo" Polk, a bright and aggressive young man who headed the corporation's acquisition-diversification program. Both traditional lines and acquisitions groups wanted support for their activities and both had friends in high places. McFarland's corporate-wide "goodness to greatness" conferences (described in earlier articles) first obtained broad agreement on growth goals and criteria for all areas.

   Out of this and the related acquisition-proposal process came two thrusts: (1) to expand—internally and through acquisitions—in food-related sectors, and (2) to acquire new growth centers based on General Mill's marketing skills. Although no formal statement was issued, there was a strong feeling that the majority of resources should be used in food-related areas. But neither group was foreclosed, and no one could suggest the new management was vindictive. As it turned out, over the next five years about $450 million was invested in new businesses, and the majority were not closely related to foods.

But such tactics do not always work. Successful executives surveyed tended to honor legitimate differences in viewpoints and noted that initial opponents often shaped new strategies in more effective directions and became supporters as new information became available. But strong-minded executives sometimes disagreed to the point where they had to be moved or stimulated to leave; timing could dictate very firm top-level decisions at key junctures. Barring crises, however, disciplinary steps usually occurred incrementally as individual executives' attitudes and competencies emerged vis-à-vis a new strategy.

Structuring Flexibility: Buffers, Slacks, and Activists

Typically there are too many uncertainties in the total environment for managers to program or control all the events involved in effecting a major change in strategic direction. Logic dictates, therefore, that managers purposely design flexibility into their organizations and have resources ready to deploy incrementally as events demand. Planned flexibility requires: (1) proactive horizon scanning to identify the general nature and potential impact of opportunities and threats the firm is most likely to encounter, (2) creating sufficient resource buffers—or slacks—to respond effectively as events actually unfurl, (3) developing and positioning "credible activists" with a psychological commitment to move quickly and flexibly to exploit specific opportunities as they occur, and (4) shortening decision lines from such people (and key operating managers) to the top for the most rapid system response. These—not precapsuled programs to respond to stimuli that never quite occur as expected—are the keys to real contingency planning.

The concept of resource buffers requires amplification. Quick access to resources is needed to cushion the impact of random events, to offset opponents' sudden attacks, or to build momentum for new strategic shifts. Some examples will indicate the form these buffers may take:

◇ For critical purchased items, General Motors maintained at least three suppliers, each with sufficient capacity to expand production should one of the others encounter a catastrophe. Thus, the company had expandable capacity with no fixed investment. Exxon set up its Exploration Group to undertake the higher risks and longer-term investments necessary to search for oil in new areas, and thus to reduce the potential impact on Exxon if there were sudden unpredictable changes in the availability of Middle East oil. Instead of hoarding cash, Pillsbury and General Mills sold off unprofitable businesses and cleaned up their financial statements to improve their access to external capital sources for acquisitions. Such access in essence provided the protection of a cash buffer without its investment. IBM's large R&D facility and its project team approach to development assured that it had a pool of people it could quickly shift among various projects to exploit interesting new technologies.

When such flexible response patterns are designed into the enterprise's strategy, it is proactively ready to move on those thrusts—acquisitions, innovations, or resource explorations—that require incrementalism.

Systematic Waiting and Trial Concepts

The prepared strategist may have to wait for events. The availability of desired acquisitions or real estate might depend on a death, divorce, fiscal crisis, management change, or an erratic stock-market break.[27] Technological advances may have to await new knowledge, inventions, or lucky accidents. Despite otherwise complete preparations, a planned market entry might not be wise until new legislation, trade agreements, or competitive shake-outs occur. Organizational moves have to be timed to retirements, promotions, management failures, and so on. Very often the specific strategy adopted depends on the timing or sequence of such random events.[28] For example:

◊ Although Continental Group's top executives had thoroughly discussed and investigated energy, natural resources, and insurance as possible "fourth legs" for the company, the major acquisition possibilities were so different that the strategic choice depended on the fit of particular candidates—e.g., Peabody Coal or Richmond Insurance—within these possible industries. The choice of one industry would have precluded the others. The sequence in which firms became available affected the final choice, and that choice itself greatly influenced the whole strategic posture of the company.

In many of the cases studied, strategists proactively launched trial concepts—Peter McColough's "architecture of information" (Xerox), Spoor's "Super Box" (Pillsbury)—in order to generate options and concrete proposals. Usually these trial balloons were phrased in very broad terms. Without making a commitment to any specific solution, the executive can activate the organization's creative abilities. This approach keeps the manager's own options open until substantive alternatives can be evaluated against each other and against concrete current realities. It prevents practical line managers from rejecting a strategic shift, as they might if forced to compare a "paper option" against well-defined current needs. Such trial concepts give cohesion to the new strategy while enabling the company to take maximum advantage of the psychological and informational benefits of incrementalism.

Solidifying Progress—Incrementally

As events move forward, executives can more clearly perceive the specific directions in which their organizations should, and realistically can, move. They can seek more aggressive movement and commitment to their new perceptions, without undermining important ongoing activities or creating unnecessary reactions to their purposes. Until this point, new strategic goals might remain broad, relatively unrefined, or even unstated except as philosophic concepts. More specific dimensions might be incrementally announced as key pieces of information fall into place, specific unanswered issues approach resolution, or significant resources have to be formally committed.

Creating Pockets of Commitment

Early in this stage, guiding executives may need to actively implant support in the organization for new thrusts. They may encourage an array of exploratory projects for each of several possible options. Initial projects can be kept small, partial, or ad hoc, neither forming a comprehensive program nor seeming to be integrated into a cohesive strategy. Executives often provide stimulating goals, a proper climate for imaginative proposals, and flexible resource support, rather than being personally identified with specific projects. In this way they can achieve organizational involvement and early commitment without focusing attention on any one solution too soon or losing personal credibility if it fails.

Once under way, project teams on the more successful programs in the sample became ever more committed to their particular areas of exploration. They became pockets of support for new strategies deep within the organization. Yet, if necessary, top managers could delay until the last moment final decisions to blend individual projects into a total strategy. Thus, they were able to obtain the best possible match among the company's technical abilities, its psychological commitments, and its changing market needs. By making final choices more effectively—as late as possible with better data, more conscientiously investigated options, and the expert critiques competitive projects allowed—these executives actually increased technical and market efficiencies of their enterprises, despite the apparent added costs of parallel efforts.[29]

In order to maintain their own objectivity and future flexibility, some executives choose to keep their own political profiles low as they build a new consensus. If they seem committed to a strategy too soon, they might discourage others from pursuing key issues which should be raised.[30] By stimulating detailed investigations several levels down, top executives can seem detached, yet can still shape both progress and ultimate outcomes by reviewing interim results and specifying the timing, format, and forums for the release of data. When reports come forward, these executives can stand above the battle and review proposals objectively, without being personally on the defensive for having committed themselves to a particular solution too soon. From this position they can more easily orchestrate a high-level consensus on a new strategic thrust. As an added benefit, negative decisions on proposals often come from a group consensus that top executives can simply confirm to lower levels, thereby preserving their personal veto for more crucial moments. In many well-made decisions people at all levels contribute to the generation, amplification, and interpretation of options and information to the extent that it is often difficult to say who really makes the decision.[31]

Focusing the Organization

In spite of their apparent detachment, top executives do focus their organizations on developing strategies at critical points in the process. While adhering to the rhetoric of specific goal setting, most executives are careful not to state new goals in concrete terms before they have built a consensus among key players. They fear that they will prematurely centralize the organization, preempt interesting options, provide a common focus for otherwise fragmented opposition, or cause the organization to act prematurely to carry out a specified commitment. Guiding executives may quietly shape the many alternatives flowing upward by using what Wrapp refers to as a "hidden hand." Through their information networks they can encourage concepts they favor, let weakly supported options die through inaction, and establish hurdles or tests for strongly supported ideas with which they do not agree but which they do not wish to oppose openly.

Since opportunities for such focusing generally develop unexpectedly, the timing of key moves is often unpredictable. A crisis, a rash of reassignments, a reorganization, or a key appointment may allow an executive to focus attention on particular thrusts, add momentum to some, and perhaps quietly phase out others.[32] Most managers surveyed seemed well aware of the notion that "if there are no other options, mine wins." Without being Machiavellian, they did not want misdirected options to gain strong political momentum and later have to be terminated in an open bloodbath. Nor did they want to send false signals that stimulated segments of their organizations to make proposals in undesirable directions. They sensed very clearly that the patterns in which proposals are approved or denied are inevitably perceived by lower echelons as precedents for developing future goals or policies.

Managing Coalitions

Power interactions among key players are important at this stage of solidifying progress. Each player has a different level of power determined by his or her information base, organizational position, and personal credibility.[33] Executives legitimately perceive problems or opportunities differently because of their particular values, experiences, and vantage points. They will promote the solutions they perceive as the best compromise for the total enterprise, for themselves, and for their particular units. In an organization with dispersed power, the key figure is the one who can manage coalitions.[34] Since no one player has all the power, regardless of that individual's skill or position, the action that occurs over time might differ greatly from the intentions of any of the players.[35] Top executives try to sense whether support exists among important parties for specific aspects of an issue and try to get partial decisions and momenta going for those aspects. As "comfort levels" or political pressures within the top group rise in favor of specific decisions, the guiding executive might, within his or her concept of a more complete solution, seek—among the various features of different proposals—a balance that the most influential and credible parties can actively support. The result tends to be a stream of partial decisions on limited strategic issues made by constantly changing coalitions of the critical power centers.[36] These decisions steadily evolve toward a broader consensus, acceptable to both the top executive and some "dominant coalition" among these centers.

As a partial consensus emerges, top executives might crystallize issues by stating some broad goals in more specific terms for internal consumption. Finally, when sufficient general acceptance exists and the timing is right, the goals may begin to appear in more public announcements. For example:

◇ As General Mills divested several of its major divisions in the early 1960s, its annual reports began to refer to these as deliberate moves "to concentrate on the company's strengths" and "to intensify General Mills's efforts in the convenience foods field." Such statements could not have been made until many of the actual divestitures were completed, and a sufficient consensus existed among the top executives to support the new corporate concept.

Formalizing Commitment by Empowering Champions

As each major strategic thrust comes into focus, top executives try to ensure that some individual or group feels responsible for its goals. If the thrust will project the enterprise in entirely new directions, executives often want more than mere accountability for its success; they want real commitment.[37] A significantly new major thrust, concept, product, or problem solution frequently needs the nurturing hand of someone who genuinely identifies with it and whose future depends on its success. For example:

◇ Once the divestiture program at General Mills was sufficiently under way. General Rawlings selected young "Bo" Polk to head up an acquisition program to use the cash generated. In this role Polk had nothing to lose. With strong senior management in the remaining consumer-products divisions, the ambitious Polk would have had a long road to the top there. In acquisitions, he provided a small political target, only a $50,000 budget in a $500 million company. Yet he had high visibility and could build his own power base, if successful. With direct access to and the support of Rawlings, he would be protected through his early ventures. All he had to do was make sure his first few acquisitions were successful. As subsequent acquisitions succeeded, his power base could feed on itself, satisfying both his ego needs and the company's strategic goals.

In some cases, top executives have to wait for champions to appear before committing resources to risky new strategies. They may immediately assign accountability for less dramatic plans by converting them into new missions for ongoing groups.

From this point on, the strategy process is familiar. The organization's formal structure has to be adjusted to support the strategy.[38] Commitment to the most important new thrusts has to be confirmed in formal plans. Detailed budgets, programs, controls, and reward systems have to reflect all planned strategic thrusts. Finally, the guiding executive has to see that recruiting and staffing plans are aligned with the new goals and that, when the situation permits, supporters and persistent opponents of intended new thrusts are assigned to appropriate positions.

Continuing the Dynamics by Eroding Consensus

The major strategic changes studied tended to take many years to accomplish. The process was continuous, often without any clear beginning or end.[39] The decision process constantly molded and modified management's concerns and concepts. Radical crusades became the new conventional wisdom, and over time totally new issues emerged. Participants or observers were often not aware of exactly when a particular decision had been made or when a subsequent consensus was created to supersede or modify it; the process of strategic change was continuous and dynamic.[40] Several GM executives described the frequently imperceptible way in which many strategic decisions evolved.[41]

We use an iterative process to make a series of tentative decisions on the way we think the market will go. As we get more data we modify these continuously. It is often difficult to say who decided something and when—or even who originated a decision. . . . Strategy really evolves as a series of incremental steps. . . . I frequently don't know when a decision is made in General Motors. I don't remember being in a committee meeting when things came to a vote. Usually someone will simply summarize a developing position. Everyone else either nods or states his particular terms of consensus.

A major strategic change in Xerox was characterized this way:

How was the overall organization decision made? I've often heard it said that after talking with a lot of people and having trouble with a number of decisions which were pending, Archie McCardell really reached his own conclusion and got Peter McColough's backing on it. But it really didn't happen quite that way. It was an absolutely evolutionary approach. It was a growing feeling. A number of people felt we ought to be moving toward some kind of matrix organization. We have always been a pretty democratic type of organization. In our culture you can't come down with mandates or ultimatums from the top on major changes like this. You almost have to work these things through and let them grow and evolve, keep them on the table so people are thinking about them and talking about them.

Once the organization arrives at its new consensus, the guiding executive has to move immediately to ensure that this new position does not become inflexible. In trying to build commitment to a new concept, individual executives often surround themselves with people who see the world in the same way. Such people can rapidly become systematic screens against other views. Effective executives therefore purposely continue the change process, constantly introducing new faces and stimuli at the top. They consciously begin to erode the very strategic thrusts they may have just created—a difficult, but essential, psychological task.

Integration of Processes and of Interests

In the large enterprises observed, strategy formulation was a continuously evolving analytical-political consensus process with neither a finite beginning nor a definite end. It generally followed the sequence described above. Yet the total process was anything but linear. It was a groping, cyclical process that often circled back on itself, with frequent interruptions and delays. Pfiffner aptly describes the process of strategy formation as being like "fermentation in biochemistry, rather than an industrial assembly line."[42]

Such incremental management processes are not abrogations of good management practice. Nor are they Machiavellian or consciously manipulative maneuvers. Instead, they represent an adaptation to the practical psychological and informational problems of getting a constantly changing group of people with diverse talents and interests to move *together* effectively in a continually dynamic environment. Much of the impelling force behind logical incrementalism comes from a desire to tap the talents and psychological drives of the whole organization, to create cohesion, and to generate identity with the emerging strategy. The remainder of that force results from the interactive nature of the random factors and lead times affecting the independent subsystems that compose any total strategy.

An Incremental—Not a Piecemeal—Process

The total pattern of action, though highly incremental, is not piecemeal in well-managed organizations. It requires constant, conscious reassessment of the total organization, its capacities, and its needs as related to surrounding environments, and it requires continual attempts by top managers to integrate these actions into an understandable, cohesive whole. How do top managers themselves describe the process? Estes, president of General Motors, said:

We try to give them the broad concepts we are trying to achieve. We operate through questioning and fact gathering. Strategy is a state of mind you go through. When you think about a little problem, your mind begins to think how it will affect all the different elements in the total situation. Once you have had all the jobs you need to qualify for this position, you can see the problem from a variety of viewpoints. But you don't try to ram your conclusions down people's throats. You try to persuade people what has to be done and provide confidence and leadership for them.

Formal-Analytical Techniques.   At each stage of strategy development, effective executives constantly try to visualize the new patterns that might exist among the emerging strategies of various subsystems. As each subsystem strategy becomes more apparent, both its executive team and top-level groups try to project implications for the total enterprise and to stimulate queries, support, and feedback from those involved in related strategies. Perceptive top executives see that the various teams generating subsystem strategies have overlapping members. They require periodic updates and reviews before higher echelon groups that can bring a total corporate view to bear. They use formal planning processes to interrelate and evaluate the resources required, benefits sought, and risks undertaken vis-à-vis other elements of the enterprise's overall strategy. Some use scenario techniques to help visualize potential impacts and relationships. Others utilize complex forecasting models to better understand the basic interactions among subsystems, the total enterprise, and the environment. Still others use specialized staffs, "devil's advocates," or "contention teams" to make sure that all important aspects of their strategies receive a thorough evaluation.

Power-Behavioral Aspects: Coalition Management.   All of the formal methodologies help, but the real integration of all the components in an enterprise's total strategy eventually takes place only in the minds of high-level executives. Each executive may legitimately perceive the intended balance of goals and thrusts differently. Some of these differences may be openly expressed as issues to be resolved when new information becomes available. Some differences may remain unstated—hidden agendas to emerge at later dates. Others may be masked by accepting so broad a statement of intention that many different views are included in a seeming consensus, when a more specific statement might be divisive. Nevertheless, effective strategies do achieve a level of understanding and consensus sufficient to focus action.

Top executives deliberately manage the incremental processes within each subsystem to create the basis for consensus. They also manage the coalitions that lie at the heart of most controlled strategy developments.[43] They recognize that they are at the confluence of innumerable pressures—from stockholders, environmentalists, government bodies, customers, suppliers, distributors, producing units, marketing groups, technologists, unions, special-issue activists, individual employees, ambitious executives, and so on—and that knowledgeable people of goodwill can easily disagree on proper actions. In response to changing pressures and coalitions among these groups, the top-management team constantly forms and reforms its own coalitions on various decisions.[44]

Most major strategic moves tend to assist some interests—and executives' careers—at the expense of others. Consequently, each set of interests serves as a check on the others and thus helps maintain the breadth and balance of strategy.[45] To avoid significant errors some managers try to ensure that all important groups have representation at or access to the top.[46] The guiding executive group may continuously adjust the number, power, or proximity of such access points in order to maintain a desired balance and focus.[47] These delicate adjustments require constant negotiations and implied bargains within the leadership group. Balancing the forces that different interests exert on key decisions is perhaps the ultimate control top executives have in guiding and coordinating the formulation of their companies' strategies.[48]

Establishing, Measuring, and Rewarding Key Thrusts

Few executives or management teams can keep all the dimensions of a complex evolving strategy in mind as they deal with the continuous flux of urgent issues. Consequently, effective strategic managers seek to identify a few central themes that can help to draw diverse efforts together in a common cause.[49] Once identified, these themes help to maintain focus and consistency in the strategy. They make it easier to discuss and monitor proposed strategic thrusts. Ideally, these themes can be developed into a matrix of programs and goals, cutting across formal divisional lines and dominating the selection and ranking of projects within divisions. This matrix can, in turn, serve as the basis for performance measurement, control, and reward systems that ensure the intended strategy is properly implemented.

Unfortunately, few companies in the sample were able to implement such a complex planning and control system without creating undue rigidities. But all did utilize logical incrementalism to bring cohesion to the formal-analytical and power-behavioral processes needed to create effective strategies. Most used some approximation of the process sequence described above to form their strategies at both subsystem and overall corporate levels. A final example demonstrates how deliberate incrementalism can integrate the key elements in more traditional approaches to strategy formulation.

◊ In the late 1970s a major nation's largest bank named as its new president and CEO a man with a long and successful career, largely in domestic operating positions. The bank's chairman had been a familiar figure on the international stage and was due to retire in three to five years. The new CEO, with the help of a few trusted colleagues, his chief planner, and a consultant, first tried to answer the questions: "If I look ahead seven to eight years to my retirement as CEO, what would I like to leave behind as the hallmarks of my leadership? What accomplishments would define my era as having been successful?" He chose the following as goals:

1. To be the country's number-one bank in profitability and size without sacrificing the quality of its assets or liabilities.
2. To be recognized as a major international bank.
3. To improve substantially the public image and employee perceptions of the bank.
4. To maintain progressive policies that prevent unionization.

5. To be viewed as a professional, well-managed bank with strong, planned management continuity.
6. To be clearly identified as the country's most professional corporate finance bank, with a strong base within the country but with foreign and domestic operations growing in balance.
7. To have women in top management and to achieve full utilization of the bank's female employees.
8. To have a tighter, smaller headquarters and a more rationalized, decentralized corporate structure.

The CEO brought back to the corporate offices the head of his overseas divisions to be COO and to be a member of the Executive Committee, which ran the company's affairs. The CEO discussed his personal views concerning the bank's future with this Committee and also with several of his group VPs. Then, to arrive at a cohesive set of corporate goals, the Executive Committee investigated the bank's existing strengths and weaknesses (again with the assistance of consultants) and extrapolated its existing growth trends seven to eight years into the future. According to the results of this exercise, the bank's foreseeable growth would require that:

1. The bank's whole structure be reoriented to make it a much stronger force in international banking.
2. The bank decentralize operations much more than it ever had.
3. The bank find or develop at least 100 new top-level specialists and general managers within a few years.
4. The bank reorganize around a "four bank" principle (international, commercial, investment, and retail banks) with entirely new linkages forged among these units.
5. These linkages and much of the bank's new international thrust be built on its expertise in certain industries, which were the primary basis of its parent country's international trade.
6. The bank's profitability be improved across the board, especially in its diverse retail banking units.

To develop more detailed data for specific actions and to further develop consensus around needed moves, the CEO commissioned two consulting studies: one on the future of the bank's home country, and the other on changing trade patterns and relationships worldwide. As these studies became available, the CEO allowed an ever wider circle of top executives to critique the studies' findings and to share their insights. Finally, the CEO and the Executive Committee were willing to draw up and agree to a statement of ten broad goals (parallel to the CEO's original goals but enriched in flavor and detail). By then, some steps were already under way to implement specific goals (e.g., the four-bank concept). But the CEO wanted further participation of his line officers in the formulation of the goals and in the strategic thrusts they represented across the whole bank. By now eighteen months had gone by, but there was widespread consensus within the top management group on major goals and directions.

The CEO then organized an international conference of some forty top officers of the bank and had a background document prepared for this meeting containing: (1) the broad goals agreed upon, (2) the ten major thrusts that the Executive Committee thought were necessary to meet these goals, (3) the key elements needed to back up each thrust, and (4) a summary of the national and economic analyses the thrusts were based upon. The forty executives had two full days to critique, question, improve, and clarify the ideas in this document. Small work groups of line executives reported their findings and concerns directly to the Executive Committee. At the end of the meeting, the Executive Committee tabled one of the major thrusts for further study, agreed to refined wording for some of the bank's broad goals, and modified details of the major thrusts in line with expressed concerns.

The CEO announced that within three months each line officer would be expected to submit his own statement of how his unit would contribute to the major goals and thrusts agreed on. Once these unit goals were discussed and negotiated with the appropriate top-executive group, the line officers would develop specific budgetary and nonbudgetary programs showing precisely how their units would carry out each of the major thrusts in the strategy. The COO was asked to develop measures both for all key elements of each unit's fiscal performance and for performance against each agreed-upon strategic thrust within each unit. As these plans came into place, it became clear that the old organization had to be aligned behind these new thrusts. The CEO had to substantially redefine the COO's job, deal with some crucial internal political pressures, and place the next generation of top managers in the line positions supporting each major thrust. The total process from concept formulation to implementation of the control system was to span three to four years, with new goals and thrusts emerging flexibly as external events and opportunities developed.

Conclusion

In recent years, there has been an increasingly loud chorus of discontent about corporate strategic planning. Many managers are concerned that, despite elaborate strategic planning systems, costly staffs for planning, and major commitments of their own time, their most elaborately analyzed strategies never get implemented. These executives and their companies generally have fallen into the trap of thinking about strategy formulation and implementation as separate, sequential processes. They rely on the awesome rationality of their formally derived strategies and the inherent power of their positions to cause their organizations to respond. When this does not occur, they become bewildered, if not frustrated and angry. Instead, successful managers in the companies observed acted logically and incrementally to improve the quality of information used in key decisions; to overcome the personal and political pressures resisting change; to deal with the varying lead times and sequencing problems in critical decisions; and to build the organizational awareness, understanding, and psychological commitment essential to effective strategies. By the time the strategies began to crystallize, pieces of them were already being implemented. Through the very processes they used to formulate their strategies, these executives had built sufficient organizational momentum and identity along with the strategies to make them flow toward flexible and successful implementation.

2

The Art of High-Technology Management

Modesto A. Maidique

Robert H. Hayes

The authors argue that, contrary to popular opinion, U.S. firms need not look overseas for models of successfully managed companies. Instead, many U.S. companies can benefit from using well-managed American high-tech firms as their guides. Through their studies of a wide range of high-technology firms, the authors identified those characteristics they believe make a company successful, and grouped them into six themes. Analysis of their findings has led them to conclude that well-managed companies have found ways to resolve a critical dilemma—the ability to manage the conflict between continuity and rapid change. *SMR.*

Over the past fifteen years, the world's perception of the competence of U.S. companies in managing technology has come full circle. In 1967, a Frenchman, J.-J. Servan-Schreiber, expressed with alarm in his book *The American Challenge* that U.S. technology was far ahead of the rest of the industrialized world.[1] This "technology gap," he argued, was continually widening because of the *superior ability of Americans to organize and manage technological development.*

Today, the situation is perceived to have changed drastically. The concern now is that the gap is reversing: the onslaught of Japanese and/or European challenges is threatening America's technological leadership. Even such informed Americans as Dr. Simon Ramo express great concern: In *America's Technology Slip,* Dr. Ramo notes the apparent inability of U.S. companies to compete technologically with their foreign counterparts.[2] Moreover, in the best seller *The Art of Japanese Management,* the authors use as a basis of

From *Sloan Management Review,* Winter 1984, Vol. 25, No. 2. Reprinted with permission.

comparison two technology-based firms: Matsushita (Japanese) and ITT (American).[3] Here, the Japanese firm is depicted as a model for managers, while the management practices of the U.S. firm are sharply criticized.

Nevertheless, a number of U.S. companies appear to be fending off these foreign challenges successfully. These firms are repeatedly included on lists of "America's best-managed companies." Many of them are competitors in the R&D intensive industries, a sector of our economy that has come under particular criticism. Ironically, some of them have even served as models for highly successful Japanese and European high-tech firms.

For example, of the forty-three companies that Peters and Waterman, Jr., judged to be "excellent" in *In Search of Excellence,* almost half were classified as "high technology," or as containing a substantial high-technology component.[4] Similarly, of the five U.S. organizations that William Ouchi described as best prepared to meet the Japanese challenge, three (IBM, Hewlett-Packard, and Kodak) were high-technology companies.[5] Indeed, high-technology corporations are among the most admired firms in America. In a *Fortune* study that ranked the corporate reputation of the 200 largest U.S. corporations, IBM and Hewlett-Packard (HP) ranked first and second, respectively.[6] And of the top ten firms, nine compete in such high-technology fields as pharmaceuticals, precision instruments, communications, office equipment, computers, jet engines, and electronics.

The above studies reinforce our own findings, which have led us to conclude that U.S. high-technology firms that seek to improve their management practices to succeed against foreign competitors need not look overseas. The firms mentioned above are not unique. On the contrary, they are representative of scores of well-managed small and large U.S. technology-based firms. Moreover, the management practices they have adopted are widely applicable. Thus, perhaps the key to stimulating innovation in our country is not to adopt the managerial practices of the Europeans or the Japanese, but to adapt some of the policies of our own successful high-technology firms.

The Study

Over the past two decades, we have been privileged to work with a host of small and large high-technology firms as participants, advisers, and researchers. We and our assistants interviewed formally and informally over 250 executives, including more than 30 CEOs, from a wide cross section of high-tech industries—biotechnology, semiconductors, computers, pharmaceuticals, and aerospace. About 100 of these executives were interviewed in 1983 as part of a large-scale study of product innovation in the electronics industry (conducted by one of this article's authors and his colleagues).[7] Our research has been guided by a fundamental question: what are the strategies, policies, practices, and decisions that result in successful management of high-technology enterprises? One of our principal findings was that no company has a monopoly on managerial excellence. Even the best run companies make big mistakes, and many smaller, less regarded companies are surprisingly sophisticated about the factors that mediate between success and failure.

It also became apparent from our interviews that the driving force behind the successes of many of these companies was strong leadership. All companies need leaders and visionaries, of course, but leadership is particularly essential when the future is blurry and when the world is changing rapidly. Although few high-tech firms can succeed for long without strong leaders, leadership itself is not the subject of this article. Rather, we accept it as given and seek to understand what strategies and management practices can reinforce strong leadership.

The companies we studied were of different sizes ($10 million to $30 billion in sales); their technologies were at different stages of maturity; their industry growth rates and product mixes were different; and their managers ranged widely in age. But they all had the same unifying thread: a rapid rate of change in the technological base of their products. This common thread, rapid technological change, implies novel products and functions and thus usually rapid growth. But even when growth is slow or moderate, the destruction of the old capital base by new technology results in the need for rapid redeployment of resources to cope with new product designs and new manufacturing processes. Thus, the two dominant characteristics of the high-technology organizations that we focused on were growth and change.

In part because of this split focus (growth and change), the companies we studied often appeared to display contradictory behavior over time. Despite these differences, in important respects, they were remarkably similar because they all confronted the same two-headed dilemma: how to unleash the creativity that promotes growth and change without being fragmented by it, and how to control innovation without stifling it. In dealing with this concern, they tended to adopt strikingly similar managerial approaches.

The Paradox: Continuity and Chaos

When we grouped our findings into general themes of success, a significant paradox gradually emerged: Some of the behavioral patterns that these companies displayed seemed to favor promoting disorder and informality, while others would have us conclude that it was consistency, continuity, integration, and order that were the keys to success. As we grappled with this apparent paradox, we came to realize that continued success in a high-technology environment requires periodic shifts between chaos and continuity.[8] Our originally static framework, therefore, was gradually replaced by a dynamic framework within whose ebbs and flows lay the secrets of success.

Six Themes of Success

The six themes that we grouped our findings into were: (1) business focus; (2) adaptability; (3) organizational cohesion; (4) entrepreneurial culture; (5) sense of integrity; and (6) "hands-on" top management. No one firm exhibits excellence in every one of these categories at any one time, nor are the less successful firms totally lacking in all. Nonetheless, outstanding high-technology firms tend to score high in most of the six categories, while less successful ones usually score low in several.[9]

1. Business Focus

Even a superficial analysis of the most successful high-technology firms leads one to conclude that they are highly focused. With few exceptions, the leaders in high-technology fields, such as computers, aerospace, semiconductors, biotechnology, chemicals, pharmaceuticals, electronic instruments, and duplicating machines, realize the great bulk of their sales either from a single product line or from a closely related set of product lines.[10] For example, IBM, Boeing, Intel, and Genentech confine themselves almost entirely to computer products, commercial aircraft, integrated circuits, and genetic engineering, respectively. Similarly, four-fifths of Kodak's and Xerox's sales come from photographic products and duplicating machines, respectively. In general, the smaller the company, the more highly focused it is. Tandon concentrates on disk drives; Tandem on high-reliability computers; Analog Devices on linear integrated circuits; and Cullinet on software products.

Closely Related Products.   This extraordinary concentration does not stop with the dominant product line. When the company grows and establishes a secondary product line, it is usually closely related to the first. Hewlett-Packard, for instance, has two product families, each of which accounts for about half of its sales. Both families—electronic instruments and data processors—are focused on the same technical, scientific, and process control markets. IBM also makes two closely related product lines—data processors (approximately 80 percent of sales) and office equipment—both of which emphasize the business market.

Companies that took the opposite path have not fared well. Two of yesterday's technological leaders, ITT and RCA, have paid dearly for diversifying away from their strengths. Today, both firms are trying to divest themselves of many of what were once highly touted acquisitions. As David Packard, chairman of the board of Hewlett-Packard, once observed, "No company ever died from starvation, but many have died from indigestion."[11]

A communications firm that became the world's largest conglomerate, ITT began to slip in the early 1970s after an acquisition wave orchestrated by Harold Geneen. When Geneen retired in 1977, his successors attempted to redress ITT's lackluster performance through a far-reaching divestment program.[12] So far, forty companies and other assets worth over $1 billion have been sold—and ITT watchers believe the program is just getting started. Some analysts believe that ITT will ultimately be restructured into three groups, with the communications/electronics group and engineered products (home of ITT semiconductors) forming the core of a "new" ITT.

RCA experienced a similar fate to ITT. When RCA's architect and longtime chairman, General David Sarnoff, retired in 1966, RCA was internationally respected for its pioneering work in television, electronic components, communications, and radar. But by 1980, the three CEOs who followed Sarnoff had turned a technological leader into a conglomerate with flat sales, declining earnings, and a $2.9 billion debt. This disappointing performance led RCA's new CEO, Thorton F. Bradshaw, to decide to return RCA to its high-technology origins.[13] Bradshaw's strategy is to now concentrate on RCA's traditional strengths—communications and entertainment—by divesting its other businesses.

Focused R&D.   Another policy that strengthens the focus of leading high-technology firms is concentrating R&D on one or two areas. Such a strategy enables these businesses to dominate the research, particularly the more risky leading-edge explorations. By spending a higher proportion of their sales dollars on R&D than their competitors do, or through their sheer size (as in the case of IBM, Kodak, and Xerox), such companies maintain their technological leadership. It is not unusual for a leading firm's R&D investment to be one and a half to two times the industry's average as a percentage of sales (8–15 percent) and several times more than any individual competitor on an absolute basis.[14]

Moreover, their commitment to R&D is both enduring and consistent, and is maintained through slack periods and recessions, because it is believed to be in the best, long-term interest of the stockholders. As the CEO of Analog Devices, a leading linear integrated-circuit manufacturer, explained in a quarterly report that noted a 30 percent decline in profits, "We are sharply constraining the growth of fixed expenses, but we do not feel it is in the best interest of shareholders to cut back further on product development . . . in order to relieve short-term pressure on earnings."[15] Similarly, when sales flattened and profit margins plummeted at Intel as the result of a recession, its management invested a record-breaking $130 million in R&D and another $150 million in plant and equipment.[16]

Consistent Priorities.   Still, another way for a company to demonstrate a strong business focus is through a set of priorities and a pattern of behavior that is continually reinforced by top management: for example, planned manufacturing improvement at Texas Instruments (TI); customer service at IBM; the concept of the entrepreneurial product champion at 3M; and the new products at HP. Belief in the competitive effectiveness of their chosen theme runs deep in each of these companies.

A business focus that is maintained over extended periods of time has fundamental consequences. By concentrating on what it does well, a company develops an intimate knowledge of its markets, competitors, technologies, employees, and of the future needs and opportunities of its customers.[17] The Stanford Innovation Project recently completed a three-year study of 224 U.S. high-technology products (half of which were successes, half of which were failures) and concluded that a continuous, in-depth, informal interaction with leading customers throughout the product-development process was the principal factor behind successful new products. In short, this coupling is the cornerstone of effective high-technology progress. Such an interaction is greatly facilitated by the longstanding and close customer relationships that are fostered by concentrating on closely related product-market choices.[18] "Customer needs," explains Tom Jones, chairman of Northrop Corporation, "must be understood *way ahead of time*" (authors' emphasis).[19]

2. Adaptability

Successful firms balance a well-defined business focus with the willingness, and the will, to undertake major and rapid change when necessary. Concentration, in short, does not mean stagnation. Immobility is the most dangerous behavioral pattern a high-technology firm can develop: technology can change rapidly, and with it the markets and customers served. Therefore, a high-technology firm must be able to track and exploit the rapid shifts and twists in market boundaries as they are redefined by new technological, market, and competitive developments.

The cost of strategic stagnation can be great, as General Radio (GR) found out. Once the proud leader of the electronic instruments business, GR almost single-handedly created many sectors of the market. Its engineering excellence and its progressive human-relations policies were models for the industry. But when its founder, Melville Eastham, retired in 1950, GR's strategy ossified. In the next two decades, the company failed to take advantage of two major opportunities for growth that were closely related to the company's strengths: microwave instruments and minicomputers. Meanwhile, its traditional product line withered away. Now all that remains of GR's once dominant instruments line, which is less than 10 percent of sales, is a small assembly area where a handful of technicians assemble batches of the old instruments.

It wasn't until William Thurston, in the wake of mounting losses, assumed the presidency at the end of 1972 that GR began to refocus its engineering creativity and develop new marketing strategies. Using the failure of the old policies as his mandate, Thurston deemphasized the aging product lines, focused GR's attention on automated test equipment, balanced its traditional engineering excellence with an increased sensitivity to market needs, and gave the firm a new name—GenRad. Since then, GenRad has resumed rapid growth and has won a leadership position in the automatic test-equipment market.[20]

The GenRad story is a classic example of a firm making a strategic change because it perceived that its existing strategy was not working. But even successful high-technology firms sometimes feel the need to be rejuvenated periodically to avoid technological stagnation. In the mid-1960s, for example, IBM appeared to have little reason for major change. The company had a near monopoly in the computer mainframe industry. Its two principal products—the 1401 at the low end of the market and the 7090 at the high end—accounted for over two-thirds of industry sales. Yet, in one move the company obsoleted both product lines (as well as others) and redefined the rules of competition for decades to come by simultaneously introducing six compatible models of the "System 360," based on proprietary hybrid-integrated circuits.[21]

During the same period, GM, whose dominance of the U.S. auto industry approached IBM's dominance of the computer mainframe industry, stoutly resisted such a rejuvenation. Instead, it became more and more centralized and inflexible. Yet, GM was also once a high-technology company. In its early days when Alfred P. Sloan ran the company, engines were viewed as high-technology products. One day, Charles F. Kettering told Sloan he believed the high efficiency of the diesel engine could be engineered into a compact power plant. Sloan's response was: "Very well—we are now in the diesel engine business. You tell us how the engine should run, and I will . . . capitalize the program."[22] Two years later, Kettering achieved a major breakthrough in diesel technology. This paved the way for a revolution in the railroad industry and led to GM's preeminence in the diesel locomotive markets.

Organizational Flexibility.   To undertake such wrenching shifts in direction requires both agility and daring. Organizational agility seems to be associated with organizational flexibility: frequent realignments of people and responsibilities as the firm attempts to maintain its balance on shifting competitive sands. The daring and the willingness to take you-bet-your-company kind of risks is a product of both the inner confidence of its members and a powerful top management—one that either has effective shareholder control or the full support of its board.

3. Organizational Cohesion

The key to success for a high-tech firm is not simply periodic renewal. There must also be cooperation in the translation of new ideas into new products and processes. As Ken Fisher, the architect of Prime Computer's extraordinary growth, puts it, "If you have the driving function, the most important success factor is the ability to integrate. It's also the most difficult part of the task."[23]

To succeed, the energy and creativity of the whole organization must be tapped. Anything that restricts the flow of ideas, or undermines the trust, respect, and sense of a commonality of purpose among individuals is a potential danger. This is why high-tech firms fight so vigorously against the usual organizational accoutrements of seniority, rank, and functional specialization. Little attention is given to organizational charts: often they don't exist.

Younger people in a rapidly evolving technological field are often as good—and sometimes even better—a source of new ideas as older ones. In some high-tech firms, in fact, the notion of a "halflife of knowledge" is used; that is, the amount of time that has to elapse before half of what one knows is obsolete. In semiconductor engineering, for example, it is estimated that the halflife of a newly minted Ph.D. is about seven years. Therefore, any practice that relegates younger engineers to secondary, non-partnership roles is considered counterproductive.

Similarly, product design, marketing, and manufacturing personnel must collaborate in a common cause rather than compete with one another, as happens in many organizations. Any policies that appear to elevate one of these functions above the others—either in prestige or in rewards—can poison the atmosphere for collaboration and cooperation.

A source of division, and one that distracts the attention of people from the needs of the firm to their own aggrandizement, are the executive "perks" that are found in many mature organizations: Pretentious job titles, separate dining rooms and restrooms for executives, larger and more luxurious offices (often separated in some way from the rest of the organization), and even separate or reserved places in the company parking lot all tend to establish "distance" between managers and doers and substitute artificial goals for the crucial real ones of creating successful new products and customers. The appearance of an executive dining room, in fact, is one of the clearest danger signals.

Good Communication.   One way to combat the development of such distance is by making top executives more visible and accessible. IBM, for instance, has an open-door policy that encourages managers at different levels of the organization to talk to department heads and vice-presidents. According to senior IBM executives, it was not unusual for a project manager to drop in and talk to Frank Cary (IBM's chairman) or John Opel (IBM's president). Likewise, an office with transparent walls and no door, such as that of John Young, CEO at HP, encourages communication. In fact, open-style offices are common in many high-tech firms.

A regular feature of 3M's management process is the monthly "technical forum" where technical staff members from the firm exchange views on their respective projects. This emphasis on communication is not restricted to internal operations. Such a firm supports and often sponsors industry-wide technical conferences, sabbaticals for staff members, and cooperative projects with technical universities.

Such forums serve to compensate partially for the loss of visibility that technologists usually experience when an organization becomes more complex and when production, marketing, and finance staffs swell. So does the concept of the dual-career ladder that is used in most of these firms; that is, a job hierarchy through which technical personnel can attain the status, compensation, and recognition accorded to a division general manager or a corporate vice-president. By using this strategy, companies try to retain the spirit of the early days of the industry, when scientists played a dominant role, often even serving as members of the board of directors.[24]

Again, a strategic business focus contributes to organizational cohesion. Managers of firms that have a strong theme/culture and that concentrate on closely related markets and technologies generally display a sophisticated understanding of their businesses. Someone who understands where the firm is going and why is more likely to be willing to subordinate the interests of his or her own unit or function in the interest of promoting the common goal.

Job Rotation.   A policy of conscious job rotation also facilitates this sense of communality. In the small firm, everyone is involved in everyone else's job, but specialization tends to creep in as size increases and boundary lines between functions appear. If left unchecked, these boundaries can become rigid and impermeable. Rotating managers in temporary assignments across these boundaries helps keep the lines fluid and informal, however. When a new process is developed at TI, for example, the process developers are sent to the production unit where the process will be implemented. They are allowed to return to their usual posts only after that unit's operations manager is convinced that the process is working properly.

Integration of Roles.   Other ways that high-tech companies try to prevent organizational, and particularly hierarchial, barriers from arising is through multidisciplinary project teams, "special venture groups," and matrixlike organizational structures. Such structures, which require functional specialists and product/market managers to interact in a variety of relatively short-term problem-solving assignments, both inject a certain ambiguity into organizational relationships and require each individual to play a variety of organizational roles.

For example, AT&T uses a combination of organizational and physical mechanisms to promote integration. The Advanced Development sections of Bell Labs are physically located on the sites of the Western Electric plants. This location creates an organizational bond between Development and Bell's basic research and an equally important spatial bond between Development and the manufacturing engineering groups at the plants. In this way, communication is encouraged among Development and the other two groups.[25]

Long-term Employment.   Long-term employment and intensive training are also important integrative mechanisms. Managers and technologists are more likely to develop satisfactory working relationships if they know they will be harnessed to each other for a good part of their working lives. Moreover, their loyalty and commitment to the firm is increased if they know the firm is continuously investing in upgrading their capabilities.

At Tandem, technologists regularly train administrators on the performance and function of the firm's products and, in turn, administrators train the technologists on personnel policies and financial operations.[26] Such a firm also tends to select college graduates who have excellent academic records, which suggest self-discipline and stability, and then encourages them to stay with the firm for most, if not all, of their careers.

4. Entrepreneurial Culture

While continuously striving to pull the organization together, successful high-tech firms also display fierce activism in promoting internal agents of change. Indeed, it has long been recognized that one of the most important characteristics of a successful high-technology firm is an entrepreneurial culture.[27]

Indeed, the ease with which small entrepreneurial firms innovate has always inspired a mixture of puzzlement and jealousy in larger firms. When new ventures and small firms fail, they usually do so because of capital shortages and managerial errors.[28] Nonetheless, time and again they develop remarkably innovative products, processes, and services with a speed and efficiency that baffle the managers of large companies. The success of the Apple II, which created a new industry, and Genentech's genetically engineered insulin are of this genre. The explanation for a small entrepreneurial firm's innovativeness is straightforward, yet it is difficult for a large firm to replicate its spirit.

Entrepreneurial Characteristics.   First, the small firm is typically blessed with excellent communication. Its technical people are in continuous contact (and often in cramped quarters). They have lunch together, and they call each other outside of working hours. Thus, they come to understand and appreciate the difficulties and challenges facing one another. Sometimes they will change jobs or double up to break a critical bottleneck; often the same person plays multiple roles. This overlapping of responsibilities results in a second blessing: a dissolving of the classic organizational barriers that are major impediments to the innovating process. Third, key decisions can be made immediately by the people who first recognize a problem, not later by top management or by someone who barely understands the issue. Fourth, the concentration of power in the leader/entrepreneurs makes it possible to deploy the firm's resources very rapidly. Last, the small firm has access to multiple funding channels, from the family dentist to a formal public offering. In contrast, the manager of an R&D project in a large firm has effectively only one source, the "corporate bank."

Small Divisions.   In order to recreate the entrepreneurial climate of the small firm, successful large high-technology firms often employ a variety of organizational devices and personnel policies. First, they divide and subdivide.

Hewlett-Packard, for example, is subdivided into fifty divisions: The company has a policy of splitting divisions soon after they exceed 1,000 employees. Texas Instruments is subdivided into more than thirty divisions and 250 "tactical action programs." Until recently, 3M's business was split into forty divisions. Although these divisions sometimes reach $100 million or more in sales, by Fortune 500 standards they are still relatively small companies.

Variety of Funding Channels.   Second, such high-tech firms employ a variety of funding channels to encourage risk taking. At Texas Instruments managers have three distinct options in funding a new R&D project. If their proposal is rejected by the centralized Strategic Planning (OST) System because it is not expected to yield acceptable economic gains, they can seek a "Wild Hare Grant." The Wild Hare program was instituted by Patrick Haggerty, while he was TI's chairman, to ensure that good ideas with long-term potential were not systematically turned down. Alternatively, if the project is outside the mainstream of the OST System, managers or engineers can contact one of dozens of individuals who hold "IDEA" grant purse strings and who can authorize up to $25,000 for prototype development. It was an IDEA grant that resulted in TI's highly successful "Speak and Spell" learning aid.

3M managers also have three choices: They can request funds from their own division, corporate R&D, or the new ventures division.[29] This willingness to allow a variety of funding channels has an important consequence: It encourages the pursuit of alternative technological approaches, particularly during the early stages of a technology's development, when no one can be sure of the best course to follow.

IBM, for instance, has found that rebellion can be good business. Arthur K. Watson, the founder's son and a longtime senior manager, once described the way the disk memory, a core element of modern computers, was developed:

[It was] not the logical outcome of a decision made by IBM management. [Because of budget difficulties] it was developed in one of our laboratories as a bootleg project. A handful of men . . . broke the rules. They risked their jobs to work on a project they believed in.[30]

At Northrop the head of aircraft design usually has at any one time several projects in progress without the awareness of top management. A lot can happen before the decision reaches even a couple of levels below the chairman. "We like it that way," explains Northrop Chairman Tom Jones.[31]

Tolerance of Failure.   Moreover, the successful high-technology firms tend to be very tolerant of technological failure. "At HP," Bob Hungate, general manager of the Medical Supplies Division, explains, "it's understood that when you try something new you will sometimes fail."[32] Similarly, at 3M, those who fail to turn their pet project into a commercial success almost always get another chance. Richard Frankel, the president of the Kevex Corporation, a $20 million instrument manufacturer, puts it this way, "You need to encourage people to make mistakes. You have to let them fly in spite of aerodynamic limitations."[33]

Opportunity to Pursue Outside Projects.   Finally, these firms provide ample time to pursue speculative projects. Typically, as much as 20 percent of a productive scientist's or engineer's time is "unprogrammed," during which he or she is free to pursue interests that may not lie in the mainstream of the firm. IBM Technical Fellows are given up to five years to work on projects of their own choosing, from high-speed memories to astronomy.

5. Sense of Integrity

While committed to individualism and entrepreneurship, at the same time successful high-tech firms tend to exhibit a commitment to long-term relationships. The firms view themselves as part of an enduring community that includes employees, stockholders, customers, suppliers, and local communities: Their objective is to maintain stable associations with all of these interest groups.

Although these firms have clearcut business objectives, such as growth, profits, and market share, they consider them subordinate to higher order ethical values. Honesty, fairness, and openness—that is, integrity—are not to be sacrificed for short-term gain. Such companies don't knowingly promise what they can't deliver to customers, stockholders, or employees. They don't misrepresent company plans and performance. They tend to be tough but forthright competitors. As Herb Dwight, president of Spectra-Physics, one of the world's leading laser manufacturers, says, "The managers that succeed here go *out of their way* to be ethical."[34] And Alexander d'Arbeloff, cofounder and president of Teradyne, states bluntly, "Integrity comes first. If you don't have that, nothing else matters."[35]

These policies may seem utopian, even puritanical, but in a high-tech firm they also make good business sense. Technological change can be dazzlingly rapid; therefore, uncertainty is high, risks are difficult to assess, and market opportunities and profits are hard to predict. It is almost impossible to get a complex product into production, for example, without solid trust between functions, between workers and managers, and between managers and stockholders (who must be willing to see the company through the possible dips in sales growth and earnings that often accompany major technological shifts). Without integrity the risks multiply and the probability of failure (in an already difficult enterprise) rises unacceptably. In such a context, Ray Stata, cofounder of the Massachusetts High Technology Council, states categorically, "You need an environment of mutual trust."[36]

This commitment to ethical values must start at the top, otherwise it is ineffective. Most of the CEOs we interviewed consider it to be a cardinal dimension of their role. As Bernie Gordon, president of Analogic, explains, "The things that make leaders are their philosophy, ethics, and psychology."[37] Nowhere is this dimension more important than in dealing with the company's employees. Paul Rizzo, IBM's vice-chairman, puts it this way, "At IBM we have a fundamental respect for the individual . . . people must be free to disagree and to be heard. Then, even if they lose, you can still marshall them behind you."[38]

Self-understanding.   This sense of integrity manifests itself in a second, not unrelated, way: self-understanding. The pride, almost arrogance, of these firms in their ability to compete in their chosen fields is tempered by a surprising acknowledgment of their limitations. One has only to read Hewlett-Packard's corporate objectives or interview one of its top managers to sense this extraordinary blend of strength and humility. Successful high-tech companies are able to reconcile their "dream" with what they can realistically achieve. This is one of the reasons why they are extremely reluctant to diversify into unknown territories.

6. "Hands-on" Top Management

Notwithstanding their deep sense of respect and trust for individuals, CEOs of successful high-technology firms are usually actively involved in the innovation process to such an extent that they are sometimes accused of meddling. Tom McAvoy, Corning's president, sifts through hundreds of project proposals each year trying to identify those that can have a "significant strategic impact on the company"—the potential to restructure the company's business. Not surprisingly, most of these projects deal with new technologies. For one or two of the most salient ones, he adopts the role of "field general," frequently visiting the line operations, receiving direct updates from those working on the project, and assuring himself that the required resources are being provided.[39]

The direct involvement of the top executive at Corning sounds more characteristic of vibrant entrepreneurial firms, such as Tandon, Activision, and Seagate, but Corning is far from unique. Similar patterns can be identified in many larger high-technology firms. Milt Greenberg, president of GCA, a $180 million semiconductor process-equipment manufacturer, stated: "Sometimes you just have to short-circuit the organization to achieve major change."[40] Tom Watson, Jr. (IBM's chairman), and Vince Learson (IBM's president) were doing just that when they met with programmers and designers and other executives in Watson's ski cabin in Vermont to finalize software design concepts for the System 360—at a point when IBM was already a $4 billion firm.[41]

Good high-tech managers not only understand how organizations, and in particular engineers, work, they understand the fundamentals of their technology and can interact directly with their people about it. This does not imply that it is necessary for the senior managers of such firms to be technologists (although they usually are, in the early stages of growth). Neither Watson nor Learson was a technologist. What appears to be more important is the ability to ask lots of questions, even "dumb" questions, and dogged patience in order to understand, in depth, such core questions as: (1) how the technology works; (2) its limits, as well as its potential (together with the limits and potential of competitors' technologies); (3) what these various technologies require in terms of technical and economic resources; (4) the direction and speed of change; and (5) the available technological options, their cost, probability of failure, and potential benefits if they prove successful.

This depth of understanding is difficult enough to achieve for one set of related technologies and markets; it is virtually impossible for one person to master many different sets. This is another reason why business focus appears to be so important in high-tech firms. It matters little if one or more perceptive scientists or technologists foresees the impact of new technologies on the firm's markets, if its top management doesn't internalize these risks and make the major changes in organization and resource allocation that are usually necessitated by a technological transition.

The Paradox of High-Technology Management

The six themes around which we arranged our findings can be organized into two apparently paradoxical groupings: Business focus, organizational cohesion, and a sense of integrity fall into one group; adaptability, entrepreneurial culture, and hands-on management fall into the other group. On the one hand, business focus, organizational cohesion, and integrity imply stability and conservatism. On the other hand, adaptability, entrepreneurial culture, and hands-on top management are synonymous with rapid, sometimes precipitous change. The fundamental tension is between order and disorder.

Half of the success factors pull in one direction; the other half tug the other way.

This paradox has frustrated many academicians who seek to identify rational processes and stable cause-effect relationships in high-tech firms and managers. Such relationships are not easily observable unless a certain constancy exists. But in most high-tech firms, the only constant is continual change. As one insightful student of the innovation process phrased it, "Advanced technology requires the collaboration of diverse professions and organizations, often with ambiguous or highly interdependent jurisdictions. In such situations, many of our highly touted rational management techniques break down."[42] One recent researcher, however, proposed a new model of the firm that attempts to rationalize the conflict between stability and change by splitting the strategic process into two loops, one that extends the past, the other that periodically attempts to break with it.[43]

Established organizations are, by their very nature, innovation resisting. By defining jobs and responsibilities and arranging them in serial reporting relationships, organizations encourage the performance of a restricted set of tasks in a programmed, predictable way. Not only do formal organizations resist innovation, they often act in ways that stamp it out. Overcoming such behavior—in much the way the human body mobilizes antibodies to overcome foreign cells—is, therefore, a core job of high-tech management.

The Paradoxical Challenge.   High-tech firms deal with this challenge in different ways. Texas Instruments, long renowned for the complex, interdependent matrix structure it used in managing dozens of product-customer centers (PCCs), recently consolidated groups of PCCs and made them into more autonomous units. "The manager of a PCC controls the resources and operations for his entire family . . . in the simplest terms, the PCC manager is to be an entrepreneur," explained Fred Bucy, TI's president.[44]

Meanwhile, a different trend is evident at 3M, where entrepreneurs have been given a free rein for decades. A recent major reorganization was designed to arrest snowballing diversity by concentrating the company's sprawling structure of autonomous divisions into four market groups. "We were becoming too fragmented," explained Vincent Ruane, vice-president of 3M's electronics division.[45]

Similarly, HP recently reorganized into five groups, each with its own strategic responsibilities. Although this simply changes some of its reporting relationships, it does give HP, for the first time, a means for integrating product and market development across generally autonomous units.[46]

These reorganizations do not mean that organizational integration is dead at Texas Instruments, or that 3M's and HP's entrepreneurial cultures are being dismantled. Rather, they signify first, that these firms recognize that both organizational integration and entrepreneurial cultures are important, and second, that periodic change is required for environmental adaptability. These three firms are demonstrating remarkable adaptability by reorganizing from a position of relative strength—not, as is far more common, in response to financial difficulties. As Lewis Lehr, 3M's president, explained, "We can change now because we're not in trouble."[47]

Such reversals are essentially antibureaucratic, in the same spirit as Mao's admonition to "let a hundred flowers blossom and a hundred schools of thought contend."[48] At IBM, in 1963, Tom Watson, Jr., temporarily abolished the corporate management committee in an attempt to push decisions downward and thus facilitate the changes necessary for IBM's great leap forward to the System 360.[49] Disorder, slack, and ambiguity are necessary for innovation, since they provide the porosity that facilitates entrepreneurial behavior, just as do geographically separated, relatively autonomous organizational subunits.

But the corporate management committee is alive and well at IBM today. As it should be. The process of innovation, once begun, is both self-perpetuating and potentially self-destructive: Although the top managers of high-tech firms must sometimes espouse organizational disorder, for the most part they must preserve order.

Winnowing Old Products.   Not all new product ideas can be pursued. As Charles Ames, former president of Reliance Electric, states, "An enthusiastic inventor is a menace to practical businessmen."[50] Older products, upon which the current success of the firm was built, at some point have to be abandoned. Just as the long-term success of the firm requires the planting and nurturing of new products, it also requires the conscious, even ruthless, pruning of other products, so that the resources they consume can be used elsewhere.

This attitude demands hard-nosed managers who are continually managing the functional and divisional interfaces of their firms. They cannot be swayed by nostalgia, or by the fear of disappointing the many committed people who are involved in the development and production of discontinued products. They must also overcome the natural resistance of their subordinates, and even their peers, who often have a vested interest in the products that brought them early personal success in the organization.

Yet firms also need a certain amount of continuity, because major change often emerges from the accretion of a number of smaller, less visible improvements. Studies of petroleum refining, rayon, and rail transportation, for example, show that half or more of the productivity gains ultimately achieved within these technologies were the result of the accumulation of minor improvements.[51] Indeed, most engineers, managers, technologists, and manufacturing and marketing specialists work on what Thomas Kuhn might have called "normal innovation,"[52] the little steps that improve or extend existing product lines and processes.

Managing Ambivalently. The successful high-technology firm, then, must be managed ambivalently. A steady commitment to order and organization will produce one-color Model T Fords. Continuous revolution will bar incremental productivity gains. Many companies have found that alternating periods of relaxation and control appear to meet this dual need. Surprisingly, such ambiguity does not necessarily lead to frustration and discontent.[53] In fact, interspersing periods of tension, action, and excitement with periods of reflection, evaluation, and revitalization is the same sort of irregular rhythm that characterizes many favorite pastimes—including sailing, which has been described as "long periods of total boredom punctuated with moments of stark terror."

Knowing when and where to change from one stance to the other, and having the power to make the shift, is the core of the art of high-technology management. James E. Webb, administrator of the National Aeronautics and Space Administration during the successful Apollo ("man on the moon") program, recalled that "we were required to fly our administrative machine in a turbulent environment, and . . . a certain level of *organizational instability was essential if NASA was not to lose control*" (authors' emphasis).[54]

In summary, the central dilemma of the high-technology firm is that it must succeed in managing two conflicting trends: continuity and rapid change. There are two ways to resolve this dilemma. One is an old idea: managing different parts of the firm differently—some business units for innovation, others for efficiency.

A second way—a way we believe is more powerful and pervasive—is to manage differently at different times in the evolutionary cycle of the firm. The successful high-technology firm *alternates* periods of consolidation and continuity with sharp reorientations that can lead to dramatic changes in the firm's strategies, structure, controls, and distribution of power, followed by a period of consolidation.[55] Thomas Jefferson knew this secret when he wrote 200 years ago, "A little revolution now and then is a good thing."

3

The Leadership Challenge—
A Call for the
Transformational Leader

Noel M. Tichy

David O. Ulrich

The authors suggest that a new brand of leadership—transformational leadership—is the key to revitalizing large U.S. corporations. Based on the premise that the pressure for basic organizational change will intensify, not diminish, over the years, they argue that transformational leaders must develop a new vision for the organization, mobilize employees to accept and work toward achieving the new vision, and institutionalize the needed changes. Unless the creation of this breed of leaders becomes a national agenda, the authors are not very optimistic about the revitalization of the U.S. economy. *SMR.*

Some optimists are heralding an age of higher productivity, a transition to a service economy, and a brighter competitive picture for U.S. corporations in world markets. We would like to believe that the future will be bright, but we feel that the years it took for most U.S. companies to get fat and flabby are not going to be reversed by a crash diet for one or two years. Our future as a world competitive economy will largely be determined by the quality of leadership in the top echelons of our business and government organizations. Thus, it is our belief that now is the time for organizations to change their corporate lifestyles.

To revitalize organizations such as General Motors, American Telephone and Telegraph, General Electric, Honeywell, Ford, Burroughs, Chase Manhattan Bank, Citibank, U.S. Steel, Union Carbide, Texas Instruments, and

From *Sloan Management Review,* Fall 1984, Vol. 26, No. 1. Reprinted with permission.

Control Data—just to mention a few companies currently undergoing major transformations—a new brand of leadership is necessary. Instead of managers who continue to move organizations along historical tracks, the new leaders must *transform* the organizations and head them down new tracks. What is required of this kind of leader is an ability to help the organization develop a vision of what it can be, to mobilize the organization to accept and work toward achieving the new vision, and to institutionalize the changes that must last over time. Unless the creation of this breed of leaders becomes a national agenda, we are not very optimistic about the revitalization of the U.S. economy.

We call these new leaders transformational leaders, for they must create something new out of something old: Out of an old vision, they must develop and communicate a new vision and get others not only to see the vision but also to commit themselves to it. Where transactional managers must make minor adjustments in the organization's mission, structure, and human-resource management, transformational leaders make major changes in these three areas and also effect fundamental changes in the basic political and cultural systems of the organization. The revamping of the political and cultural systems is what best distinguishes the transformational leader from the transactional one.

Lee Iacocca: A Transformational Leader

One of the most dramatic examples of transformational leadership and organizational revitalization in the early 1980s has been the leadership of Lee Iacocca, the chairman of Chrysler Corporation, who led the company from the brink of bankruptcy to profitability. He created a vision of success and mobilized large factions of key employees toward enacting that vision, while simultaneously downsizing the workforce by 60,000 employees. As a result of Iacocca's leadership, by 1984 Chrysler had earned record profits, had attained high levels of employee morale, and had helped employees generate a sense of meaning in their work.

Until Lee Iacocca took over at Chrysler, the basic internal political structure had been unchanged for decades. It was clear who reaped what benefits from the organization, how the pie was to be divided, and who could exercise what power. Nonetheless, Mr. Iacocca knew that he needed to alter these political traditions, starting with a new definition of Chrysler's link to external stakeholders. Therefore, the government was given a great deal of control over Chrysler in return for the guaranteed loan that staved off bankruptcy. Modification of the political system required other adjustments, including the trimming of fat in the management ranks, limiting financial rewards for all employees, and receiving major concessions for the UAW. An indicator of a significant political shift was the inclusion of Douglas Frazer on the Chrysler Board of Directors as part of UAW concessions.

Equally dramatic was the change in the organization's cultural system. First, the company had to recognize its unique status as a recipient of a federal bailout. This bailout came with a stigma; thus Iacocca's job was to change the company's cultural values from a loser's to a winner's feeling. Still, he realized that employees were not going to be winners unless they could, in cultural norms, be more efficient and innovative than their competitors. The molding and shaping of the new culture was clearly and visibly led by Mr. Iacocca, who not only used internal communication as a vehicle to signal change but also used his own personal appearance in Chrysler ads to reinforce these changes. Quickly, the internal culture was transformed to that of a lean and hungry team looking for victory. Whether Chrysler will be able to sustain this organizational phenomenon over time remains to be seen. If it does, it will provide a solid corporate example of what Burns referred to as a transforming leader.[1]

Lee Iacocca's high visibility may be the important missing element in management today.

Organizational Dynamics of Change

Assumption One: Trigger Events Indicate Change Is Needed

Organizations do not change unless there is a trigger that indicates change is needed. This trigger can be as extreme as the Chrysler impending bankruptcy or as moderate as an abstract future-oriented fear that an organization may lose its competitiveness. For example, General Electric's trigger for change is a view that by 1990 the company will not be world competitive unless major changes occur in productivity, innovation, and marketing. Thus, Chairman Jack Welch sees his role as that of transforming GE, even though it does not face imminent doom. Nonetheless, the trick for him is to *activate* the trigger; otherwise, complacency may prevail. Similarly, for AT&T, technological, competitive, and political forces have led it to undertake its massive transformation. For General Motors, economic factors of world competition, shifting consumer preferences, and technological change have driven it to change.

In a decade of increased information, international competition, and technological advances, triggers for change have become commonplace and very pressing. However, not all potential trigger events lead to organizational responses, and not all triggers lead to change. Nonetheless, the trigger must create a felt need in organizational leaders. Without this felt need, the "boiled frog phenomenon" is likely to occur.

The Boiled Frog.   This phenomenon is based on a classic experiment in biology. A frog that is placed in a pan of cold water but that still has the freedom to jump out can be boiled to death if the temperature change is gradual, for the frog is not aware of the barely detectable changing heat threshold. In contrast, a frog dropped into a pot of boiling water will immediately jump out: It has a felt need to survive. In a similar vein, many organizations that are insensitive to gradually changing organizational thresholds are likely to become "boiled frogs"; they act in ignorant bliss of environmental triggers and are doomed to eventual failure. This failure, in part, is a result of the organization having no felt need to change.

Assumption Two: A Change Unleashes Mixed Feelings

A felt need for change unleashes a mix of forces, both a positive impetus for change as well as a strong negative individual and organizational resistance. These forces of resistance are generated in each of three interrelated systems—technical, political, and cultural—that must be managed in the process of organizational transitions (see Table 3.1).[2] Individual and organizational resistance to change in these three systems must be overcome if an organization is to be revitalized.[3]

Managing technical systems refers to managing the coordination of technology, capital, information, and people in order to produce products or services desired and used in the external marketplace. Managing political systems refers to managing the allocation of organizational rewards, such as money, status, power, and career opportunities, and to exercising power so employees and departments perceive equity and justice. Managing cultural systems refers to managing the set of shared values and norms that guides the behavior of members of the organization.

When a needed change is perceived by the organizational leaders, the dominant group in the organization must experience a dissatisfaction with the status quo. For example, in the late 1970s John DeButts, chairman and chief executive officer of AT&T, was not satisfied with the long-term viability of AT&T as a regulated telephone monopoly in the age of computers and satellite communication systems. Likewise, when Roger Smith became CEO at General Motors in the early 1980s, he could hardly be satisfied with presiding over GM's first financial loss since the depression. In these two cases, the felt need provided the impetus for transition; yet, such impetus is not uniformly positive.

Table 3.1 Technical, Political, and Cultural System Resistances

Technical System Resistances include:

Habit and inertia. Habit and inertia cause task-related resistance to change. Individuals who have always done things one way may not be politically or culturally resistant to change, but may have trouble, for technical reasons, changing behavior patterns. Example: some office workers may have difficulty shifting from electric typewriters to word processors.

Fear of the unknown or loss of organizational predictability. Not knowing or having difficulty predicting the future creates anxiety and hence resistance in many individuals. Example: the introduction of automated office equipment has often been accompanied by such resistances.

Sunk costs. Organizations, even when realizing that there are potential payoffs from a change, are often unable to enact a change, because of the sunk costs of the organizations' resources in the old way of doing things.

Political System Resistances include:

Powerful coalitions. A common threat is the conflict between the old guard and the new guard. One interpretation of the exit of Archie McGill, former president of the newly formed AT&T American Bell, is that the backlash of the old-guard coalition exacted its price on the leader of the new-guard coalition.

Resource limitations. In the days when the economic pie was steadily expanding and resources were regarded as virtually unlimited, change was easier to enact, for every part could gain. Such was the nature of labor-management agreements in the auto industry for decades. Now that the pie is shrinking, decisions need to be made as to who shares the smaller set of resources. These zero-sum decisions are politically difficult. As more and more U.S. companies deal with productivity, downsizing, and divestiture, political resistance will be triggered.

Indictment quality of change. Perhaps the most significant resistance to change comes from leaders having to indict their own past decisions and behaviors to bring about a change. Example: Roger Smith, chairman and CEO of GM, must implicitly indict his own past behavior as a member of senior management when he suggests changes in GM's operations. Psychologically, it is very difficult for people to change when they were party to creating the problems they are trying to change. It is much easier for a leader from the outside, such as Lee Iacocca, who does not have to indict himself every time he points out what is wrong with the organization.

Cultural System Resistances include:

Selective perception (cultural filters). An organization's culture may highlight certain elements of the organization, making it difficult for members to conceive of other ways of doing things. An organization's culture channels that which people perceive as possible; thus, innovation may come from outsiders or deviants who are not so channeled in their perceptions.

Security based on the past. Transition requires people to give up the old ways of doing things. There is security in the past, and one of the problems is getting people to overcome the tendency to want to return to the "good old days." Example: today, there are still significant members of the white-collar workforce at GM who are waiting for the "good old days" to return.

Lack of climate for change. Organizations often vary in their conduciveness to change. Cultures that require a great deal of conformity often lack much receptivity to change. Example: GM with its years of internally developed managers must overcome a limited climate for change.

The technical, political, and cultural resistances are most evident during early stages of an organizational transformation. At GM the early 1980s were marked by tremendous uncertainty concerning many technical issues such as marketing strategy, production strategy, organization design, factory automation, and development of international management. Politically, many powerful coalitions were threatened. The UAW was forced to make wage concessions and accept staffing reductions. The white-collar workers saw their benefits being cut and witnessed major layoffs within the managerial ranks. Culturally, the once dominant managerial style no longer fit the environmental pressures for change: the "GM way" was no longer the right way.

One must be wary of these resistances to change as they can lead to organizational stagnation rather than revitalization. In fact, some managers at GM in late 1983 were waiting for the "good old days" to return. Such resistance exemplifies a dysfunctional reaction to the felt need. As indicated in Figure 3.1, a key to whether resistant forces will lead to little or inadequate change and hence organizational decline or revitalization lies in an organization's leadership. Defensive, transactional leadership will not rechannel the resistant forces. A case in point is International Harvester, which appears to have had a defensive transactional leadership that, in the early 1980s, lacked a new vision to inspire employees to engage in new behaviors. In contrast, Lee Iacocca has been a transformational leader at Chrysler by creating a vision, mobilizing employees, and working toward the institutionalization of Chrysler's transition.

Assumption Three: Quick-Fix Leadership Leads to Decline

Overcoming resistance to change requires transformational leadership, not defensive, transactional managers in search of the one-minute quick fix. The transformational leader needs to avoid the trap of simple, quick-fix solutions to major organizational problems. Today, many versions of this quick-fix mentality abound: The *One Minute Manager* has become a best-seller in companies in need of basic transformation.[4] Likewise, *In Search of Excellence* is a virtual cookbook for change.[5] In fact, a number of CEOs have taken the eight characteristics of the "excellent" companies and are trying to impose them on their organizations without first examining their appropriateness. Some faltering organizations have tried to copy such company practices as Hewlett-Packard's (HP) statement of company values. Because they read that HP has a clearly articulated statement of company values—the HP equivalent of the ten commandments—they want to create their own list of ten commandments. A scenario carried out in many major U.S. firms in the

Organization Dynamics:

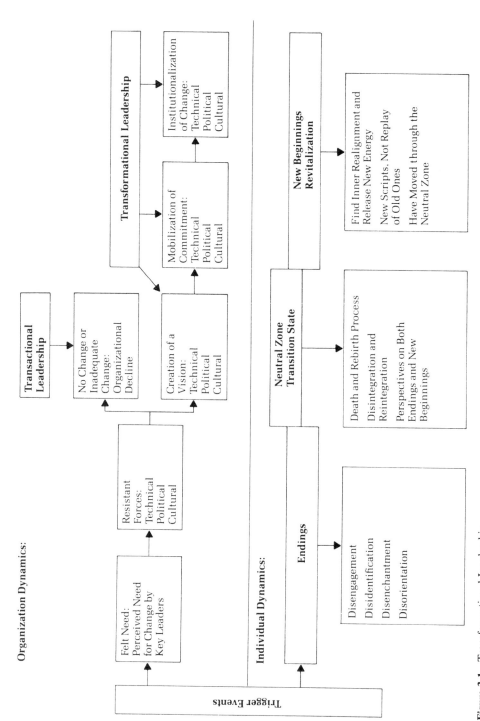

Figure 3.1 Transformational Leadership

64

past year goes something like this: The CEO wants to develop the company value statement, so he organizes an off-site meeting in order to spend a couple of days doing so. The session is usually quite enlightening: Managers become thoughtful, and soul-searching takes place. At the end of the session, the group is able to list the company's "ten commandments," and the CEO, delighted that the firm is now well on the way to a major cultural change, brings the ten commandments back to headquarters, where he calls in the staff to begin the communication program in which all company employees can learn the new cultural values. This about ends the transformational process.

The problem with the ten-commandments quick fix is that the CEOs tend to overlook the lesson Moses learned several thousand years ago: Getting the ten commandments written down and communicated is the easy part; getting them implemented is the challenge. Transformational leadership is different from defensive, transactional leadership. Lee Iacocca did not have to read about what others did to find a recipe for his company's success.

Assumption Four: Revitalization Requires Transformational Leadership

There are three identifiable programs of activity associated with transformational leadership.

1. Creation of a Vision. The transformational leader must provide the organization with a vision of a desired future state. While this task may be shared with other key members of the organization, the vision remains the core responsibility of the transformational leader. The leader needs to integrate analytic, creative, intuitive, and deductive thinking. Each leader must create a vision that gives direction to the organization while being congruent with the leader's and the organization's philosophy and style.

For example, in the early 1980s at GM, after several years of committee work and staff analysis, a vision of the future was drafted that included a mission statement and eight objectives for the company. This statement was the first articulation of a strategic vision for General Motors since Alfred Sloan's leadership. This new vision was developed consistently with the leadership philosophy and style of Roger Smith. Many people were involved in carefully assessing opportunities and constraints for General Motors. Meticulous staff work culminated in committee discussions to evoke agreement and commitment to the mission statement. Through this process a vision was created that paved the way for the next phases of the transformation at GM.

At Chrysler, Lee Iacocca developed a vision without committee work or heavy staff involvement. Instead, he relied more on his intuitive and directive leadership, philosophy, and style. Both GM and Chrysler ended up with a new vision, because transformational leaders proactively shaped a new organization mission and vision. The long-term challenge to organizational revitalization is not "how" the visions are created, but the extent to which the visions correctly respond to environmental pressures and transitions within the organization.

2. Mobilization of Commitment.   Here, the organization, or at least a critical mass of it, accepts the new mission and vision and makes it happen. At General Motors, Roger Smith took his top 900 executives on a five-day retreat to share and discuss the vision. The event lasted five days not because it takes that long to share a one-paragraph mission statement and eight objectives, but because the process of evolving commitment and mobilizing support requires a great deal of dialogue and exchange. It should be noted that mobilization of commitment must go well beyond five-day retreats; nevertheless, it is in this phase that transformational leaders get deeper understanding of their *followers*. Maccoby acknowledges that leaders who guide organizations through revitalization are distinct from previous leaders and gamesmen who spearheaded managers to be winners in the growth days of the 1960s and early 1970s. Today, Maccoby argues:

> The positive traits of the gamesman, enthusiasm, risk taking, meritocratic fairness, fit America in a period of unlimited economic growth, hunger for novelty, and an unquestioned career ethic. The negative traits for manipulation, seduction, and the perpetual adolescent need for adventure were always problems, causing distrust and unnecessary crises. The gamesman's daring, the willingness to innovate and take risks are still needed. Companies that rely on conservative company men in finance to run technically based organizations (for example, auto and steel) lose the competitive edge. But unless their negative traits are transformed or controlled, even gifted gamesmen become liabilities as leaders in a new economic reality. A period of limited resources and cutbacks, when the team can no longer be controlled by the promise of more, and one person's gains may be another's loss, leadership with values of caring and integrity and a vision of self-development must create the trust that no one will be penalized for cooperation and that sacrifice as well as rewards are equitable.[6]

After transformational leaders create a vision and mobilize commitment, they must determine how to institutionalize the new mission and vision.

3. Institutionalization of Change.   Organizations will not be revitalized unless new patterns of behavior within the organization are adopted. Transformational leaders need to transmit their vision into reality, their mission into action, their philosophy into practice. New realities, action, and practices must be shared throughout the organization. Alterations in communication, decision making, and problem-solving systems are tools through which transitions are shared so that visions become a reality. At a deeper level, institutionalization of change requires shaping and reinforcement of a new culture that fits with the revitalized organization. The human-resource systems of selection, development, appraisal, and reward are major levers for institutionalizing change.

Individual Dynamics of Change

The previous section outlined requisite processes for organizational revitalization. Although organizational steps are necessary, they are not sufficient in creating and implementing change. In managing transitions, a more problematic set of forces that focuses on individual psychodynamics of change must be understood and managed. Major transitions unleash powerful conflicting forces in people. The change invokes simultaneous positive and negative personal feelings of fear and hope, anxiety and relief, pressure and stimulation, leaving the old and accepting a new direction, loss of meaning and new meaning, threat to self-esteem and new sense of value. The challenge for transformational leaders is to recognize these mixed emotions, act to help people move from negative to positive emotions, and mobilize and focus energy that is necessary for individual renewal and organizational revitalization.

Figure 3.1 provides a set of concepts for understanding the individual dynamics of transitions. The concepts, drawn from the work by Bridges, propose a three-phase process of individual change: first come endings, followed by neutral zones, and then new beginnings.[7] During each of these phases, an identifiable set of psychological tasks can be identified that individuals need to complete successfully in order to accept change.

The Three-Phase Process

Endings.   All individual transitions start with endings. Endings must be accepted and understood before transitions can begin. Employees who refuse to accept the fact that traditional behaviors have ended will be unable to adopt new behaviors. The first task is to disengage, which often accompanies a physical transaction. For example, when transferring from one job to another, individuals must learn to accept the new physical setting and disengage from the old position: when transferred employees continually return to visit former colleagues, this is a sign that they have inadequately disengaged. The second task is to disidentify. Individual self-identity is often tied to a job position in such a way that when a plant manager is transferred to corporate staff to work in the marketing department, he or she must disidentify with the plant and its people and with the self-esteem felt as a plant manager. At a deeper personal level, individual transactions require disenchantment. Disenchantment entails recognizing that the enchantment or positive feelings associated with past situations will not be possible to replicate in the future. Chrysler, GM, AT&T, and U.S. Steel employees who remember the "good old days" need to become disenchanted with those feelings: The present reality is different and self-worth cannot be recaptured by longing for or thinking about the past. A new enchantment centered on new circumstances needs to be built. Finally, individuals need to experience and work through the disorientation that results from the loss of familiar trappings. As mature organizations become revitalized, individuals must disengage, disidentify, disenchant, and disorient with past practices and discover in the new organizations a new sense of worth or value.

To help individuals cope with endings, transformational leaders need to replace past glories with future opportunities. However, leaders must also acknowledge individual resistances and senses of loss in a transitional period, while encouraging employees to face and accept failures as learning opportunities. Holding on to past accomplishments and memories without coming to grips with failure and the need to change may be why companies such as W.T. Grant, International Harvester, and Braniff were unsuccessful at revitalization. There is a sense of dying in all endings, and it does not help to treat transactions as if the past can be buried without effort. Yet, one should see the past as providing new directions.

Neutral Zone.   The key to individuals being able to change fully may be in the second phase, which Bridges terms the neutral zone.[8] The neutral zone is seemingly an unproductive "time out," when individuals feel disconnected from people and things of the past and emotionally unconnected with the present. In reality, it is a time of reorientation, when individuals complete endings and begin new patterns of behavior. Often Western culture, especially in the U.S., avoids this experience and treats the neutral zone like a busy street, to be crossed as fast as possible—certainly not a place to contemplate and experience. However, dashing across the neutral zone does not allow a proper ending to occur, nor the new beginning to start properly. A death and rebirth process is necessary, so that organizational members can work through the disintegration and reintegration. To pass through the neutral zone requires taking the time and thought to gain perspective on both the ending—what went wrong, why it needs to be changed, and what must be overcome in both attitude and behavioral change—and the new beginning—what the new priorities are, why they are needed, and what new attitudes and behaviors will be required. It is in this phase that the most skillful transformational leadership is called upon.

A timid bureaucratic leader who often reels in the good old days will not provide the needed support to help individuals cross the neutral zone. On the other hand, the militaristic dictatorial leader who tries to force a "new beginning" and does not allow people to work through their own feelings and emotions may also fail to bring about change. The purported backlash toward the "brash" Archie McGill at American Bell in June 1983 may have been an example of trying to force people through the neutral zone in order to get to a new beginning. Archie McGill was known to rant and rave about the stodgy, old fashioned, and noninnovative "bell-shaped men" at AT&T. This was his way of trying to help and lead individuals to become innovative and marketing oriented, but it was not a way that allowed them to accept the endings inherent in the transition. Although his enthusiasm may have been well placed, he may have lacked the sensitivity to individual endings and neutral phases of transactions.

Failure to lead individuals through the neutral zone may result in aborted new beginnings. In 1983, International Harvester appeared to be stuck in the neutral zone. In order for International Harvester to make a new beginning, it had to enable its employees to find a new identification with the future organization while accepting the end of the old organization. Such a transformation has successfully occurred at Chrysler Corporation, where morale and esprit de corps grew with the new vision implanted by Lee Iacocca. In the end, organizational revitalization can occur only if individuals accept past failures and engage in new behaviors and attitudes.

New Beginnings.   After individuals accept endings by working through neutral zones, they are able to work with new enthusiasm and commitment. New beginnings are characterized by employees learning from the past rather than reveling in it, looking for new scripts rather than acting out old ones, and being positive and excited about current and future work opportunities rather than dwelling on past successes or failures. When Iacocca implemented his vision at Chrysler, many long-term employees discovered new beginnings. They saw the new Chrysler as an opportunity to succeed, and they worked with a renewed vigor.

What Qualities Do Transformational Leaders Possess?

What does it take to transform an organization's technical, political, and cultural systems? The transformational leader must possess a deep understanding, whether it be intuitive or learned, of organizations and their place both in society at large and in the lives of individuals. The ability to build a new institution requires the kind of political dialogue our founding fathers had when Jefferson, Hamilton, Adams, and others debated issues of justice, equity, separation of powers, checks and balances, and freedom. This language may sound foreign to corporate settings, but when major organization revitalization is being undertaken, all of these concepts merit some level of examination. At Chrysler, issues of equity, justice, power, and freedom underlay many of Iacocca's decisions. Thus, as a start, transformational leaders need to understand concepts of equity, power, freedom, and the dynamics of decision making. In addition to modifying systems, transformational leaders must understand and realign cultural systems.

They must also make difficult decisions quickly. Leaders need to know when to push and when to back off. Finally, transformational leaders are often seen as creators of their own luck. These leaders seize opportunities and know when to act. Casual observers may perceive luck as a plausible explanation for their success, but in reality it is a transformational leader who knows when to jump and when not to jump. Again, Lee Iacocca can be viewed either as a very lucky person or as the possessor of a great ability to judge when to act and when not to act.

The Significance of Corporate Cultures

Much has been written about organizational cultures in recent years.[9] We suggest that every organization has a culture, or a patterned set of activities that reflects its underlying values. Cultures don't occur randomly. They occur because leaders spend time on and reward some behaviors and practices more than others. These practices become the foundation of the organization's culture. At HP, for example, Bill Hewlett and Dave Packard spent time wandering around, informally meeting with and talking to employees. Such leadership behavior set the HP cultural tone of caring about and listening to people. Similarly, Tom Watson, Sr., at IBM spent a great deal of time with customers. His practice led to a company culture of commitment to customers. Indeed, corporate cultures exist. Leaders can shape cultures by carefully monitoring where and how they spend their time and by encouraging and rewarding employees to behave in certain ways.

Culture plays two central roles in organizations. First, it provides organizational members with a way of understanding and making sense of events and symbols. Thus, when employees are confronted with certain complex problems, they "know" how to approach them the "right" way. Like the

Eskimos who have a vocabulary that differentiates among five types of snow, organizations create vocabularies to describe how things are done in the organization. At IBM, it is very clear to all insiders how to form a task force and to solve problems, since task forces and problem solving are a way of life in IBM's culture.

Second, culture provides meaning. It embodies a set of values that helps justify why certain behaviors are encouraged at the exclusion of other behaviors. Companies with strong cultures have been able to commit people to the organization and have them identify very personally and closely with the organization's success. Superficially, this is seen in the "hoopla" activities associated with an IBM sales meeting, a Tupperware party, or an Amway distributor meeting. Outsiders often ridicule such activities, yet they are part of the process by which some successful companies manage cultural meaning. On one level, corporate culture is analogous to rituals carried out in religious groups. The key point in assessing culture is to realize that, in order to transform an organization, the culture that provides meaning must be assessed and revamped. The transformational leader needs to articulate new values and norms and then to use multiple change levers, ranging from role modeling, symbolic acts, creation of rituals, and revamping of human-resource systems and management processes, to support new cultural messages.

Conclusion

Based on the premise that the pressure for basic organizational change will intensify and not diminish, we strongly believe that transformational leadership, not transactional management, is required for revitalizing our organizations. Ultimately, it is up to our leaders to choose the right kind of leadership and corporate lifestyle.

4

Does Japanese Management Style Have a Message for American Managers?

Edgar H. Schein

Many managers and observers, concerned about U.S. market share and productivity and impressed with Japanese success in these areas, have developed a sudden preoccupation with Japanese management methods. In this article, the author addresses the fundamental issue of what American managers can really learn from the Japanese through an analysis of two current best-sellers on Japanese management. He finds that the books fail to answer the critical question: Can management methods embedded in one culture be effectively transferred to another? As he explains, so little is understood about culture and its relationship to management methods that it is risky to assume that a method that works well in Japan will also work well here. *SMR.*

One of the greatest strengths of U.S. society is our flexibility, our ability to learn. When we see a problem, we tinker with it until we have it solved, and we seem to be willing to try anything and everything. One of our greatest weaknesses, on the other hand, is our impatience and short-run orientation. This leads to fads, a preoccupation with instant solutions, a blind faith that if we put in enough effort and money anything is possible, and an inability or unwillingness to see the long-range consequences of some of the quick fixes we try. Complicated solutions that require long-range planning, resolute implementation, and patience in the face of short-run difficulties are harder for us to implement.[1]

The tension between flexibility and faddism can be seen clearly in the current preoccupation with Japanese management. Two recent books, Ou-

From *Sloan Management Review*, Fall 1981, Vol. 23, No. 1. Reprinted with permission.

chi's *Theory Z* and Pascale and Athos's *The Art of Japanese Management,* are currently on the New York Times best-seller list.[1a] Why this sudden interest, and what are the implications of it for management theory? I would like to examine some of the theses of these two books and put these theses into a historical perspective. From this perspective I will draw some tentative conclusions about cultural themes in the U.S. and the implications for U.S. management.

Some Historical Perspective: Indoctrination

In 1961 I published an article called "Management Development as a Process of Influence" attempting to show that many of the socialization methods used by some of our largest corporations (such as IBM and General Electric) were essentially similar to processes of indoctrination that one could observe in many other settings.[2] Such socialization methods were under strong attack by W.H. Whyte (in *The Organization Man*) and others who saw in them a tendency to create "men in grey flannel suits" who would cease to think for themselves and just parrot the corporate line, thus reducing the innovative and creative capacity of the organization and the individuality of the employee.[3] Ironically, the companies that had built such indoctrination centers (such as IBM at Sands Point, N.Y., and General Electric at Crotonville, N.Y.) were very proud of the spirit and common way of thinking that they could induce in their employees and managers. Such spirit was viewed as one of the key sources of strength of these enterprises.

But the pendulum swung hard during the 1960s, and it became the fashion to move away from producing conformity toward stimulating self-actualization.[4] "Indoctrination" either moved underground, was relabeled, or was replaced by "development" programs that emphasized opportunities for the integration of individual goals with organizational goals. Models of development shifted from the engineering model of "molding or shaping people to fit the organization" to more agricultural models of permitting people to flourish according to their innate potential; the obligation of the organization was to provide sunshine, nutrients, water, and other environmental supports. (Little was said in this model about pruning, transplanting, and uprooting, by the way.) The IBM songbook was put away, and managers who used to be proud of their ability to motivate people by inspiring them through common rituals and activities were made to feel ashamed of using "manipulative" tactics.

In the 1970s we discovered the concept of "organizational culture" and have begun to rethink the issue once again.[5] Even if a company does not deliberately and consciously indoctrinate its new employees, its important

beliefs, values, and ways of doing things will, in any case, powerfully social-
ize anyone who remains in the organization and wishes to move upward and
inward in it.[6] Such socialization processes and their effects in producing
either conformity or innovation have been described and analyzed, and the
tactics which stimulate innovation have received special attention.[7]

Now, with the "discovery" that some Japanese companies are effective
because of their ability to involve and motivate people, and the assertion
that such involvement results from socialization tactics that induce a high
degree of loyalty and conformity, we may be headed back toward the ideology of indoctrination so forcefully put aside a mere twenty years ago.

Human Relations and Participation

A similar pendulum swing can be identified with respect to two other
human-relations values: whether or not one should treat people holistically,
and whether or not one should make decisions from the bottom up by
participation and consensus mechanisms. Many Americans have grown up
with a tradition of bureaucracy, of strong bosses, of hiring people as
"hands" to provide certain activities in return for certain pay and benefits.
But most students of industrial-relations systems note that there has been a
historical trend in such systems from a period of autocracy through a period
of paternalism toward the present more consultative and participative models.[8] In the paternalistic phase American companies have treated employees
very holistically: building company towns; funding company sports activities;
providing country clubs, counseling services, day-care centers, medical facilities, uniforms, and so on. Indeed, one of Ralph Nader's most powerful films
deals with the town of Kannapolis, N.C., where the Cannon Mills Co. not
only provides lifetime employment but owns all of the housing, uses its own
security force as the town police force, and provides all the services needed
by the town. What alarmed Nader was the possibility that the citizens of this
town were not developing any skills in self-government, which would leave
them very vulnerable if the company should move or cease to be so totally
paternalistic.

We may also recall that one of the major results of the now historic
studies of the Hawthorne plant of the Western Electric Company was the
recognition that employees were whole people who brought their personal
problems with them to their place of work. In the 1930s the company
launched a counseling program that involved company-employed counselors
to help employees deal with any personal problems on a totally confidential
basis.[9] Though it has been a tradition in our military services that officers
not fraternize with the men (presumably because it might be difficult to be

objective when individuals must be sent into dangerous situations), there is no such tradition in industry generally. Office parties, company picnics, and other forms of fraternization have been considered legitimate and desirable in many organizations and by many managers, though they are clearly not so institutionalized in the U.S. as they are in Latin America and Japan.

The human-relations training programs for foremen that were rampant in the 1940s were clearly aimed at teaching managers to treat their employees as whole people, to consider their needs, to fight for them when necessary, and to build strong loyalty and team spirit. The leadership and sensitivity training that flourished in the 1960s was similarly aimed at truly understanding the needs and talents of subordinates, peers, and bosses, so that appropriate levels of participation could be used in solving increasingly complex problems in organizations.[10] The writings of McGregor on Theory Y showed the importance of trust and faith in people; the writings of Argyris showed the necessity of permitting people in organizations to function as adults instead of reducing them to dependent children.[11] Likert argued cogently for System 4, a more participative form of organization in which consensus management plays a big role; and Maslow first introduced the idea of Theory Z, a self-actualizing organization.[12]

Many managers saw the point immediately, and either felt reinforced for what they were already doing or began to retrain themselves and their organization toward some of the new values and technologies of participative decision making. But as a total ideology this approach clearly has not taken hold. Many organizations discovered:

- That high morale did not necessarily correlate with high productivity.
- That autocratic systems could outproduce democratic systems (at least in the short run).
- That high productivity even when achieved by autocratic methods could build high morale.
- That the costs in terms of time and effort which participation entailed were often not affordable in certain kinds of environments.

Human Relations Japanese Style

Now the pendulum appears to be swinging once again on the issue of paternalism, managing the whole worker, and creating worker involvement through participation. We are told that the Japanese are extremely paternalistic and holistic in their approach to employees, that they tend to employ people for life, and that supervisors take care of the personal as well as the work needs of subordinates (sometimes even helping an employee find a wife). The Japanese use bottom-up consensual decision making and encourage high levels of trust across hierarchical and functional boundaries.

Theory Z

Ouchi has for some time been arguing that the essential differences between American (Theory A) and Japanese (Theory J) management systems lie in some key *structural* issues and *cultural* values that make it possible for certain kinds of management styles to flourish. Specifically, he points out that major Japanese companies:

- Employ their key people for "life" (i.e., until forced retirement at the age of fifty-five to sixty).
- Rotate them through various functions.
- Promote them very slowly and according to more of a seniority than a merit system.
- Place responsibility on groups rather than on individuals (a value of the Japanese culture).

These determinants make it possible for Japanese companies:

- To treat their employees as total people.
- To build the kind of trust that facilitates bottom-up consensual decision making.
- To control employees in a subtle, indirect manner.

In contrast, Ouchi points out, the bureaucratic model often associated with pure American management methods emphasizes:

- Employment contracts that last only as long as the individual is contributing.
- Specialization of function with rotation reserved only for people on a managerial track.
- Little concern for the total person.
- Rapid feedback and promotion.
- Explicit formal control systems.
- Individual responsibility (a strong cultural value in the U.S.).
- Individual top-down decision making.

The crucial insight Ouchi provides is to identify another model, which he calls Theory Z, that is found in many American companies, that fits into our culture, and that combines certain features of the A and J models. Such companies have:

- Lifetime employment.
- Slower rates of promotion.
- Somewhat more implicit, less formal control systems.
- More concern for the total person.
- More cross-functional rotation and emphasis on becoming a generalist.
- Some level of participation and consensual decision making.
- A continued emphasis on individual responsibility as a core value.

Though he does not give much evidence in his book, Ouchi has shown in other papers that a U.S. company that approximates the Theory Z criteria generated higher morale, higher loyalty, and generally more healthy, positive feelings at all levels of the hierarchy than did a comparable Theory A company. What is missing, however, is convincing evidence that those companies fitting the Theory Z model are more *effective* than comparable companies operating more on the Theory A bureaucratic model. Furthermore, Ouchi acknowledges that the Theory Z companies he has studied generate less professionalism, have a harder time integrating mavericks into their ranks because they generate strong conformity pressures (leading them to be sexist and racist), and may only be adaptive for certain kinds of technological or economic environments. In fact, the only way a Theory Z company can manage the instabilities inherent in running a successful business in a turbulent environment is to limit lifetime employment to a small cadre of key people and to keep a large percentage of the labor force in a temporary role, policies that resemble more closely the bureaucratic A model. In order to survive, it may be necessary for Theory Z companies to subcontract much of their work or to rely on a set of satellite companies to absorb the instabilities. (The latter is the typical Japanese pattern.)

Implications of Theory Z

After describing how this notion of an industrial "clan" can facilitate certain kinds of long-range involvement on the part of employees, Ouchi argues strongly that U.S. companies should think seriously about becoming more like clans, and lays out a program of how they might do it. Neither the argument that a company should be more like Z, nor the proposed steps for how to get there, are at all convincing, however. The theoretical sophistication displayed in the analysis of types of organizational control is followed by naive and superficial prescriptions about how one might think about a change program designed to help a company to become more like a clan (if, indeed, this is even possible). In effect, the manager is invited to be more open and trusting and to involve his or her people more. Little attention is given to the issue of why a given organization would be less trusting and participative in the first place, or to the problem of transferring managerial values from a culture in which they fit very well to one in which the fit is not at all clear.

But Ouchi makes a strong sales pitch, and it is here that our tendency to embrace the quick fix may get us into trouble. If someone tells us that Theory Z is closer to the Japanese model, and that the Japanese are getting a lot of mileage out of their model, do we all get on the bandwagon and give our employees tenure, push decision making down the hierarchy, and slow down promotions? Do we turn everyone into a generalist, throw out formal control systems, and treat each person as a total human being? If we do, will our productivity shoot right back up, so that we can regain our once dominant economic position? Sounds too simplistic, does it not? Unfortunately, that is just what it is, because it takes into account neither the uniqueness of Japanese culture, the uniqueness of U.S. culture, nor the technological and environmental conditions that ultimately will dictate whether an A, a Z, or some other form will be the most effective in a given situation. What the Ouchi book leaves out, unfortunately, are criteria to help a manager decide whether or not a Z, an A, or some other form is appropriate.

On the positive side, the analysis focuses on the importance of the human factor, and Ouchi's seven criterion categories are certainly important in assessing the options for managing people. The identification of the clan mechanism as a way of organizing and controlling people brings us back to what many companies know intuitively—"we are one big family in this organization"—and legitimizes the kind of indoctrination that used to be more common. We can see more clearly that between autocracy and democracy there lies a full range of choices, and that a high degree of paternalism is not necessarily incompatible with bottom-up, consensual, participative decision making. The manager can also see that the way people feel about an organization can be explicitly managed even if the relationship to long-range effectiveness is not completely clear. As Etzioni noted long ago, a person can be involved in an organization in a variety of ways, ranging from the "alienated prisoner" or calculative employee to the participating member who is fully and morally involved.[13] Two serious questions to consider are whether U.S. economic organizations can claim moral involvement (as some Japanese firms apparently do) and whether such levels of involvement are even desirable in our culture.

The Ouchi analysis closes with a useful reminder that what ties the Japanese company together is a *company philosophy,* dominant values that serve as criteria for decisions. What permits bottom-up consensual decision making to occur is the wide sharing of a common philosophy that guarantees a similarity of outlook with respect to the basic goals of the organization. Ouchi provides some case examples and displays a method by which a company can determine its own philosophy.

Integrating the Seven S's

Pascale and Athos make their argument at a different level of analysis, though they also stress the importance of managing *people* as key resources and the importance of superordinate goals, sense of spirit, or company philosophy. Ouchi is more the social scientist, presenting a theoretically grounded sociological argument for a structural approach to human resource management. Pascale and Athos are less theoretical and more didactic. They are the teachers/consultants, distilling some of the wisdom from the analysis of the Japanese experience, and they try to transmit that wisdom through a more down-to-earth writing style. The managerial reader will learn more from this book, while the social scientist will learn more from the Ouchi book.

As already indicated, Ouchi has seven basic criteria for distinguishing A from J. Pascale and Athos (with due apologies for the gimmicky quality of the scheme) draw on a formulation developed by the McKinsey Co. that includes the following seven basic variables:

1. Superordinate goals.
2. Strategy.
3. Structure.
4. Systems.
5. Staff (the concern for having the right sort of people to do the work).
6. Skills (training and developing people to do what is needed).
7. Style (the manner in which management handles subordinates, peers, and superiors).

Within this structure, Pascale and Athos identify what they term the "soft S's" and the "hard S's," and explain that the superordinate goals are critical in tying everything together. They argue that Japanese companies are effective because of their attention to such integration and their concern for those variables which have to do with the human factor, the soft S's. These are the factors American managers allegedly pay too little attention to: staff, skills, and, most important, style. The hard S's are strategy, structure, and systems.

Through a detailed comparison of the Matsushita Corp. and ITT under Geneen, the authors bring out the essential contrast between Japanese attention to the soft S's and Geneen's more "American" preoccupation with very tight controls, autocratic decision making, and concern for the bottom line. Yet the Geneen story also illustrates that a system that is as internally consistent as ITT's was can be very effective. Its weakness lay in its inability to survive without the personal genius of a Geneen to run it.

The Japanese Style

Following this dramatic contrast, Pascale and Athos analyze the Japanese management style and explain how a culture that values "face" and is collective in its orientation can breed managerial behavior that makes the most of ambiguity, indirection, subtle cues, trust, interdependence, uncertainty, implicit messages, and management of process (instead of attempting to develop complete openness, explicitness, and directness in order to minimize ambiguity and uncertainty). "Explicit communication is a cultural assumption; it is not a linguistic imperative," they remind us.[14]

The lesson for American managers is diametrically opposite in the two books. Ouchi's proposal for how to get to Theory Z is to be more open; Pascale and Athos imply (from their positive case examples of U.S. managers who use indirection, implicit messages, and nondecision as strategies) that we might do well to learn more of the arts of how to be less open. Though we in the U.S. often imply that to worry about "face" is a weakness and that it is better to "put all the cards on the table," in fact, there is ample evidence that Americans no less than Japanese respond better to helpful face-saving hints than to sledgehammers. "When feedback is really clear and bad, it's usually too late."[15] "The inherent preferences of organizations are clarity, certainty, and perfection. The inherent nature of human relationships involves ambiguity, uncertainty, and imperfection. How one honors, balances, and integrates the needs of both is the real trick of management."[16]

The analysis of face-to-face communication, drawn from an article by Pascale called "Zen and the Art of Management," is full of valuable insights on the subtleties of how and why indirection, tact, and concern for face are not merely niceties but necessities in human relations. It is crucial to recognize, of course, the distinction between *task* relevant information (about which one should be as open as possible in a problem-solving situation) and *interpersonal* evaluative information (about which it may be impossible to be completely open without running the risk of permanently damaging relationships).[17] Sensitivity training in which people attempted to tell each other what they thought of each other only worked in so-called stranger groups, where people did not know each other before and knew that they would not have to work or live with each other after the program.[18]

Interdependence

Pascale and Athos supplement their analysis of face-to-face relations with an excellent analysis of groups and the dilemmas of interdependence. Noting that the American tradition is one of independence and that the Japanese tradition (based on their limited space and the technology of rice farming) is one of interdependence, they show how groups and meetings can work in this context by members being more restrained, self-effacing, and trusting. As Ouchi points out, getting credit in the *long-run,* instead of worrying (as Americans often do) about being recognized immediately for any and all accomplishments, is made possible by the knowledge of lifetime employment, i.e., if people have to work with each other for a long time, true contribution will ultimately be recognized. Both books indicate that such group relationships combined with lack of specialization of careers give the Japanese company the ability to integrate better across key functional interfaces, because everyone has more empathy and understanding for other functions.

Superior-Subordinate Relationships

Long-term relationships and a culture in which everyone knows his or her place in the status hierarchy lead to a different concept of superior-subordinate relationships in Japan. The boss is automatically more of a mentor, teaching through subtle cues, rather than blunt feedback, exercising great patience while the subordinate learns how to interpret cues and to develop his or her own skills, and reinforcing the basic company philosophy as a conceptual source that helps subordinates to decide what to do in any given situation. This point is critical, because it highlights one of the most important functions of superordinate goals or organizational philosophy. If everyone understands what the organization is trying to do and what its values are for how to do things, then every employee who truly understands the philosophy can figure out what his or her course of action should be in an ambiguous situation. No directives or explicit control systems are needed because the controls are internalized.

Individualism and Authority

Pascale and Athos take the issues of power and authority into the cultural realm in a more subtle fashion than does Ouchi, who merely lables J companies as having collective responsibility and A and Z companies as having individual responsibility. But we must ask what individual or collective responsibility means in each culture. Can we assume that the American model of individual rights, independence, equal opportunity under the law, and related values and norms is in any sense the opposite of or even on the same dimension with the Japanese notion of group responsibility? Is the issue simply that the group would be sacrificed for the individual in the U.S., whereas the individual would be sacrificed for the group in Japan?

A more appropriate formulation is to assume that in every culture and in every individual there is a core conflict about how self-seeking or self-effacing to be for the sake of one's group or organization. At the extremes where either nationalism or anarchy is involved, the conflict is easier to reduce, but in a pluralistic society it is a genuine dilemma. (This is exemplified in U.S. sports organizations, which try to create a team while maximizing the individual talents of the players.) In a recent analysis of individualism, Waterman has indicated that in political and social science writings there have always been two versions of individualism: one focuses on selfishness and takes advantage of the group, and one focuses on self-actualization in the interest of maximizing for both the individual and the group the talents latent in the members.[19] Those writers who argue for a humanistic solution to organizational problems are espousing the second definition, which assumes that integration is possible.

In my experience the effective organization is neither individualistic nor collective; rather, it attempts to create norms and procedures that extol stardom and teamwork equally. The manager's job (just like the good coach's) is to find a way to weld the two forces together. The Japanese solution to this dilemma appears to be aided immensely by the fact that basic traditions and cultural values strongly favor hierarchy and the subordination of the individual to those above. However, this solution has potentially negative consequences, because it reduces the creative talent available to the organization. One might suspect, however, that the effective organization in Japan finds ways of dealing with this dilemma, and that the highly talented individual is not as pressured to conform as the less talented individual.[20]

The Japanese company in the Ouchi model could be expected to be more innovative on those tasks requiring group solutions, while the American company could be expected to be more innovative on those tasks that require a high level of individual expertise and creativity. Company effectiveness would then depend on the nature of the tasks facing it, its ability to diagnose accurately what those tasks are, and its flexibility in transforming itself—what I have termed an "adaptive coping cycle."[21] Whatever its human virtues and in spite of its ability to integrate better, a Theory Z organization might have *more* trouble both in seeing changes in its environment and in making the necessary transformations to adapt to those changes. Because of its strong commitment to a given philosophy and the pressure for everyone to conform, it is more likely to produce rigid paradigms for dealing with problems.

Implications for U.S. Management

Both books call for a reexamination of U.S. paradigms of how to organize and how to manage. While one can only applaud this challenge and use the models the books present to gain perspective for such reexamination, one must be concerned about the glibness of the lessons, recommendations, and advice, given the meager data base on which they are based. Neither book makes much of an effort to decipher what may be happening in our own culture and society that would explain our tendency toward Theory A (if, indeed, it can be shown that such a tendency exists). Why do we have difficulty with some of the solutions the Japanese apparently find natural and easy? And, most important, what are the strengths in the U.S. system that should be preserved and built upon?

For example, Ouchi is quick to point out the negative consequences of the American tendency to try to quantify everything. Most of us would agree that for managing the human system of the organization, quantification may be more of a trap than a help, but one might also argue that our desire to quantify reflects some of the best traditions of Western science and rationalism. The trick is to learn what to quantify and to know why quantification is helpful. In designing quality-control programs or in setting sales targets, it may be crucial to state a goal in quantifiable form in order to measure progress toward the goal. On the other hand, attempting to quantify managerial traits as part of a performance-appraisal system may distort communication and reduce the effectiveness of the whole system, because people would begin to feel like "mere numbers." The effective manager in any cultural system would be the one who knows what to quantify.

Many of the formal control systems that have become associated with the concept of bureaucracy (and that are seen by Ouchi, Pascale, and Athos as dysfunctional relative to the more indirect controls associated with the Japanese style) imply that all organizations face similar control problems. One suspects, however, that controlling the design and building of a large aerospace system might require more formal control mechanisms than the control of an R&D organization in a high-technology industry. Ouchi's comparison of formal bureaucratic with informal clan mechanisms misses the point that Galbraith made so effectively: As any organization evolves, it develops organizational structures that are needed at *that stage* to deal with its information-processing and control problems. A geographically dispersed organization dealing with local variants of a given market has different problems from a high-technology company that has standard products that work more or less in any market. Galbraith's analysis reveals at least six or seven variants of control systems from simple rules to complex matrix structures.[22]

But the most important issue to examine before we race into new organizational paradigms is whether or not we even have the right explanation for Japanese success. Neither Ouchi nor Pascale and Athos presents much evidence to justify the premise that the Japanese organizations cited are successful because of the management system described. In addition, no evidence is shown that such organizations are, indeed, the most successful ones in Japan. For example, it may well be that both Japanese productivity and management style are the reflection of some other common historical, economic, and/or sociocultural factor(s) in Japan.[23] Neither book tells us enough about the following important issues:

- The role of postwar reconstruction.
- The opportunity to modernize the industrial base.
- The close collaboration between industry and government.
- The strong sense of nationalism that produces high levels of motivation in all workers.
- That lifetime employment is possible for roughly one-third of the employees in some Japanese organizations, because of the system of temporary employment for the rest of the employees and the existence of satellite companies that absorb some of the economic fluctuations.
- That all employees retire fairly early by U.S. standards (in their mid- to late fifties).
- That many of the best companies are family dominated and their strong company philosophies may be a reflection of founder values that might be hard to maintain as these companies age.
- That the cultural traditions of duty, obedience, and discipline strongly favor a paternalistic clan form of organization.

Neither book refers to the growing literature that compares managerial style and beliefs in different countries and that contradicts directly some of the books' assertions about U.S. and Japanese management approaches.[24] For example, although both books extol the virtues of Japanese indirection, subtlety, and ability to live with uncertainty and ambiguity, Hofstede found in a sample of forty countries that U.S. managers reported the highest levels of tolerance of ambiguity, while Japanese managers reported some of the lowest levels. On many dimensions U.S. and Japanese managers are surprisingly similar in their orientation, which suggests that the real answer to organizational effectiveness may be to find those combinations of strategy, structure, and style that are either "culture free" or adaptable within a wide variety of cultures.

Knowing What Is Cultural

If we are to have a theory of organizations or management that is culture free or adaptable within any given culture, we must first know what culture is. This is surprisingly difficult, because we are all embedded in our own culture. What can we learn from Japanese managers if we cannot decipher how their behavior is embedded in their culture? Can we attempt to adapt managerial methods developed in other cultures without understanding how they would fit into our own?

The first and perhaps the most important point is that we probably *cannot really understand another culture* at the level of its basic world view. The only one we can really understand is our own. Even understanding our own culture at this level requires intensive analysis and thought. One cannot suddenly become aware of something and understand it if one has always taken it completely for granted. The true value of looking at other cultures is, therefore, to gain perspective for studying one's own culture. By seeing how others think about and do things, we become more aware of how we think about and do things, and that awareness is the first step in analyzing our own cultural assumptions and values. We can use analyses of Japanese management methods and their underlying cultural presumptions to learn about the hidden premises of U.S. managerial methods and our own cultural presumptions.

If we can grasp and become aware of our own premises and values, we can then examine analytically and empirically what the strengths and weaknesses of our own paradigm may be. This process of self-analysis is subtle and difficult. Not enough research has been done on managerial practices in our own culture; thus, the methods of analysis and tentative conclusions presented below should be treated as a rough first cut at analyzing our own cultural terrain.[25]

Levels of Culture

In thinking about culture, one should distinguish surface manifestations from the essential underlying premises that bind the elements of any given culture. As shown in Figure 4.1, there are at least three interconnected levels:

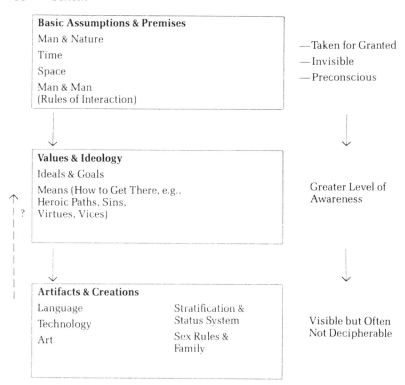

Figure 4.1   The Levels of Culture

1. *Artifacts and creations* are the visible manifestations of a culture (which include its language, art, architecture, technology, and other material outputs) and its visible system of organizing interpersonal relationships, status levels, sex roles, age roles, etc. Though this level is visible, it is often not decipherable in the sense that the newcomer to the culture cannot figure out "what is really going on," what values or assumptions tie together the various visible manifestations.

2. *Values and ideology* are the rules, principles, norms, values, morals, and ethics that guide both the ends of a given society (group) and the means by which to accomplish them. Values and ideological statements usually define what national goals, intergroup relationships, and interpersonal relationships are appropriate to strive for. They are taught to children and reinforced in adults. Generally the level of culture we first encounter is how to achieve the goals (i.e., we encounter the appropriate rules of conduct that govern relationships between nations, groups, and individuals within the society). This is also where differences are felt most

strongly, because of the penalties associated with behaving inappropriately. This level of culture, although partly conscious and partly unconscious, can be revealed if people reflect analytically about their own behavior.

3. *Basic assumptions and premises* are the underlying and typically unconscious assumptions about the nature of truth and reality, the nature of human nature, "man's" relationship to nature, "man's" relationship to "man," the nature of time, and the nature of space.[26] These assumptions create the cultural core or essence, provide the key to deciphering the values and artifacts, and create the patterning that characterizes cultural phenomena. This level is hardest to examine, because it is taken for granted and, hence, outside of awareness.

If we analyze U.S. culture and managerial assumptions in terms of some of the categories around which basic assumptions are built, what perspective does this provide, and how does this help us to learn from Japanese managerial practices?

Some Key Assumptions of U.S. Culture

"Man's" Relationship to Nature: Proactive Optimism

It is a premise of most Western societies (particularly of the U.S.) that nature can and should be conquered, that "man" is ultimately perfectible, and that anything is ultimately possible if we put enough effort into it. The philosophy "Where there's a will there's a way," buttressed by "Every day we do difficult things; the impossible just takes a little longer," sets the tone for how we approach tasks. We feel constrained by the environment only if we do not have the knowledge or technology to control or alter it, and then we proactively seek whatever knowledge or technology is necessary to overcome the obstacle.

Such proactive optimism underlies the values surrounding equality of opportunity in that we take it for granted that anyone might be able to accomplish anything, if given the opportunity. In other words, man is ultimately perfectible, as the thousands of self-help books in book stores proclaim. The notion of accepting one's "fate" (limiting one's aspirations according to one's social position or some other nontechnological constraint) is simply not part of the underlying ideology, however much empirical data might argue to the contrary.[27]

Given this core assumption, what kinds of organizational forms are possible in the U.S.? Can an industrial clan (a Theory Z organization) with its intrinsic conservative orientation survive in a cultural environment that emphasizes change, progress, innovation, and novelty? Or would this cultural orientation begin to erode the very core of such an organization—the stability that produces the comfort?

Similarly, can a culture that encourages people to find better ways to do things independently, to resist arbitrary authority if it interferes with pragmatic problem solving, and to value individual accomplishment produce an integrated system like the Pascale/Athos Seven S model? Perhaps the most notable characteristic of U.S. managerial practice is that we are never satisfied and are forever tinkering to find a better way. This will always undermine efforts toward integration. For many U.S. managers, integration equals stagnation. I have observed repeatedly that as soon as a system becomes routine, managers begin to think about "reorganization." Perhaps we deeply mistrust stability and are culturally "pot stirrers."

"Man's" Relationship to "Man": Individualistic Egalitarianism

Every society or group must resolve the issue between individualism and collectivism. The underlying U.S. assumption appears to be that the individual always does and should do what is best for himself or herself, and is constrained only by respect for the law and the rights of others. The rule of law implies that there are no philosophical and moral principles that can ultimately determine when another's rights have been violated, and, therefore, the legislative and judicial process must decide this on a case-by-case basis through a confronting, problem-solving process judged by a jury of peers. Buried in these assumptions is a further assumption that the world can be known only through successive confrontations with natural phenomena and other people; that the nature of truth resides in empirical experience, not in some philosophical, moral, or religious system; and that the ultimate "philosophy," therefore, might as well be one of pragmatism. Ambition, maximizing one's opportunities, and fully utilizing one's capacities become the moral imperatives.

These assumptions, in turn, are related to the Western rational scientific tradition, which emphasizes experimentation; learning from experience; open debate of facts; and a commitment to truth, accuracy, measurement, and other aids to establish what is "real." The openness and pluralism that so many commentators on America emphasize are closely related to the assumption that truth can be discovered only through open confrontation and can come from anyone. The lowliest employee has as good a chance to solve a key problem as the president of the company, and one of the worst sins is *arbitrary* authority ("Do it because I am the boss, even if you think it is wrong" or "If I'm the boss, that makes me right").

Yet teamwork is an important value in U.S. sports and organizational life. It is not clear to me how to reconcile the need for teamwork with the assumptions of individualism, and neither Ouchi nor Pascale and Athos offers much guidance on how consensual methods can be fitted to the notions of individual responsibility that U.S. managers take for granted. One of the greatest fears U.S. managers have of groups is that responsibility and accountability will become diffused. We need to be able to identify who is accountable for what, even when the realities of the task make shared responsibility more appropriate. According to Ouchi and Pascale and Athos, the Japanese deliberately blur individual responsibility and adapt their decision making to such blurring. If that is so, their version of the consensus method may have little to teach us.

Participatory methods can work in the U.S., but they must be based on a different premise: the premise that teamwork and participation are better ways to solve problems, because knowledge, information, and skills are distributed among a number of people. We must, therefore, involve those people who have relevant information and skills. But the goal in terms of U.S. assumptions is better problem solving and more efficient performance, not teamwork, consensus, or involvement per se. Unless Japanese consensus methods are built on the same premise of effective problem solving, they are in many senses culturally irrelevant.

Similarly, the Japanese concern for the whole person may be based on premises and assumptions that simply do not fit our core assumptions of individualism and self-help. U.S. managers are scared of paternalism and excessive involvement with subordinates, because they see them as "invasions of privacy." If an individual is taken care of by an organization, he or she may lose the ability to fight for himself or herself. Our whole system is based on the assumptions that one must "be one's own best friend" and that the law is there to protect each and every one of us. Dependency, security orientation, and allowing others to solve our problems are viewed as signs of failure and lack of ambition and are considered to be undeserving of sympathy. On the other hand, if it is necessary to take care of the whole family in an overseas transfer in order to enable the primary employee to function effectively, then we do it. "Pragmatism, necessity, and efficiency override issues of what would be more humane, because of the underlying belief that we cannot philosophically agree on basic standards of what is "best" for everyone. What is best for people must be decided on the basis of negotiation and experience (ultimately expressed in laws, safety codes, and quality of work-life standards).

A culture based on such premises sounds harsh and cold, and the things we are told we should do to "humanize" organizations sound friendly and warm. But cultures are neither cold nor warm, because within any given culture both warmth and coldness have their own meaning. We may not like certain facets of our culture once we discover their underlying premises, and we may even set out to change our culture. However, we cannot produce such change simply by pointing to another culture and saying that some of the things they do *there* would be neat *here*. We have not yet begun to understand our own culture and the managerial paradigms it has created. This article is a beginning attempt to stimulate such self-understanding, which is a prerequisite for any "remedial" action.

5

Entering New Businesses:
Selecting Strategies
for Success

Edward B. Roberts

Charles A. Berry

Selective use of the alternative strategies available for entering new businesses is a key issue for diversifying corporations. The approaches include internal development, acquisition, licensing, joint ventures, and minority venture-capital investments. Using the existing literature, the authors devise a matrix of company "familiarity" with relevant market and technological experiences. Through a case study of a successful diversified technological firm, they demonstrate how the familiarity matrix can be applied to help a company select optimum entry strategies. *SMR.*

Entry into new product-markets, which represents diversification for the existing firm, may provide an important source of future growth and profitability. Typically, such new businesses are initiated with low-market share in high-growth markets and require large cash inflows to finance growth. In addition, many new product-market entries fail, draining additional cash resources and incurring high opportunity costs to the firm. Two strategic questions are thus posed: (1) Which product markets should a corporation enter? and (2) How should the company enter these product markets to avoid failure and maximize gain?

Although these questions are fundamentally different, they should not be answered independently of one another. Entering a new business may be achieved by a variety of mechanisms, such as internal development, acquisition, joint ventures, and minority investments of venture capital. As Roberts

From *Sloan Management Review*, Spring 1985, Vol. 26, No. 3. Reprinted with permission.

indicates, each of these mechanisms makes different demands upon the corporation.[1] Some, such as internal development, require a high level of commitment and involvement. Others, such as venture-capital investment, require much lower levels of involvement. What are the relative benefits and costs of each of these entry mechanisms? When should each be used?

This article attempts to analyze and answer these questions, first by proposing a framework for considering entry issues, second by a review of relevant literature, third by application of this literature to the creation of a matrix that suggests optimum entry strategies, and finally by a test of the matrix through a case analysis of business development decisions by a successful diversified corporation.

Entry Strategy: A New Selection Framework

New business development may address new markets, new products, or both. In addition, these new areas may be ones that are familiar or unfamiliar to a company. Let us first define "newness" and "familiarity":

- Newness of a Technology or Service: the degree to which that technology or service has not formerly been embodied within the products of the company.
- Newness of a Market: the degree to which the products of the company have not formerly been targeted at that particular market.
- Familiarity with a Technology: the degree to which knowledge of the technology exists within the company, but is not necessarily embodied in the products.
- Familiarity with a Market: the degree to which the characteristics and business patterns of a market are understood within the company, but not necessarily as a result of participation in the market.

If the businesses in which a company currently competes are its *base* businesses, then market factors associated with the new business area may be characterized as *base, new familiar,* or *new unfamiliar.* Here, "market factors" refers not only to particular characteristics of the market and the participating competitors, but also includes the appropriate pattern of doing business that may lead to competitive advantage. Two alternative patterns are performance-premium price and lowest-cost producer. Similarly, the technologies or service embodied in the product for the new business area may be characterized on the same basis. Figure 5.1 illustrates some tests that may be used to distinguish between "base" and "new" areas. Table 5.1 lists questions that may be used to distinguish between familiar

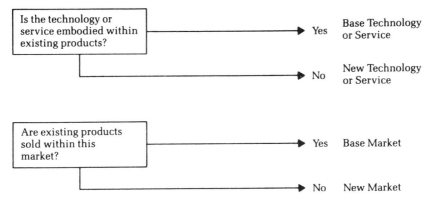

Figure 5.1 Tests of Newness

and unfamiliar technologies. (Equivalent tests may be applied to services.) Questions to distinguish between familiar and unfamiliar markets are given in Table 5.2.

The application of these tests to any new business development opportunity enables it to be located conceptually on a 3 × 3 technology/market *familiarity matrix* as illustrated in Figure 5.2. The nine sectors of this matrix may be grouped into three regions, with the three sectors that comprise any one region possessing broadly similar levels of familiarity.

Table 5.1 Tests of Technological Familiarity

	Decreasing Familiarity
1. Is the technological capability used within the corporation without being embodied in products, e.g., required for component manufacture (incorporated in processes rather than products)?	
2. Do the main features of the new technology relate to or overlap with existing corporate technological skills or knowledge, e.g., coating of optical lenses and aluminizing semiconductor substrates?	
3. Do technological skills or knowledge exist within the corporation without being embodied in products or processes, e.g., at a central R&D facility?	
4. Has the technology been systematically monitored from within the corporation in anticipation of future utilization, e.g., by a technology-assessment group?	
5. Is relevant and reliable advice available from external consultants?	

Table 5.2   Tests of Market Familiarity

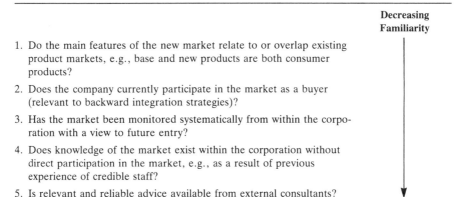

	Decreasing Familiarity
1. Do the main features of the new market relate to or overlap existing product markets, e.g., base and new products are both consumer products?	
2. Does the company currently participate in the market as a buyer (relevant to backward integration strategies)?	
3. Has the market been monitored systematically from within the corporation with a view to future entry?	
4. Does knowledge of the market exist within the corporation without direct participation in the market, e.g., as a result of previous experience of credible staff?	
5. Is relevant and reliable advice available from external consultants?	

Literature Review: Alternative Strategies

Extensive writings have focused on new business development and the various mechanisms by which it may be achieved. Much of this literature concentrates on diversification, the most demanding approach to new business development, in which both the product and market dimensions of the business area may be new to a company. Our review of the literature supports and provides details for the framework shown in Figure 5.2, finding that familiarity of a company with the technology and market being addressed is the critical variable that explains much of the success or failure in new business development approaches.

Rumelt's pioneering 1974 study of diversification analyzed company performance against a measure of the relatedness of the various businesses forming the company.[2] Rumelt identified nine types of diversified companies, clustered into three categories: dominant business companies, related business companies, and unrelated business companies. From extensive analysis Rumelt concluded that related business companies outperformed the averages on five accounting-based performance measures over the period 1949 to 1969.

Rumelt recently updated his analysis to include Fortune 500 companies' performances through 1974 and drew similar conclusions: The related constrained group of companies was the most profitable, building on single strengths or resources associated with their original businesses.[3] Rumelt, as well as Christensen and Montgomery, also found, however, that the performance in part reflected effects of concentrations in certain categories of

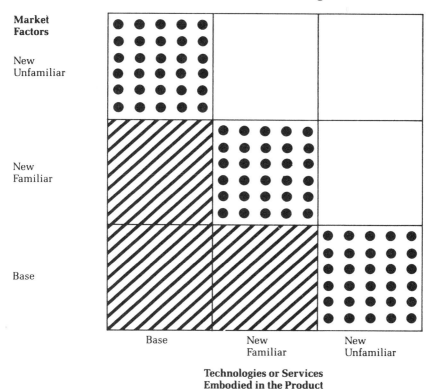

Figure 5.2 appears with the following labels:

Market Factors

New Unfamiliar

New Familiar

Base

Technologies or Services Embodied in the Product

Base   New Familiar   New Unfamiliar

Key:

Increasing Corporate Familiarity

Figure 5.2   The Familiarity Matrix

industrial market clusters.[4] While some (e.g., Bettis and Hall)[5] have questioned Rumelt's earlier conclusions, others (e.g., Holzmann, Copeland, and Hayya)[6] have supported the findings of lower returns by unrelated business firms and highest profitability for the related constrained group of firms.

Peters supports Rumelt's general conclusions on the superior performance of related business companies.[7] In his study of thirty-seven "well-managed" organizations, he found that they had all been able to define their strengths and build upon them: They had not moved into potentially attractive new business areas that required skills they did not possess. In their recent book Peters and Waterman termed this "sticking to the knitting."[8]

Even in small high-technology firms similar effects can be noted. Recent research by Meyer and Roberts on ten such firms revealed that the most successful in terms of growth had concentrated on one key technological area and introduced product enhancements related to that area.[9] In contrast, the poorest performers had tackled "unrelated" new technologies in attempts to enter new product-market areas.

The research discussed above indicates that in order to ensure highest performance, new business development should be constrained within areas related to a company's base business—a very limiting constraint. However, no account was taken of how new businesses were in fact entered and the effect that the entry mechanism had on subsequent corporate performance. As summarized in Table 5.3, the literature identifies a wide range of approaches that are available for entering new business areas, and highlights various advantages and disadvantages.

Table 5.3 Entry Mechanisms: Advantages and Disadvantages

New Business Development Mechanisms	Major Advantages	Major Disadvantages
Internal developments	Use existing resources	Time lag to break even tends to be long (on average eight years); Unfamiliarity with new markets may lead to errors
Acquisitions	Rapid market entry	New business area may be unfamiliar to parent
Licensing	Rapid access to proven technology; Reduced financial exposure	Not a substitute for internal technical competence; Not proprietary technology; Dependent upon licensor
Internal ventures	Use existing resources; May enable a company to hold a talented entrepreneur	Mixed record of success; Corporation's internal climate often unsuitable
Joint ventures or alliances	Technological/marketing unions can exploit small/large company synergies; Distribute risk	Potential for conflict between partners
Venture capital and nurturing	Can provide window on new technology or market	Unlikely alone to be a major stimulus of corporate growth
Educational acquisitions	Provide window and initial staff	Higher initial financial commitment than venture capital; Risk of departure of entrepreneurs

New Business Development Mechanisms

Internal Developments.   Companies have traditionally approached new business development via two routes: internal development and acquisition. Internal development exploits internal resources as a basis for establishing a business new to the company. Biggadike studied Fortune 500 companies that had used this approach in corporate diversification.[10] He found that, typically, eight years were needed to generate a positive return on investment, and performance did not match that of a mature business until a period of ten to twelve years had elapsed. However, Weiss asserts that this need not be the case.[11] He compared the performance of internal corporate developments with comparable businesses newly started by individuals and found that the new independent businesses reached profitability in half the time of corporate effort—approximately four years versus eight years. Although Weiss attributes this to the more ambitious targets established by independent operations, indeed the opposite may be true. Large companies' overhead-allocation charges or their attempts at large-scale entry and other objectives that preclude early profitability may be more correct explanations for the delayed profitability of these ventures.

Miller indicates that forcing established attitudes and procedures upon a new business may severely handicap it, and he suggests that success may not come until the technology has been adapted, new facilities established, or familiarity with the new markets developed.[12] Miller stresses this last factor. Gilmore and Coddington also believe that lack of familiarity with new markets often leads to major errors.[13]

Acquisitions.   In contrast to internal development, acquisition can take weeks rather than years to execute. This approach may be attractive not only because of its speed, but because it offers a much lower initial cost of entry into a new business or industry. Salter and Weinhold point out that this is particularly true if the key parameters for success in the new business field are intangibles, such as patents, product image, or R&D skills, which may be difficult to duplicate via internal developments within reasonable costs and time scales.[14]

Miller believes that a diversifying company cannot step in immediately after acquisition to manage a business it knows nothing about.[15] It must set up a communication system that will permit it to understand the new business gradually. Before this understanding develops, incompatibility may exist between the managerial judgment appropriate for the parent and that required for the new subsidiary.

Licensing.   Acquiring technology through licensing represents an alternative to acquiring a complete company. J. P. Killing has pointed out that licensing avoids the risks of product development by exploiting the experience of firms who have already developed and marketed the product.[16]

Internal Ventures.   Roberts indicates that many corporations are now adopting new venture strategies in order to meet ambitious plans for diversification and growth.[17] Internal ventures share some similarities with internal development, which has already been discussed. In this venture strategy, a firm attempts to enter different markets or develop substantially different products from those of its existing base business by setting up a separate entity within the existing corporate body. Overall, the strategy has had a mixed record, but some companies such as 3M have exploited it with considerable success. This was due in large part to their ability to harness and nurture entrepreneurial behavior within the corporation. More recently, IBM's Independent Business Units (especially its PC venture) and Du Pont's new electronic-materials division demonstrate the effectiveness of internal ventures for market expansion and/or diversification. Burgelman has suggested that corporations need to "develop greater flexibility between new venture projects and the corporation," using external as well as internal ventures.[18]

   The difficulty in successfully diversifying via internal ventures is not a new one. Citing Chandler,[19] Morecroft comments on Du Pont's failure in moving from explosive powders to varnishes and paints in 1917:

[C]ompeting firms, though much smaller and therefore lacking large economies of scale and production, were nonetheless profitable. . . . Their sole advantage lay in the fact that they specialized in the manufacture, distribution, and sale of varnishes and paints. This focus provided them with clearer responsibilities and clearer standards for administering sales and distribution.[20]

Joint Ventures or Alliances.   Despite the great potential for conflict, many companies successfully diversify and grow via joint ventures. As Killing points out, when projects get larger, technology more expensive, and the cost of failure too large to be borne alone, joint venturing becomes increasingly important.[21] Shifts in national policy in the United States are now encouraging the formation of several large research-based joint ventures involving many companies. But the traditional forms of joint ventures, involving creation of third corporations, seem to have limited life and/or growth potential.

   Hlavacek et al. and Roberts believe one class of joint venture to be of particular interest—"new style" joint ventures in which large and small companies join forces to create a new entry in the market place.[22] In these efforts of "mutual pursuit," usually without the formality of a joint-venture company, the small company provides the technology, the large company provides marketing capability, and the venture is synergistic for both parties. Recent articles have indicated how these large company/small company "alliances," frequently forged through the creative use of corporate venture capital, are growing in strategic importance.[23]

Venture Capital and Nurturing.   The venture strategy that permits some degree of entry, but the lowest level of required corporate commitment, is that associated with external venture-capital investment. Major corporations have exploited this approach in order to become involved with the growth and development of small companies as investors, participants, or even eventual acquirers. Roberts points out that this approach was popular as early as the mid-to-late 1960s with many large corporations, such as Du Pont, Exxon, Ford, General Electric, Singer, and Union Carbide.[24] Their motivation was the so-called window on technology, the opportunity to secure closeness to and possibly later entry into new technologies by making minority investments in young and growing high-technology enterprises. However, few companies in the 1960s were able to make this approach alone an important stimulus of corporate growth or profitability. Despite this, ever-increasing numbers of companies today are experimenting with venture capital, and many are showing important financial and informational benefits.

Studies carried out by Greenthal and Larson[25] show that venture capital investments can indeed provide satisfactory and perhaps highly attractive returns, if they are properly managed, although Hardymon et al.[26] essentially disagree. Rind distinguishes between direct venture investments and investment into pooled funds of venture-capital partnerships.[27] He points out that although direct venture investments can be carried out from within a corporation by appropriate planning and organization, difficulties are often encountered because of a lack of appropriately skilled people, contradictory rationales between the investee company and parent, legal problems, and an inadequate time horizon. Investment in a partnership may remove some of these problems, but if the investor's motives are something other than simply maximizing financial return, it may be important to select a partnership concentrating investments in areas of interest. Increasingly, corporations are trying to use pooled funds to provide the "windows" on new technologies and new markets that are more readily afforded by direct investment, but special linkages with the investment-fund managers are needed to implement a "window" strategy. Fast cites 3M and Corning as companies that have invested as limited partners in venture-capital partnerships.[28] This involvement in business-development financing can keep the company in touch with new technologies and emerging industries as well as provide the guidance and understanding of the venture-development process necessary for more effective internal corporate venturing.

In situations where the investing company provides managerial assistance to the recipient of the venture capital, the strategy is classed "venture nurturing" rather than pure venture capital. This seems to be a more sensible entry toward diversification objectives as opposed to a simple provision of funds, but it also needs to be tied to other company diversification efforts.

Educational Acquisitions.   Although not discussed in the management literature, targeted small acquisitions can fulfill a role similar to that of a venture-capital minority investment and, in some circumstances, may offer significant advantages. In an acquisition of this type, the acquiring firm immediately obtains people familiar with the new business area, whereas in a minority investment, the parent relies upon its existing staff to build familiarity by interacting with the investee. Acquisitions for educational purposes may therefore represent a faster route to familiarity than the venture capital "window" approach. Staff acquired in this manner may even be used by the parent as a basis for redirecting a corporation's primary product-market thrust. Harris Corporation (formerly Harris-Intertype) entered the computer and communication-systems industry using precisely this mechanism: It acquired internal skills and knowledge through its acquisition of Radiation Dynamics, Inc. Procter & Gamble recently demonstrated similar behavior in citing its acquisition of the Tender Leaf Tea brand as an "initial learning opportunity in a growing category of the beverage business."[29]

One potential drawback to this acquisition approach is that it usually requires a higher level of financial commitment than minority investment and therefore increases risk. In addition, it is necessary to ensure that key people do not leave soon after the acquisition as a result of the removal of entrepreneurial incentives. A carefully designed acquisition deal may be necessary to ensure that incentives remain. When Xerox acquired Versatec, for example, the founder and key employees were given the opportunity to double their "sellout" price by meeting performance targets over the next five years.

Though not without controversy, major previous research work on large U.S. corporations indicated that the highest performers had diversified to some extent but had constrained the development of new business within areas related to the company's base business. The range of mechanisms employed for entering new businesses, previously displayed in Table 5.3, is divided in Figure 5.3 into three regions, each requiring a different level of corporate involvement and commitment. No one mechanism is ideal for all new business development. It may be possible, therefore, that selective use

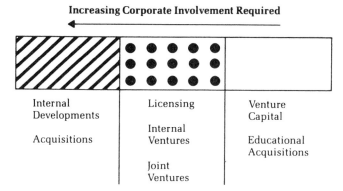

Increasing Corporate Involvement Required

Internal Developments	Licensing	Venture Capital
Acquisitions	Internal Ventures	Educational Acquisitions
	Joint Ventures	

Figure 5.3   Spectrum of Entry Strategies

of entry mechanisms can yield substantial benefits over concentration on one particular approach. If this presumption is valid, then careful strategy selection can reduce the risk associated with new business development in unrelated areas.

Determining Optimum Entry Strategies

How can the entry strategies in Figure 5.3 be combined with the conceptual framework in Figure 5.2? Which entry strategies are appropriate in the various regions of the familiarity matrix? The literature provides some useful guides.

In his discussion of the management problems of diversification, Miller proposes that acquisitive diversifiers are frequently required to participate in the strategic and operating decisions of the new subsidiary before they are properly oriented to the new business.[30] In this situation the parent is "unfamiliar" with the new business area. It is logical to conclude that if the new business is unfamiliar *after* acquisition, it must also have been unfamiliar *before* acquisition. How then could the parent have carried out comprehensive screening of the new company before executing the acquisition? In a situation in which familiarity was low or absent, preacquisition screening most probably overlooked many factors, turning the acquisition into something of a gamble from a portfolio standpoint. Similar arguments can be applied to internal development in unfamiliar areas, and Gilmore and Coddington specifically stress the dangers associated with entry into unfamiliar markets.[31]

This leads to the rather logical conclusion that entry strategies requiring high corporate involvement should be reserved for new businesses with familiar market and technological characteristics. Similarly, entry mechanisms requiring low corporate input seem best for unfamiliar sectors. A recent discussion meeting with a number of chief executive officers suggested that, at most, 50 percent of major U.S. corporations practice even this simple advice.

The three sections of the Entry Strategy Spectrum in Figure 5.3 can now be aligned with the three regions of the familiarity matrix in Figure 5.2. Let us analyze this alignment for each region of the matrix, with particular regard for the main factors identified in the literature.

Region 1: Base/Familiar Sectors

Within the base/familiar sector combinations illustrated in Figure 5.4, a corporation is fully equipped to undertake all aspects of new business development. Consequently, the full range of entry strategies may be considered, including internal development, joint venturing, licensing, acquisition, or minority investment of venture capital. However, although all of these are valid from a corporate familiarity standpoint, other factors suggest what may be the optimum entry approach.

The potential of conflict between partners may reduce the appeal of a joint venture, and minority investments offer little benefit, since the investee would do nothing that could not be done internally.

The most attractive entry mechanisms in these sectors probably include internal development, licensing, and acquisition. Internal development may be appropriate in each of these sectors, since the required expertise already exists within the corporation. Licensing may be a useful alternative in the base market/new familiar technology sector, since it offers fast access to proven products. Acquisition may be attractive in each sector but, as indicated by Shanklin, may not be feasible for some companies in the base/base sector as a result of antitrust legislation.[32] For example, although IBM was permitted to acquire ROLM Corporation, the Justice Department did require that IBM divest ROLM's MIL-SPECS Division because of concern for concentration in the area of military computers.

It may therefore be concluded that in these base/familiar sectors, the optimum-entry strategy range may be limited to internal development, licensing, and acquisition as illustrated in Figure 5.4. In all cases a new business developed in each of these sectors is immediately required to fulfill a conventional sales/profit role within the corporate business portfolio.

Finally, since new businesses within the base market/new familiar technology and new familiar market/base technology sectors immediately enter the

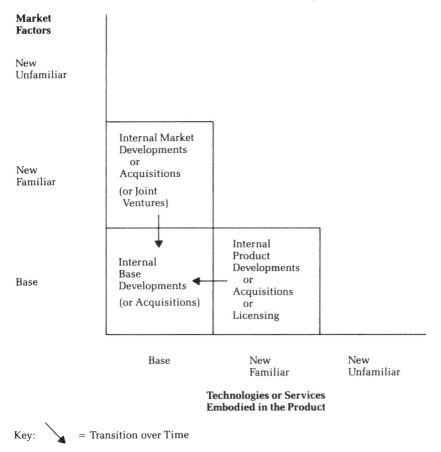

**Market
Factors**

New
Unfamiliar

New
Familiar

Base

Internal Market
Developments
or
Acquisitions
(or Joint
Ventures)

Internal
Base
Developments
(or Acquisitions)

Internal
Product
Developments
or
Acquisitions
or
Licensing

Base

New
Familiar

New
Unfamiliar

**Technologies or Services
Embodied in the Product**

Key: = Transition over Time

Figure 5.4 Preferred Entry Mechanisms in Base/Familiar Sectors

portfolio of ongoing business activities, they transfer rapidly into the base/
base sector. These expected transitions are illustrated by the arrows in Figure 5.4.

Region 2: Familiar/Unfamiliar Sectors

Figure 5.5 illustrates the sectors of lowest familiarity from a corporate standpoint. It has already been proposed that a company is potentially competent
to carry out totally appropriate analyses only on those new business opportunities that lie within its own sphere of familiarity. Large-scale entry decisions outside this sphere are liable to miss important characteristics of the
technology or market, reducing the probability of success. This situation
frequently generates unhappy and costly surprises. Furthermore, if the unfa-

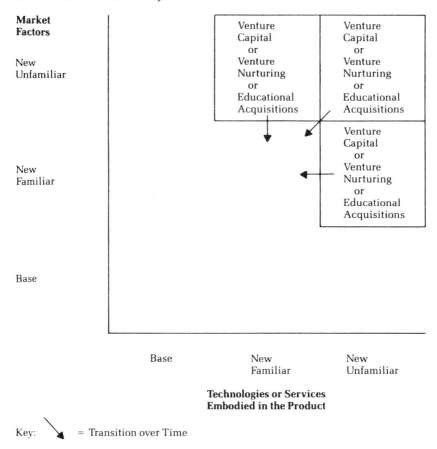

Figure 5.5   Preferred Entry Mechanisms in Familiar/Unfamiliar Sectors

miliar parent attempts to exert strong influence on the new business, the probability of success will be reduced still further.

These factors suggest that a two-stage approach may be best when a company desires to enter unfamiliar new business areas. The first stage should be devoted to building corporate familiarity with the new area. Once this has been achieved, the parent is then in a position to decide whether to allocate more substantial resources to the opportunity and, if appropriate, select a mechanism for developing the business.

As indicated earlier, venture capital provides one possible vehicle for building corporate familiarity with an unfamiliar area. With active nurturing of a venture-capital minority investment, the corporation can monitor, firsthand, new technologies and markets. If the investment is to prove worthwhile, it is essential for the investee to be totally familiar with the technology/market being monitored by the investor. The technology and market must therefore be the investee's base business. Over time active involvement with the new investment can help the investor move into a more familiar market/technology region, as illustrated in Figure 5.5, from which the parent can exercise appropriate judgment on the commitment of more substantial resources.

Similarly, educational acquisitions of small young firms may provide a more transparent window on a new technology or market, and even on the initial key employees, who can assist the transition toward higher familiarity. It is important, however, that the performance of acquisitions of this type be measured according to criteria different from those used to assess the "portfolio" acquisitions discussed earlier. These educational acquisitions should be measured initially on their ability to provide increased corporate familiarity with a new technology or market, and not on their ability to perform immediately a conventional business-unit role of sales and profits contributions.

Region 3: Marginal Sectors

The marginal sectors of the matrix are the two base/new unfamiliar combinations plus the new familiar market/new familiar technology area, as illustrated in Figure 5.6. In each of the base/new unfamiliar sectors, the company has a strong familiarity with either markets or technologies, but is totally unfamiliar with the other dimension of the new business. In these situations joint venturing may be very attractive to the company and prospective partners can see that the company may have something to offer. However, in the new familiar technology/market region the company's base business strengths do not communicate obvious familiarity with that new technology or market. Hence, prospective partners may not perceive that a joint-venture relationship would yield any benefit for them.

In the base market/new unfamiliar technology sector the "new style" joint venture or alliance seems appropriate. The large firm provides the marketing channels, and the small company provides the technological capability, forming a union that can result in a very powerful team.[33] The complement of this situation may be equally attractive in the new unfamiliar market/base technology sector, although small companies less frequently have strong marketing/distribution capabilities to offer a larger ally.

The various forms of joint ventures not only provide a means of fast entry into a new business sector, but offer increased corporate familiarity over time, as illustrated in Figure 5.6. Consequently, although a joint venture may be the optimum entry mechanism into the new business area, future development of that business may be best achieved by internal development

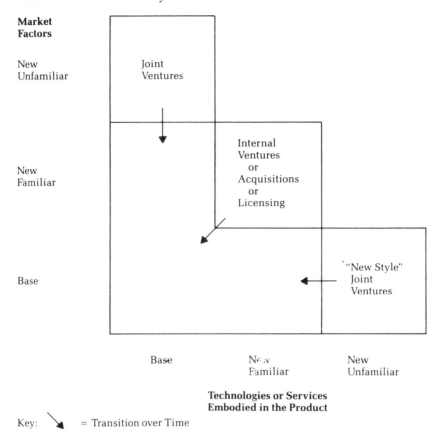

Key: ⬊ = Transition over Time

Figure 5.6   Preferred Entry Mechanisms in Marginal Sectors

or acquisition, as discussed in the earlier base/familiar sectors section of this article.

In the new familiar market/new familiar technology sector, the company may be in an ideal spot to undertake an internal venture. Alternatively, licensing may provide a useful means of obtaining rapid access to a proven product embodying the new technology. Minority investments can also succeed in this sector but, since familiarity already exists, a higher level of corporate involvement and control may be justifiable.

Acquisitions may be potentially attractive in all marginal sectors. However, in the base/new unfamiliar areas this is dangerous, since the company's lack of familiarity with the technology or market prevents it from carrying out comprehensive screening of candidates. In contrast, the region of new familiar market/new familiar technologies does provide adequate familiarity to ensure that screening of candidates covers most significant factors. In this instance an acquisitive strategy is reasonable.

Sector Integration: Optimum Entry Strategies

The above discussion has proposed optimum entry strategies for attractive new business opportunities based on their position in the familiarity matrix. Figure 5.7 integrates these proposals to form a tool for selecting entry strategies based on corporate familiarity.

Testing the Proposals

In testing the proposed entry strategies, Berry studied fourteen new business development episodes that had been undertaken within one highly successful

Market Factors	Base	New Familiar	New Unfamiliar
New Unfamiliar	Joint Ventures	Venture Capital or Venture Nurturing or Educational Acquisitions	Venture Capital or Venture Nurturing or Educational Acquisitions
New Familiar	Internal Market Developments or Acquisitions (or Joint Ventures)	Internal Ventures or Acquisitions or Licensing	Venture Capital or Venture Nurturing or Educational Acquisitions
Base	Internal Base Developments (or Acquisitions)	Internal Product Developments or Acquisitions or Licensing	"New Style" Joint Ventures

**Technologies or Services
Embodied in the Product**

Figure 5.7   Optimum Entry Strategies

diversified technological corporation.[34] These episodes were all initiated within the period 1971 to 1977, thus representing relatively recent activity, while still ensuring that sufficient time had elapsed for performance to be measurable.

The sample comprised six internal developments (three successful, three unsuccessful); six acquisitions (three successful, three incompatible); and two successful minority investments of venture capital. These were analyzed in order to identify factors that differentiated successful from unsuccessful episodes, measured in terms of meeting very high corporate standards of growth, profitability, and return on investment. Failures had not achieved these standards and had been discontinued or divested. The scatter of these episodes on the familiarity matrix is illustrated in Figure 5.8. Internal developments are represented by symbols A to F, acquisitions by symbols G to L, with symbols M and N showing the location of the minority investments.

The distribution of success and failure on the matrix gives support to the entry strategy proposals that have been made in this article. All high corporate-involvement mechanisms (internal development and regular "portfolio" acquisitions) in familiar sectors were successful. However, in unfamiliar areas, only one of this category of entry mechanism, acquisition G, succeeded. This acquisition was a thirty-year-old private company with about 1,000 employees, producing components for the electronics and computer industries. Company G was believed to offer opportunities for high growth, although it was unrelated to any area of the parent's existing business. The deal was completed after an unusually long period of two years of candidate evaluation carried out from within the parent company. The only constraint imposed upon Company G following acquisition was the parent's planning and control system, and in fact the acquired company was highly receptive to the introduction of this system. This indicated that Company G was not tightly integrated with the parent and that any constraints imposed did not severely disrupt the established operating procedures of the company.

All factors surrounding the acquisition of Company G—its size, growth market, low level of constraints, and low disruption by the parent—suggest that Company G might have continued to be successful even if it had not been acquired. Representatives of the parent agreed that this might be the case, although they pointed out that the levels of performance obtained following acquisition might not have occurred if Company G had remained independent. Hence, if an acquired company is big enough to stand alone and is *not* tightly integrated with the parent, its degree of operational success is probably independently determined.

It is important to point out that despite the success that occurred in

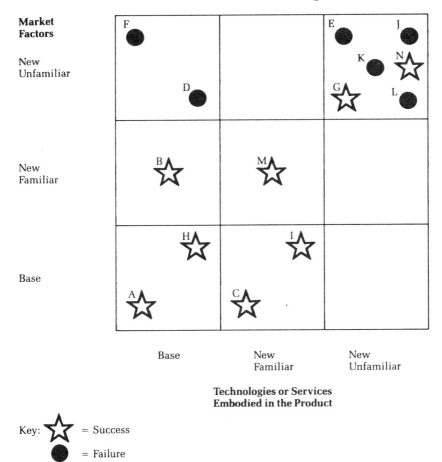

**Market
Factors**

New
Unfamiliar

New
Familiar

Base

Base   New   New
              Familiar   Unfamiliar

**Technologies or Services
Embodied in the Product**

Key: ☆ = Success

      ⬤ = Failure

Figure 5.8   Episode Scatter on the Familiarity Matrix

instance G, an acquisition of this type in unfamiliar areas must carry some degree of risk. The parent is liable to overlook many subtle details while screening candidates. Furthermore, when an established company is acquired and continues to operate with a high degree of independence, identification of synergy becomes difficult. Synergy must exist in any acquisitive development, if economic value is to be created by the move.[35] Consequently, an acquisition of this type not only carries risk, but may also be of questionable benefit to shareholders, especially if a high price was required because of an earlier good performance record.

The other success in an unfamiliar area, episode N, is a minority investment of venture capital. By the very nature of minority investments, corporate involvement is limited to a low level. Although some influence may be exerted via participation on the board of directors of the investee, again, the investee is not tightly bound to the parent. Consequently, the success of the investee tends to be determined to a large extent by its own actions.

Detailed examination of episodes G and N suggests a good reason for the subject companies' success despite their location in unfamiliar sectors: The companies did not require significant input from the unfamiliar parent in the decision-making process. This suggests that new-business-development success rates in unfamiliar areas may be increased by limiting corporate input to the decision-making process to low levels until corporate familiarity with the new area has developed. These experiences support the entry proposals already outlined in this article.

Some companies have already adopted entry strategies that seem to fit the proposals of this article, and Monsanto represents one of the best examples. Monsanto is now committed to significant corporate venturing in the emerging field of biotechnology. Its first involvement in this field was achieved with the aid of its venture-capital partnership, Innoven, which invested in several small biotechnology firms, including Genentech. During this phase Monsanto interacted closely with the investees, inviting them in-house to give seminars to senior management on their biotechnology research and opportunities. Once some internal familiarity with the emerging field had developed, Monsanto decided to commit substantial resources to internal research-based ventures. Monsanto used venture capital to move from an unfamiliar region to an area of more familiar technology and market and is currently continuing those venture-capital activities to seek new opportunities in Europe. Joint ventures with Harvard Medical School and Washington University of St. Louis are further enhancing its familiarity with biotechnology, while producing technologies that Monsanto hopes to market. Contract research leading to licenses from small companies, primarily those in which it holds minority investments, is another strategy Monsanto is employing. Although the outcome is far from determined, Monsanto seems to be effectively entering biotechnology by moving from top right to bottom left across the familiarity matrix of Figure 5.7.

Conclusion

A spectrum of entry strategies was presented in this article, ranging from those that require high corporate involvement, such as internal development or acquisition, to those that require only low involvement, such as venture capital. These were incorporated into a new conceptual framework designed to assist in selecting entry strategies into potentially attractive new business areas. The framework concentrates on the concept of a corporation's "familiarity" with the technology and market aspects of a new business area, and a matrix was used to relate familiarity to optimum entry strategy.

In this concept, no one strategy is ideal. Within familiar sectors virtually any strategy may be adopted; internal development or acquisition is probably most appropriate. However, in unfamiliar areas these two high involvement approaches are very risky, and greater familiarity should be built *before* they are attempted. Minority investments and small targeted educational acquisitions form ideal vehicles for building familiarity and are therefore the preferred entry strategies in unfamiliar sectors.

Early in this article, research results from the literature were outlined that indicated that, in order to ensure highest performance, new business development should be constrained within areas related to a company's base business. However, this research did not account for alternative entry mechanisms. This article proposes that a multifaceted approach, encompassing internal developments, acquisitions, joint ventures, and venture-capital minority investments, can make available a much broader range of business development opportunities, at lower risk than would otherwise be possible.

6

Strategic Human Resource Management

Noel M. Tichy

Charles J. Fombrun

Mary Anne Devanna

To solve our productivity problems, we may not need to look to the Japanese for answers as much as we need to examine the congruence between human resource systems and our firms' strategies. The authors maintain that, just as different strategies require different structures, so must human resource management suit a particular strategy. Focusing primarily on the human resource system's impact at the management level, the authors show how the system can be linked to the strategic plan to facilitate successful implementation. In so doing, they develop a framework for analyzing human resource management, and they show how it applies through specific case examples. *SMR.*

Technological, economic, and demographic changes are pressuring organizations to use more effective human resource management. While sagging productivity and worker alienation have popularized management tools such as quality circles and profit-sharing plans, the long-run competitiveness of American industry will require considerably more sophisticated approaches to deal with the strategic role of human resources in organizational performance.

Recent attacks on American business have stressed the short-run financial outlook of its management and its distinctly callous treatment of workers. The Japanese organization, on the other hand, is seen as the prototype of the future, as its planning systems center on worker loyalty.

From *Sloan Management Review*, Winter 1982, Vol. 23, No. 2. Reprinted with permission.

This article, however, argues that we should not evaluate the Japanese organization per se. Rather, we should focus on human resource management in terms of its strategic role in both the formulation and the implementation of long-run plans. The strategic human resource concepts and tools needed are fundamentally different from the stock in trade of traditional personnel administration. This article, therefore, stresses the strategic level of human resource management at the expense of some of the operational concerns of the standard personnel organization. Several companies are described as examples of sophisticated American organizations that have instituted strategic human resource management as an integral component of their management process. Specifically, this article presents a framework for conceptualizing human resource management; links human resource management to general strategic management; and describes some current applications of human resource management as a strategic tool in achieving corporate objectives.

Strategic Management

Three core elements are necessary for firms to function effectively:

1. *Mission and Strategy.* The organization has to have a reason for being, a means for using money, material, information, and people to carry out the mission.
2. *Organization Structure.* People are organized to carry out the mission of the organization and to do the necessary tasks.
3. *Human Resource Management.* People are recruited into the organization to do the jobs defined by the division of labor. Performance must be monitored, and rewards must be given to keep individuals productive.

Figure 6.1 presents these basic elements as interrelated systems embedded in the work environment. In the past, human resource management has been largely missing from the general strategic management process. Thus, our aim here is to help make human resource management an integral part of the strategic arena in organizations.

Strategy is defined as a process through which the basic mission and objectives of the organization are set and a process through which the organization uses its resources to achieve its objectives. In turn, structure reflects the "organization of work into roles such as production, finance, marketing, and so on; the recombining of the roles into departments or divisions around functions, products, regions, or markets and the distribution of power across this role structure."[1] The structure of the organization embodies the funda-

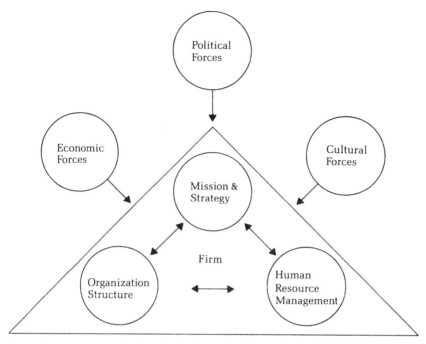

Figure 6.1   Strategic Management and Environmental Pressures

mental division of labor, describes the basic nature of the jobs to be done, and aggregates them into groups, functions, or businesses. It also defines the degree of centralized control that top management holds over the operating units.

Strategy Follows Structure

In his historical study of American industry, Chandler provided a convincing argument that the structure of an organization follows from its strategy.[2] He identified four major strategies that resulted in structural or organizational design changes. They are: (1) expansion of volume; (2) geographic dispersion; (3) vertical integration; and (4) product diversification. Each of these strategies is followed by a structural transformation from function through to product forms. But while Chandler's work focused attention on the structural supports needed to drive a strategy and on the use of the organization's formal design in the implementation of a strategy, he did not discuss the role of the human resource systems in the implementation process.

Strategy, Structure, and Human Resource Management

The addition of human resource management to the strategic arena was presented by Galbraith and Nathanson who expanded on Chandler's analysis.[3] They focused on such issues as fitting performance measures to the strategy and structure as well as to rewards, career paths, and leadership styles. Table 6.1 modifies and expands upon their work to illustrate how strategy, structure, and human resource management systems fit together: the fundamental strategic management problem is to keep the strategy, structure, and human resource dimensions of the organization in direct alignment. In the rest of this article, we will discuss some of the human resource management concepts and tools that are needed to describe completely the strategic management role.

Human Resource Policies: A Context

A number of fundamental organizational policies provide the context for considering human resource management. These policies vary from organization to organization and tend to limit or constrain the actual design of a human resource system. While they are not the focus of this article, they are identified as important contextual issues that organizations must consider along the way. These policies are:

1. Management Philosophy.   A basic policy that influences the overall design of a human resource system is the organization's management philosophy, i.e., its "psychological contract" with employees. An organization typically specifies the nature of the exchange with its employees. On one end of the spectrum is a "fair day's work for a fair day's pay," a purely extrinsic quid pro quo contract. Many U.S. blue-collar jobs fit this description. At the other extreme is the contract that stresses "challenging, meaningful work in return for a loyal, committed, and self-motivated employee," an intrinsically oriented contract. Some of the Scandinavian companies committed to quality of work life are positioned at this end of the spectrum. Such organizations typically develop people from within and seldom go to the external labor market to fill job openings.

A second policy decision involving management philosophy is the extent to which the organization is top-down or bottom-up driven. In a top-down organization, the human resource system centralizes all key selection, appraisal, and reward and development decisions. A bottom-up system encourages widespread participation in all activities.

Table 6.1 Human Resource Management Links to Strategy and Structure

		Human Resource Management			
Strategy	Structure	Selection	Appraisal	Rewards	Development
1. Single product	Functional	Functionally oriented: subjective criteria used	Subjective: measure via personal contact	Unsystematic and allocated in a paternalistic manner	Unsystematic largely through job experiences: single function focus
2. Single product (vertically integrated)	Functional	Functionally oriented: standardized criteria used	Impersonal: based on cost and productivity data	Related to performance and productivity	Functional specialists with some generalists: largely through job rotation
3. Growth by acquisition (holding company) of unrelated businesses	Separate self-contained businesses	Functionally oriented, but varies from business to business in terms of how systematic	Impersonal: based on return on investment and profitability	Formula-based and includes return on investment and profitability	Cross-functional but not cross-business
4. Related diversification of product lines through internal growth and acquisition	Multidivisional	Functionally and generalist oriented: systematic criteria used	Impersonal: based on return on investment, productivity, and subjective assessment of contribution to overall company	Large bonuses: based on profitability and subjective assessment of contribution to overall company	Cross-functional, cross-divisional, and cross-corporate/ divisional: formal
5. Multiple products in multiple countries	Global organization (geographic center and worldwide)	Functionally and generalist oriented: systematic criteria used	Impersonal: based on multiple goals such as return on investment, profit tailored to product and country	Bonuses: based on multiple planned goals with moderate top management discretion	Cross-divisional and cross-subsidiary to corporate: formal and systematic

Table adapted from J. Galbraith and D. Nathanson, *Strategy Implementation: The Role of Structure and Process* (St. Paul, MN: West Publishing, 1978).

116

2. Reliance on Development or Selection.   Organizations vary in the degree to which they weight the impact of these two factors of performance. Some companies do almost no training or development. Other companies, such as AT&T, invest heavily in development. A company such as GE ascribes to a management philosophy that stresses both careful selection and development.

3. Group versus Individual Performance.   The human resource systems can be geared toward collective, group-based performance or individual performance, or toward some mixture of the two. When the emphasis is on group performance, the selection must take into account social compatibility; the appraisal system must be group focused; and rewards must provide incentives for the work group.

The Human Resource Cycle

In light of these policies, we may now focus on four generic processes or functions that are performed by a human resource system in all organizations—selection, appraisal, rewards, and development. These four processes reflect sequential managerial tasks. Figure 6.2 represents them in terms of a human resource cycle. Clearly the dependent variable in Figure 6.2 is performance: the human resource elements are designed to impact performance at both the individual and the organizational levels.

Performance, in other words, is a function of all the human resource components: selecting people who are best able to perform the jobs defined by the structure; motivating employees by rewarding them judiciously; training and developing employees for future performance; and appraising em-

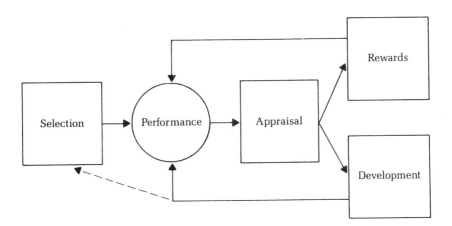

Figure 6.2   The Human Resource Cycle

ployees in order to justify the rewards. In addition, performance is a function of the organizational context and resources surrounding the individual. Thus, strategy and structure also impact performance through the ways jobs are designed, through how the organization is structured, and through how well services or products are planned to meet environmental threats and opportunities.

In order to put these functions in the various contexts of the organization, we rely upon Robert Anthony's distinction among the three levels of managerial work: the strategic level, the managerial level, and the operational level.[4]

The strategic level deals with policy formulation and overall goal setting: Its objective is to position effectively the organization in its environment. The managerial level is concerned with the availability and allocation of resources to carry out the strategic plan. To be in the business(es) specified by the strategic plan, the company must decide what its capital, informational, and human resource needs are. At the operational level, the day-to-day management of the organization is carried out. (Operational activities are ideally carried out under the umbrella of the managerial plan.)

Table 6.2 illustrates the kinds of activities associated with these three levels for each generic component of the human resource cycle. For example, in the selection placement area, operational-level activities include the annual staffing and recruitment plans. Managerial selection is more concerned with manpower planning for the intermediate future. For instance, a company that is about to open two plants in different parts of the country would want to know the kinds of people the company will need and how it should go about finding the people to run the plants. Strategic selection is concerned with identifying who can best run the business(es) in the long run.

Selection, Promotion, and Placement Process

The selection, promotion, and placement process includes all those activities related to the internal movement of people across positions and to the external hiring into the organization. The essential process is one of matching available human resources to jobs in the organization. It entails defining the organization's human needs for particular positions and assessing the available pool of people to determine the best fit.

Three strategic selection concerns are particularly salient. The first involves devising an organization-wide selection and promotion system that supports the organization's business strategy. For example, if a company will be diversifying over a ten-year period, it is most likely that the types of people needed to run the new business will be different from in the past.

Table 6.2 Human Resource Activities

Management Level	Selection	Appraisal	Rewards (Compensation and Fringe Benefits)	Development
Strategic	Specify characteristics of people needed to run business in long term Alter internal and external systems to reflect future	In long term, what should be valued? Develop means to appraise future dimensions Early identification of potential	In world as it might be in long term, how will work force be rewarded? Link to the long-term business strategy	Plan developmental experiences for people running business of the future Systems with flexibility to adjust to change Develop long-term career paths
Managerial	Longitudinal validation of selection criteria Development of recruitment marketing plan New markets	Validated systems linking current and future potential Assessment centers for development	Five-year compensation plans for individuals Cafeteria-style fringe packages	General management development programs Organization development Foster self-development
Operational	Staffing plans Recruitment plans Day-to-day monitoring systems	Annual or more frequent appraisal system(s) Day-to-day control systems	Wage and salary administration Benefit packages	Specific job skill training On-the-job training

Thus, a redesigned selection process will be required. This process is taking place in the oil industry as it launches its twenty-year diversification effort.

The second strategic concern requires creating internal flows of people that match the business strategy. Companies that diversify or change their strategic direction need to alter traditional promotional patterns in order to move new types of people into key positions. AT&T's move into the competitive electronic communication and knowledge business has necessitated their developing internal promotion systems for profit-driven people who are able to innovate and deal with competitive markets. This is a major change from the regulated telephone monopoly that was service oriented, low on innovation, and not managed competitively where profit was regulated.

The third strategic concern is matching key executives to the business's strategy. There is a growing interest in meshing strategic planning with executive skills. This is especially true in companies that are using a product-portfolio-analysis approach to strategic management. The Boston Consulting Group's (BCG's) portfolio matrix is the most common and simplest formulation. In the BCG approach, a set of business practices is prescribed for managing each type of business. Several examples of companies already committed to using senior-executive selection as a strategic management tool are presented below:

General Electric.   GE uses a more complex portfolio matrix with nine cells. Yet the underlying concepts are based on the same product-life-cycle notions represented in the BCG matrix. GE defines its products in terms of the kinds of management practices required for success. Thus, its products are defined as "growers" for wildcats, "defenders" for stars, "harvesters" for cash cows, and "undertakers" for dogs:

> Its [GE] general managers are being classified by personal style or orientation as "growers," "caretakers," and "undertakers." . . . They [GE] have a shortage of growers but they are making a great effort to remove the undertaker types who are heading up growth businesses. The lighting business is mainly mature but we [GE] just designated international operations as a growth area to our five year forecast. . . . John D. Hamilton, the manager responsible for manpower planning, says he and the executive manpower staff at corporate headquarters looked at the whole pool of corporate talent. They decided to move in a manager who had an industrial rather than a lighting background, but who seemed to show entrepreneurial flair.[5]

Corning Glass Company.   At Corning, an extensive effort is under way to assess the company's top 100 executives for such qualities as entrepreneurial flair. The goal is to have a clearer profile of the organization's pool of executive talent specified in terms of capabilities for managing different parts of the BCG matrix. An example of this process occurred in December 1979:

Corning reshaped its electronic strategy, deciding that the market was starting to expand again, and that it needed a growth-oriented manager. It placed a manufacturing specialist who had shown a great deal of flair in working with customers in the top marketing slot for electronics, and says Shafer, "It looks like he's turning it around."[6]

Chase Manhattan Bank. During the period between 1975 and 1980, the bank underwent major managerial changes. A key to the bank's successful turnaround from a troubled bank in the mid-1970s was its careful strategic-level selection and placement of executives. Historically, at Chase, as is the case with banking in general, senior-level positions were filled on the historical precedent: The old-boy networks played a major role. Furthermore, the tradition was to reward those with banker skills and not those with managerial skills, which were implicitly considered to be of less importance. But under the stress of serious performance problems, Chase Manhattan Bank reexamined these practices. As a result, a systematic effort was launched to strategically manage senior selection and placement decisions. For example, "When the trust manager retired, corporate management decided that the department, whose operation had been essentially stable, should focus on a more aggressive growth strategy. Instead of seeking a veteran banker, Chase hired a man whose experience had been with IBM," because it was felt that he would bring the strong marketing orientation to the trust department that the new strategy required.[7]

Texas Instruments. At TI, there is an explicit attempt to match management style to product life cycles. "As a product moves through different phases of its life cycle, different kinds of management skills become dominant."[8] The mismatch of managerial style to the product life cycle can be quite serious. For example, a risk-taking entrepreneurial manager who is in charge of a cash-cow business is likely to reduce the profitability of the business by trying to "grow" the business and take risks. On the other hand, putting a cost-cutting, efficiency-oriented manager in charge of a growth business can stifle innovation and prevent the business from acquiring market share. TI feels that, in the past, it did not pay adequate attention to the match between product life cycle and managerial style. As a result, TI feels it lost its early lead in integrated circuits. During the growth stage, TI had a "cash-cow manager in charge rather than a grower or entrepreneurial type."[9] The result was that "tighter controls were introduced, but TI failed to recognize that a research orientation was really what the Integrated Department needed at the growth stage. TI has since redoubled its efforts to match management orientation with job needs. Bucy, now president, personally reviews the records of the top TI managers."[10]

Reward Processes

Performance follows the selection process. Once people are in their jobs, they need to be rewarded for good performance. The rewards that exist in organizational settings are many. Among them are:

- Pay in its various forms: salary, bonuses, stock options, benefits, and perquisites.
- Promotion: both upward mobility and lateral transfers into desirable positions.
- Management praise.
- Career opportunities: a long-term chance for growth and development.
- Appreciation from customers and/or clients of the organization.
- Personal sense of well-being: feeling good about oneself for accomplishing objectives.
- Opportunity to learn: a chance to expand one's skills and knowledge base.
- Security: a sense of job and financial security.
- Responsibility: providing individuals with a sense of organizational responsibility.
- Respect from coworkers.
- Friendship from coworkers.

Most organizations, however, do not do a very good job of managing these rewards to produce desired organizational behaviors. As a result, the reward system is one of the most underutilized and mishandled managerial tools for driving organizational performance. As can be seen from the human resource cycle in Figure 6.2, rewards are a major factor in influencing performance. Assuming that the organization can appraise performance, which is not always a good assumption, the organization then has a rationale for allocating rewards based on how well people perform: Many organizations think of rewards only in terms of managing pay.

Thus, a major strategic issue concerning the reward system is how to use it to overcome the tendency toward short-sighted management. The rewards for this year's profits generally turn out to be both financial incentives and promotions. Motivation of senior executives toward long-term strategic goals is difficult, given that the reward system often encourages short-term achievement at the expense of long-term goals:

Though bonuses based on achieving sales or earning goals have long been common, the emphasis on long term is a new element. Top corporate executives, under pressure from Wall Street and stockholders, have been rewarded with bonuses and stock options when immediate profits spurt. The auto industry, for example, is notable for its short-term rewards.[11]

It is unreasonable and unwise to recommend that managers be rewarded only for long-term strategic goals, as businesses must perform in the present to succeed in the future. Thus, the reward system should provide balanced support to short-term and long-term strategic goals.

Balancing Long- and Short-Term Goals

Texas Instruments.   TI has thought long and hard about the use of its reward system for driving the company's short- and long-term goals.

One major part of TI's strategy since the early 1960s has been to adhere rigidly to the "learning curve theory." Simply put, it states that "manufacturing costs can be brought down by a fixed percentage, depending on the product, each time cumulative volume is doubled."[12] The strategy involves constant redesign improvement of the product and of the processes of production, so that prices can drop as fast as possible. This strategy was implemented by organizing Product Customer Centers (PCCs), decentralized profit centers that can be closely monitored for cost performance. The reward system was closely tied to the PCCs, so that managers worked hard to make the learning-curve theory operative. However, there were some problems.

The Product Customer Centers and associated reward systems worked against another organizational strategy: the development of innovations for future products. The rewards were structured to drive managers to be overly concerned with short-run efficiencies and not with long-term strategic goals.

The solution to this dilemma was to design another organization and to drape it over the existing PCC structure. The new organization, called Objectives, Strategies, and Tactics (OST), was created to supplement the PCCs, which remained intact. The OST structure was used for the formulation and implementation of strategic long-range plans, and it consisted of the same managers as that of the PCC organization.

Thus, the top managers at TI wear two hats. Wearing one hat, they are bottom-line, efficiency-focused managers who work to drive the PCC system and who are rewarded and evaluated for accomplishing the efficiency objectives. Wearing the OST hat, the managers are involved in working toward a strategic objective that may have a ten- to twenty-year time horizon. Separate monitoring and appraisal systems tied to the OST organization are used to drive performance in the long-term strategic area. For example, a manager may be responsible for PCC efficiency, while at the same time he may work in the OST structure toward a strategic objective in the development of products in the computerized auto industry of the future. If 60 percent of his time is allocated to the PCCs and 40 percent of his time to OST, then his compensation is split to reflect the short- and long-term aspects of the job.

TI also uses the reward system to encourage another set of desired strategic behaviors. When it discovered that managers tended to set low-risk objectives in order to enhance their chances of receiving a bigger bonus, and thereby stifled their creativity and innovativeness, TI altered the reward system through a "wild hare" program that provides funding for more speculative programs. Under this program, managers are asked to rank speculative projects on a separate basis. The bonus system is then tied into this process.

Another strategic reward mechanism for fostering organizational innovation is to provide organization members with a chance to obtain a grant from a pool containing several million dollars set up to fund innovative projects. The result has been the emergence of informal groups who apply for grants from the innovation pool, called IDEA. These groups then attempt to turn their ideas into viable products.

Management Development

Activities designed to ensure that individuals are properly equipped with skills and knowledge to carry out their jobs fall into the management-development category. These activities range from simple job training for lower-level employees to long-term development of senior executives. The three major areas of the developmental process are (1) job improvement: the development of specific job skills and competencies; (2) career planning: a longitudinal focus on individual growth and development in relation to organizational opportunities; and (3) succession planning: the organizational focus on ensuring an adequate supply of human resource talent for projected needs in the future based on strategic plans.

At the long-term strategic level, the developmental process includes such activities as management education, job assignments, and the use of mentor relationships. Some of the strategic-level developmental concerns are discussed briefly.

Ensuring that the organization has an adequate supply of human resource talent at all levels is no easy task, especially when the organization is undergoing rapid strategic changes. The key to this concern is to have a human resource planning system that makes accurate forecasts of needs and of resources available to meet those needs. Such systems, however, are not easily built, and even though most large companies have manpower planning systems, they are often very inadequate as a result of two basic flaws.

The first flaw is that the data about people that are fed into the system are unreliable because managers generally do not appraise employees well. As it now stands, the appraisal process that provides these data is the weakest link in the human resource cycle. Thus, planning systems that are built on these data are also inadequate. In order to plan for the future, it is necessary to have an inventory of current human resources that includes an assessment of both current performance and of the future potential of key individuals.

The second basic flaw is that there is a missing link between human resource planning systems and business strategy. Although many organizations have given lip service to this missing link, the reality is that it has been treated as an afterthought that has usually been delegated to the human resource staff without any line management involvement. As a result, the human resource plan is a paper exercise that is not utilized by the strategic decision makers.

A handful of U.S. companies have strategically managed the development of senior executive talent. At General Motors, Exxon, General Electric, Texas Instruments, IBM, and Procter & Gamble, the emphasis has been on carefully developing managers by following such principles as:

1. Sustained interest in and support for management development and succession planning on the part of top management.
2. Efforts to identify young professionals deemed to have potential for top-level management positions.
3. Comprehensive and systematic rewards used for managerial performance.
4. The appraisal includes data from multiple sources and is used in making decisions about management development.
5. Special recruiting efforts to provide appropriate raw materials for general managers of the future.
6. Opportunities for capable young professionals to develop managerial skills early in their careers.
7. Compensation policies and salary administration to help stimulate management development and retain key personnel.
8. Clear developmental objectives and career plans for managers at all levels.
9. Effective coaching from personnel's superiors.
10. Stressing results in the performance appraisal process.

Some companies have been very strategic in developing managers. For example:

Exxon. The Compensation and Executive Development (COED) system at Exxon is designed to ensure a disciplined approach to the development of managerial talent for the company. The system is directed from the top, where the COED committee is headed by the CEO, Clifford Garvin, and is made up of members of Exxon's Board. The committee is in charge of reviewing the development and placement of the top 250 Exxon executives. Meeting nearly every Monday, the COED committee carefully reviews the performance of executives and examines their developmental needs. To ensure that there is a continual flow of managerial talent for the company and that all positions have back-up candidates, the committee then compares the performances of all the executives and makes decisions according to future developmental needs.

There is also a COED system within each of the Exxon subsidiaries, where the president of each subsidiary has his or her own COED committee, similar to the one Mr. Garvin heads. Each subsidiary also has a senior level staff for the COED committee: This enables the COED system to reach the top 2,000 or so managers at Exxon.

In discussions with senior Exxon managers, it is rather striking to hear the universal acclaim given the system. Most agree that the system accounts for Exxon's overall success and that it is an excellent system for developing managers.

General Motors.   General Motors is another company with an equally strong tradition of management development that dates back to Alfred Sloan.

> At General Motors, the supreme court of executive review in recent years included the top six executives in the company. . . . During the week-long sessions in the Board room of Detroit headquarters each February and July, they spend long days and nights listening to analysis of more than 600 managers from each of GM's ten vice-presidents and group executives. . . . A variety of questions are covered to get an accurate picture of where the individual stands in his career development. . . . We don't have jobs at GM, we have careers. Along with performance, the probing is centered on just what kind of potential the executive may have. Here are some examples. Does the executive seem to be developing at the rate expected? What is the job contributing to the person's ability? Is it rounding out the person as we intended? What should be the next job for this executive? Should it be in another division or involve greater responsibility? If so, who would we put in this executive's place?[13]

Chase Manhattan Bank.   A more targeted use of management development took place at Chase Manhattan Bank. A management-development program was designed to support the company's first formal strategic-planning process. The two-week program for the top officers of the bank focused on awareness and frameworks needed to support the new process. The program had the involvement of the then chairman, David Rockefeller, and the then president, Willard Butcher. Both symbolically and substantively, the program strongly reinforced the importance of the new strategic-planning process.

Appraisal Process

Perhaps the least liked managerial activity is the annual performance appraisal. The activity is often only a perfunctory paper exercise. Performance appraisals are like seat belts: Everyone agrees that they are important and that they save lives, yet no one uses them. Similarly, the problem with appraisal systems includes poorly designed procedures, a psychological resistance of managers to give negative evaluations, and a perceived invalidity. The appraisal system, nonetheless, is central to the human resource cycle. It contributes to three essential processes:

1. Rewards can be allocated in relation to performance only through the use of an appraisal system by which performance can be measured. Such appraisal systems range from subjective personal evaluations to impersonal criteria based on profitability, return on investment, market share, and other quantitative measures.
2. Human resource planning relies on valid appraisals. A current inventory of talent can be made only through a valid appraisal process that shows those who have been performing well and those who have not. In addition, future human resource projections must be based on an assessment of the potential of the employees, which is indicated by the appraisal process. Without the data provided by a valid appraisal, such forecasting is impossible, as there is no basis for making predictions.
3. The development process is also built on the appraisal process. Based on an assessment of an individual's performance and potential, both the individual and the organization can plan for future training and development. A weak data base leads to a hit-or-miss training program and retards the development process.

Relationship to Strategy

A strategic concern for companies is to develop appraisal processes that are supportive of the business strategy. A study by Lorsch and Allen indicated that such a link influences total performance.[14] In this study, the authors compared the appraisal systems in diversified companies to those in integrated companies. They found that the diversified companies placed more emphasis on objective and result measures such as productivity, profit, volume, etc. The integrated firms, however, tended to rely more on operating and intermediate measures, as well as on more subjective evaluation of abilities such as "planning," "controlling," "organizing," and "leadership." The diversified appraisal system worked better because the divisions were more self-contained, having little interdivisional or corporate contact. The integrated companies, on the other hand, had greater interdivisional contact and greater sharing of resources, which made it hard for them to decide who exactly was responsible for how much of the end results. These two simple examples underscore some of the strategic issues involved in matching an appraisal process to the business strategy.

The key to an effective appraisal system at the strategic level is the commitment of quality managerial time to systematic examination and evaluation of executive talent. The descriptions of the Exxon and GM development systems are in part descriptions of their appraisal systems, as the two systems are interrelated. The company with the best strategic appraisal system is probably General Electric, where much time and staff work go into appraising the top 600 executives.

General Electric.   The diversification of GE makes the appraisal of managers more complex than that of most other companies. Unlike GM or Exxon, which have one major line of business, GE has more than 240 businesses. As a result, GE has developed elaborate approaches to handling the appraisal of key managers.

An example of this is the slate system. The top 600 positions at GE are carefully managed and monitored by the chairman. A special human resource staff under the direction of a senior vice-president reviews these key executives. This staff works with line managers to develop slates of acceptable candidates for key managerial positions in the company. Positions must be filled from among those on the approved slate; that is, a business head cannot select his own vice-president of marketing unless the individual is among those on the official slate list for the position. Although a manager may select an individual who is not on the slate, the decision must ultimately be kicked up the hierarchy at GE to the chairman. However, this kind of selection is frowned upon, and very few people who are not on the slate are selected for key managerial positions.

One of the services the human resource staff provides in developing the data base for the slate system is an in-depth executive review of key managers. Highly trained personnel spend several weeks preparing a report on a single executive. The process involves interviews with subordinates, peers, bosses, and even customers of GE to get a composite picture of the individual's strengths, weaknesses, accomplishments, failures, and potentials.

These reviews estimate the expected future progress of the individual at GE and give extensive suggestions for futher development. The completed report is reviewed by the individual, who can voice disagreement with it. It then becomes part of the individual's file. (Only forty of these reviews are conducted a year.)

Implementing Strategic Human Resource Management

In another article, we discussed a methodology for moving a human resource function into the strategic arena.[15] The approach is based on a human resource audit that provides the organization with data on the internal capacity of the human resource function and data from the line concerning the kind of services the organization needs at the operational, managerial, and strategic levels. As a result of our conducting these audits in several large companies, we developed the following suggestions for making the human resource function more strategic:

The Internal Organization of the Human Resource Function. The first area of focus is on how to properly organize, staff, and manage the human resource function. This involves four steps:

Step 1. Identify the portfolio of human resource tasks at the strategic, managerial, and operational level for each human resource element.

Step 2. Reorganize the human resource function to reflect the operational, managerial, and strategic needs of the business. The *operational level* is best served by a tradtional functional personnel department where there are separate units carrying out recruitment, compensation, development, etc. The *managerial level* must be organized to cut across the subfunctions identified at the operational level (recruitment, development, compensation, etc.) by using such design tools as liaison managers, teams, or, under limited conditions, a matrix organizational design. The *strategic level* activities require an elite senior human resource management (individual or team, depending on the size of the organization) supported by strong managerial human resource services.

Step 3. The human resource staff must be trained in the more strategically focused organization. At the operational level, the function must be staffed with technically focused professional personnel and/or with MBAs who are starting out in their careers and who need to learn the nuts and bolts of personnel. At the managerial level, individuals who possess a more general managerial orientation and background either through actual work experience or through an MBA degree should be selected from the operational level. Finally, at the strategic level, the aim should be to select human resource executives who have political skills, a broad business orientation, and a broad human resource management background. A proactive stance toward the strategic future of the organization is also required.

Step 4. The reward and control systems must be altered to support the strategic human resource function. Rewards and controls should reflect specific tasks at each of the three levels. Most personnel reward and control systems are geared toward operational-level activities: These should be expanded to reward and control people in terms of the new strategic and managerial-level activities.

Linking the Human Resource Function to the Line Organization.   Major changes are also required to link the human resource function to the user organization. Most personnel functions are linked to the operational business activities. With the addition of new managerial and strategic activities, new linking mechanisms will be required:

Step 1. Provide the business with good human resource data bases. These include environmental scanning of labor markets and social and economic issues that impact the long-term human resource context of the organization. In addition, data on the internal labor pool are required in both a present and a future context. Internal marketing data on the human resource needs of various user groups in the organization are especially helpful.

Step 2. Alter the senior management role when it comes to human resource management issues, so that these concerns receive quality attention. The managers need to be committed to weighing human resource issues with the same level of attention as that of other functions, such as finance, marketing, and production.

Step 3. The line organization must alter its incentive and control systems, so that the overall human resource function is managed. It will also be necessary for the organization to have ways of measuring the overall performance of the human resource function at the strategic, managerial, and operational levels. This will entail ongoing audits of the human resource function to determine how well it is doing in providing services to its clients. Also adjustments must be made in budgeting for human resource services, as some of these adjustments will require new sources of corporate funding.

These steps are illustrative of what is involved in developing a more strategic human resource function. Obviously, every organization must develop its own answers and a tailored strategic stance in terms of its human resources.

Summary and Conclusions

Human resource management is a major force in driving organizational performance. Thus, when business is castigated and when American industry is unfavorably compared to that of Japan or West Germany, two major factors are underscored: (1) our lack of a long-term perspective in management; and (2) our lack of skill in managing people. Both of these factors can be changed only with a concomitant change in the human resource activities inside our organizations; that is, it requires changes in the way people think and behave. In the final analysis, three concluding points should be made about human resource management:

1. Human resource activities have a major impact on individual performance and hence on productivity and organizational performance.
2. The cycle of human resource activities is highly interdependent. The human resource system is therefore only as strong as its weakest link.
3. Effective strategic management requires effective human resource management.

7

Increasing Organizational Effectiveness Through Better Human Resource Planning and Development

Edgar H. Schein

Planning for and managing human resources is emerging as an increasingly important determinant of organizational effectiveness. It is an area all too often ignored by line managers. As organizations evolve, the complexity of the environments within which they operate will cause increased dependence upon the very people making up the organization. This article focuses upon two key issues: the increasing importance of human resource planning and development in organizational effectiveness, and how the major components of a human resource planning and development system should be coordinated for maximum effectiveness. The author concludes that these multiple components must be managed by both line managers and staff specialists as part of a total system to be effective. *SMR*.

In this article I would like to address two basic questions. First, why is human resource planning and development becoming increasingly important as a determinant of organizational effectiveness? Second, what are the major components of a human resource planning and career development system, and how should these components be linked for maximum organizational effectiveness?

The field of personnel management has for some time addressed issues such as these, and much of the technology of planning for and managing human resources has been worked out to a considerable degree.[1] Nevertheless there continues to be in organizations a failure, particularly on the part of line managers and functional managers in areas other than personnel, to recognize the true importance of planning for and managing human re-

From *Sloan Management Review*, Fall 1977, Vol. 19, No. 1. Reprinted with permission.

sources. This article is not intended to be a review of what is known, but rather a kind of position paper for line managers to bring to their attention some important and all too often neglected issues. These issues are important for organizational effectiveness, quite apart from their relevance to the issue of humanizing work or improving the quality of working life.[2]

The observations and analyses made below are based on several kinds of information:

- Formal research on management development, career development, and human development through the adult life cycle conducted in the Sloan School and at other places for the past several decades.[3]
- Analysis of consulting relationships, field observations, and other involvements over the past several decades with all kinds of organizations dealing with the planning for and implementation of human resource development programs and organization development projects.[4]

Why is Human Resource Planning and Development Increasingly Important?

The Changing Managerial Job

The first answer to the question is simple, though paradoxical. Organizations are becoming more dependent upon people, because they are increasingly involved in more complex technologies and are attempting to function in more complex economic, political, and sociocultural environments. The more different technical skills there are involved in the design, manufacture, marketing, and sales of a product, the more vulnerable the organization will be to critical shortages of the right kinds of human resources. The more complex the process, the higher the interdependence among the various specialists. The higher the interdependence, the greater the need for effective integration of all the specialities, because the entire process is only as strong as its weakest link.

In simpler technologies, managers could often compensate for the technical or communication failures of their subordinates. General managers today are much more dependent upon their technically trained subordinates, because they usually do not understand the details of the engineering, marketing, financial, and other decisions that their subordinates are making. Even the general manager who grew up in finance may find that, since his day, the field of finance has outrun him, and his subordinates are using models and methods he cannot entirely understand.

What all this means for the general manager is that he cannot any longer safely make decisions by himself; he cannot get enough information digested within his own head to be the integrator and sole decision maker. Instead, he finds himself increasingly having to manage the *process* of decision making, bringing the right people together around the right questions or problems, stimulating open discussion, ensuring that all relevant information surfaces and is critically assessed, managing the emotional ups and downs of his prima donnas, and ensuring that, out of all this human and interpersonal process, a good decision will result.

As I have watched processes like these in management groups, I have often been struck by the fact that the decision emerges out of the interplay. It is hard to pin down who had the idea and who made the decision. The general manager in this setting is accountable for the decision, but rarely would I describe the process as one where he or she actually made the decision, except in the sense of recognizing when the right answer was achieved, ratifying that answer, announcing it, and following up on its implementation.

If the managerial *job* is increasingly moving in the direction I have indicated, managers of the future will have to be much more skilled in how to:

1. Select and train their subordinates.
2. Design and run meetings and groups.
3. Deal with conflict between strong individuals and groups.
4. Influence and negotiate from a low power base.
5. Integrate the efforts of diverse technical specialists.

If the above image of what is happening to organizations has any generality, it will force the field of human resource management increasingly to center stage. The more complex organizations become, the more they will be vulnerable to human error. They will not necessarily employ more people, but they will employ more sophisticated highly trained people, both in managerial and in individual-contributor staff roles. The price of low motivation, turnover, poor productivity, sabotage, and intraorganizational conflict will be higher in such an organization. Therefore it will become a matter of economic necessity to improve human resource planning and development systems.

Changing Social Values

A second reason why human resource planning and development will become more central and important is that changing social values regarding the role of work will make it more complicated to manage people. Several kinds of research findings and observations illustrate this point.

First, my own longitudinal research of a panel of Sloan School graduates of the 1960s strongly suggests that we have put much too much emphasis on the traditional success syndrome of "climbing the corporate ladder."[5] Some alumni indeed want to rise to high-level general-manager positions, but many others want to exercise their particular technical or functional competence and rise only to levels of functional management or senior staff roles with minimal managerial responsibility. Some want security, others are seeking nonorganizational careers as teachers or consultants, while a few are becoming entrepreneurs. I have called these patterns of motivation, talent, and values "career anchors" and believe that they serve to stabilize and constrain the career in predictable ways. The implication is obvious—organizations must develop multiple ladders and multiple reward systems to deal with different types of people.[6]

Second, studies of young people entering organizations in the last several decades suggest that work and career are not so central a life preoccupation as they once were. Perhaps because of a prolonged period of economic affluence, people see more options for themselves and are increasingly exercising those options. In particular, one sees more concern with a balanced life in which work, family, and self-development play more equal roles.[7]

Third, closely linked to the above trend is the increase in the number of women in organizations, which will have its major impact through the increase of dual-career families. As opportunities for women increase, we will see more new life-styles in young couples that will affect the organization's options as to moving people geographically, joint employment, joint career management, family support, etc.[8]

Fourth, research evidence is beginning to show that personal growth and development is a life-long process and that predictable issues and crises come up in every decade of our lives. Organizations will have to be much more aware of what these issues are, how work and family interact, and how to manage people at different ages. The current "hot button" is mid-career crisis, but the more research we do the more we find developmental crises at all ages and stages.[9]

An excellent summary of what is happening in the world of values, technology, and management is provided in a recent text by Elmer Burack:

The leading edge of change in the future will include the new technologies of information, production, and management, interlaced with considerable social dislocation and shifts in manpower inputs. These developments are without precedent in our industrial history.

Technological and social changes have created a need for more education, training, and skill at all managerial and support levels. The lowering of barriers to employment based on sex and race introduces new kinds of manpower problems for management officials. Seniority is coming to mean relatively less in relation to the comprehension of problems, processes, and approaches. The newer manpower elements and work technologies have shifted institutional arrangements: The locus of decision making is altered, role relationships among workers and supervisors are changed (often becoming more collegial), and the need to respond to changing routines has become commonplace. . . .

These shifts have been supported by more demanding customer requirements, increasing government surveillance (from product-quality to antipollution measures), and more widespread use of computers, shifting power bases to the holders of specialized knowledge skills.[10]

In order for human resource planning and development (HRPD) systems to become more responsive and capable of handling such growing complexity, they must contain all the necessary components, must be based on correct assumptions, and must be adequately integrated.

Components of a Human Resource Planning and Development System

The major problem with existing HRPD systems is that they are fragmented, incomplete, and sometimes built on faulty assumptions about human or organizational growth.

Human growth takes place through successive encounters with one's environment. As the person encounters a new situation, he or she is forced to try new responses to deal with that situation. Learning takes place as a function of how those responses work out and the results they achieve. If they are successful in coping with the situation, the person enlarges his repertory of responses; if they are not successful the person must try alternate responses until the situation has been dealt with. If none of the active coping responses work, the person sometimes retreats from the new situation, or denies there is a problem to be solved. These responses are defensive and growth limiting.

For growth to occur, people basically need two things: *new challenges* that are within the range of their coping responses, and *knowledge of results*—information on how their responses to the challenge have worked out. If the tasks and challenges are too easy or too hard, the person will be demotivated and cease to grow. If the information is not available on how well the person's responses are working, the person cannot grow in a systematic, valid direction but is forced into guessing or trying to infer information from ambiguous signals.

Organizational growth similarly takes place through successful coping with the internal and external environment.[11] But since the organization is a complex system of human, material, financial, and informational resources, one must consider how each of those areas can be properly managed toward organizational effectiveness. In this article I will deal only with human resources.

In order for the organization to have the capacity to perform effectively over a period of time it must be able to plan for, recruit, manage, develop, measure, dispose of, and replace human resources as warranted by the tasks to be done. The most important of these functions is the planning function, since task requirements are likely to change as the complexity and turbulence of the organization's environment increase. In other words, a key assumption underlying organizational growth is that the nature of jobs will change over time, which means that such changes must be continuously monitored in order to ensure that the right kinds of human resources can be recruited or developed to do those jobs. Many of the activities such as recruitment, selection, performance appraisal, and so on presume that some planning process has occurred that makes it possible to assess whether or not those activities are meeting organizational needs, quite apart from whether they are facilitating the individual's growth.

In an ideal HRPD system, one would seek to match the organization's needs for human resources with the individual's needs for personal career growth and development. One can then depict the basic system as involving both individual and organizational planning, and a series of matching activities designed to satisfy mutual needs. If we further assume that both individual and organizational needs change over time, we can depict this process as a developmental one, as in Figure 7.1.

In the right-hand column we show the basic stages of the individual career through the life cycle. While not everyone will go through these stages in the manner depicted, there is growing evidence that, for organizational careers in particular, these stages reasonably depict the movement of people through their adult lives.[12]

Given those developmental assumptions, the left-hand side of the diagram shows the organizational planning activities that must occur if human resources are to be managed in an optimal way, and if changing job requirements are to be properly assessed and continuously monitored. The middle column shows the various matching activities that have to occur at various career stages.

The components of an effective HRPD system now can be derived from the diagram. First, there have to be in the organization the overall planning components shown on the left-hand side of Figure 7.1. Second, there have to be components that ensure an adequate process of staffing the organization. Third, there have to be components that plan for and monitor growth and development. Fourth, there have to be components that facilitate the

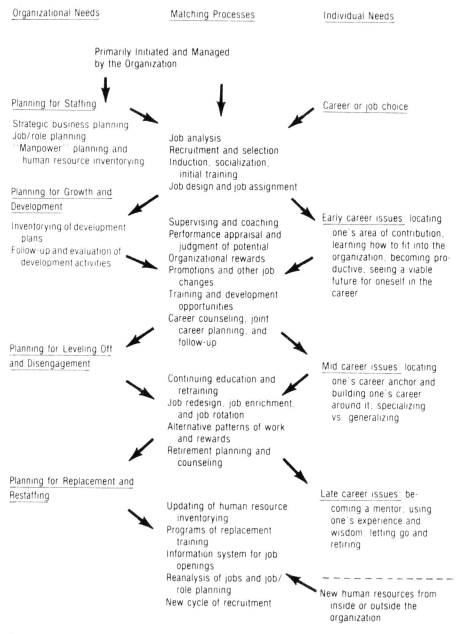

Organizational Needs   Matching Processes   Individual Needs

Primarily Initiated and Managed
by the Organization

Planning for Staffing

Strategic business planning
Job/role planning
"Manpower" planning and
   human resource inventorying

Job analysis
Recruitment and selection
Induction, socialization,
   initial training
Job design and job assignment

Career or job choice

Planning for Growth and
Development

Inventorying of development
   plans
Follow-up and evaluation of
   development activities

Supervising and coaching
Performance appraisal and
   judgment of potential
Organizational rewards
Promotions and other job
   changes
Training and development
   opportunities
Career counseling, joint
   career planning, and
   follow-up

Early career issues: locating
   one's area of contribution,
   learning how to fit into the
   organization, becoming productive, seeing a viable
   future for oneself in the
   career

Planning for Leveling Off
and Disengagement

Continuing education and
   retraining
Job redesign, job enrichment,
   and job rotation
Alternative patterns of work
   and rewards
Retirement planning and
   counseling

Mid career issues: locating
   one's career anchor and
   building one's career
   around it, specializing
   vs. generalizing

Planning for Replacement and
Restaffing

Updating of human resource
   inventorying
Programs of replacement
   training
Information system for job
   openings
Reanalysis of jobs and job/
   role planning
New cycle of recruitment

Late career issues: be-
   coming a mentor, using
   one's experience and
   wisdom; letting go and
   retiring

New human resources from
   inside or outside the
   organization

Figure 7.1   A Developmental Model of Human Resource Planning and Development

138

actual process of the growth and development of the people who are brought into the organization; this growth and development must be organized to meet both the needs of the organization and the needs of the individuals within it. Fifth, there have to be components that deal with decreasing effectiveness, leveling off, obsolescence of skills, turnover, retirement, and other phenomena that reflect the need for either a new growth direction or a process of disengagement of the person from his or her job. Finally, there have to be components that ensure that, as some people move out of jobs, others are available to fill those jobs and, as new jobs arise, that people are available with the requisite skills to fill them.

In the remainder of this article I would like to comment on each of these six sets of components and indicate where and how they should be linked to each other.

Overall Planning Components

The function of these components is to ensure that the organization has an adequate basis for selecting its human resources and developing them toward the fulfillment of organizational goals.

Strategic Business Planning.   These activities are designed to determine the organization's goals, priorities, future directions, products, market growth rate, geographical location, and organization structure or design. This process should lead logically into the next two planning activities, but it is often disconnected from them, because it is located in a different part of the organization or is staffed by people with different orientations and backgrounds.

Job/Role Planning.   These activities are designed to determine what actually needs to be done at every level of the organization (up through top management) to fulfill the organization's goals and tasks. This activity can be thought of as a dynamic kind of job analysis, where a continual review is made of the skills, knowledge, values, etc., currently needed in the organization and that will be needed in the future. The focus is on the predictable consequences of the strategic planning for managerial roles, specialist roles, and skill mixes that may be needed to get the mission accomplished. If the organization already has a satisfactory system of job descriptions, this activity would concern itself with how those jobs will evolve and change, and what new jobs or roles will evolve in the future.[13]

This component is often missing completely in organizations or is carried out only for lower level jobs. From a planning point of view it is probably most important for the highest level jobs—how the nature of general and functional management will change as the organization faces new technologies, new social values, and new environmental conditions.

"Manpower Planning" and Human Resource Inventorying.   These activities draw on the job/role descriptions generated in job/role planning and assess the capabilities of the present human resources against those plans or requirements. These activities may be focused on the numbers of people in given categories and are often designed to ensure that under given assumptions of growth there will be an adequate supply of people in those categories. Or the process may focus more on how to ensure that certain scarce skills that will be needed will in fact be available, leading to more sophisticated programs of recruitment or human resource development. For example, the inventorying process at high levels may reveal the need for a new type of general manager with broad integrative capacities, which may further reveal the need to start a development program to ensure that such managers will be available five to ten years down the road.

These first three component activities are all geared to identifying the organization's needs in the human resource area. They are difficult to do, and tools are only now beginning to be developed for job/role planning.[14] In most organizations I have dealt with, the three areas, if they exist at all, are not linked to each other organizationally. Strategic planning is likely to exist in the Office of the President. Job/role planning is likely to be an offshoot of some management-development activities in Personnel. And human resource inventorying is likely to be a specialized subsection within Personnel. Typically, no one is accountable for bringing these activities together, even on an ad hoc basis.

This situation reflects an erroneous assumption about growth and development: The assumption is, if the organization develops its *present* human resources, it will be able to fill whatever job demands may arise in the future. Thus we do find in organizations elaborate human resource planning systems, but they plan for the present people in the organization, not for the organization per se. If there are no major changes in job requirements as the organization grows and develops, this system will work. But if jobs themselves change, it is no longer safe to assume that today's human resources, with development plans based on *today's* job requirements, will produce the people needed in some future situation. Therefore, I am asserting that more job/role planning must be done, independent of the present people in the organization.

The subsequent components to be discussed, which focus on the matching of individual and organizational needs, all assume that some sort of basic planning activities such as those described have been carried out. They may not be very formal, or they may be highly decentralized (e.g., every supervisor who has an open slot might make his own decision of what sort of person to hire based on his private assumptions about strategic business planning and job/role planning). Obviously, the more turbulent the environment, the greater the vulnerability of the organization if it does not centralize and coordinate its various planning activities—and generate its HRPD system from those plans.

Staffing Processes

The function of these processes is to ensure that the organization acquires the human resources necessary to fulfill its goals.

Job Analysis. If the organizational planning has been done adequately, the next component of the HRPD system is to specify what jobs need to be filled and what skills, etc., are needed to do those jobs. Some organizations go through this process very formally, others do it in an informal unprogrammed manner, but in some form it must occur in order to specify what kind of recruitment to undertake and how to select people from among the recruits.

Recruitment and Selection. This activity involves the actual process of going out to find people to fulfill jobs and developing systems for deciding which of those people to hire. These components may be very formal, including testing, assessment, and other aids to the selection process. If this component is seen as part of a total HRPD system, it will alert management to the fact that the recruitment-selection system communicates to future employees something about the nature of the organization and its approach to people. All too often this component sends incorrect messages or turns off future employees or builds incorrect stereotypes that make subsequent supervision more difficult.[15]

Induction, Socialization, and Initial Training. Once the employee has been hired, there ensues a period during which he or she learns the ropes, learns how to get along in the organization, how to work, how to fit in, how to master the particulars of the job, and so on. Once again, it is important that these activities are seen as part of a total process with long-range consequences for the attitudes of the employee.[16] The goal should be to facilitate the employee's becoming a productive and useful member of the organization both in the short run and in terms of long-range potential.

Job Design and Job Assignment.   One of the most crucial components of staffing is the actual design of the job given to the new employee and the manner in which the assignment is made. The issue is how to provide *optimal challenge,* a set of activities neither too hard nor too easy for the new employee, and neither too meaningless nor too risky from the point of view of the organization. If the job is too easy or too meaningless, the employee may become demotivated; if the job is too hard and/or involves too much responsibility and risk from the point of view of the organization, the employee may become too anxious, frustrated, or angry to perform at an optimal level. Some organizations have set up training programs for supervisors to help them to design optimally challenging work assignments.[17]

These four components are geared to ensuring that the work of the organization will be performed. They tend to be processes that have to be performed by line managers and personnel staff specialists together. Line managers have the basic information about jobs and skill requirements; personnel specialists have the interviewing, recruiting, and assessment skills to aid in the selection process. In an optimal system these functions will be closely coordinated, particularly to ensure that the recruiting process provides to the employee accurate information about the nature of the organization and the actual work that he or she will be doing in it. Recruiters also need good information on the long-range human resource plans, so that these can be taken into account in the selection of new employees.

Development Planning

It is not enough to get good human resources in the door. Some planning activities have to concern themselves with how employees who may be spending thirty to forty years of their total life in a given organization will make a contribution for all of that time, will remain motivated and productive, and will maintain a reasonable level of job satisfaction.

Inventorying of Development Plans.   Whether or not the process is highly formalized, there is in most organizations some effort to plan for the growth and development of all employees. The planning component that is often missing is some kind of pulling together of this information into a centralized inventory that permits coordination and evaluation of the development activities. Individual supervisors may have clear ideas of what they will do with and for their subordinates, but this information may never be collected, making it impossible to determine whether the individual plans of supervisors are connected in any way. Whether it is done by department, division, or total company, some effort to collect such information and to think through its implications is of great value to furthering the total development of employees at all levels.

Follow-up and Evaluation of Development Activities.   I have observed two symptoms of insufficient planning in this area: One, development plans are made for individual employees, are written down, but are never implemented; and two, if they are implemented they are never evaluated either in relation to the individual's own needs for growth or in relation to the organization's needs for new skills. Some system should exist to ensure that plans are implemented and that activities are evaluated against both individual and organizational goals.

Career Development Processes

This label is deliberately broad to cover all of the major processes of managing human resources during their period of growth and peak productivity, a period that may be several decades in length. These processes must match the organization's needs for work with the individual's needs for a productive and satisfying work career. The system must provide for some kind of forward movement for the employee through some succession of jobs, whether these involve promotion, lateral movement to new functions, or simply new assignments within a given area.[18] The system must be based both on the organization's need to fill jobs as they open up and on employees' needs to have some sense of progress in their working lives.

Supervision and Coaching.   By far the most important component in this area is the actual process of supervising, guiding, coaching, and monitoring. It is in this context that the work assignment and feedback processes that make learning possible occur, and it is the boss who plays the key role in molding the employee to the organization. There is considerable evidence that the first boss is especially crucial in giving new employees a good start in their careers,[19] and that training of supervisors in how to handle new employees is a valuable organizational investment.

Performance Appraisal and Judgment of Potential.   This component is part of the general process of supervision but stands out as such an important part of that process that it must be treated separately. In most organizations there is some effort to standardize and formalize a process of appraisal above and beyond the normal performance feedback expected on a day-to-day basis. Such systems serve a number of functions—to justify salary increases, promotions, and other formal organizational actions with respect to the employee; to provide information for human resource inventories or at least written records of past accomplishments for the employee's personnel folder; and to provide a basis for annual or semiannual formal reviews between boss and subordinate to supplement day-to-day feedback and to facilitate information exchange for career planning and counseling. In some organizations so little day-to-day feedback occurs that the *formal* system bears the burden of providing the employees with knowledge of how they are doing and what they can look forward to. Since knowledge of results, of how one is doing, is a crucial component of any developmental process, it is important for organizations to monitor how well and how frequently feedback is actually given.

One of the major dilemmas in this area is whether to have a single system that provides both feedback for the growth and development of the employee and information for the organization's planning systems. The dilemma arises because the information the planning system requires (e.g., "how much potential does this employee have to rise in the organization?") may be the kind of information neither the boss nor the planner wants to share with the employee. The more potent and more accurate the information, the less likely it is to be fed back to the employee in anything other than very vague terms.

On the other hand, the detailed work-oriented, day-to-day feedback the employee needs for growth and development may be too cumbersome to record as part of a selection-oriented appraisal system. If hundreds of employees are to be compared, there is strong pressure in the system toward more general kinds of judgments, traits, rankings, numerical estimates of ultimate potential, and the like. One way of resolving this dilemma is to develop two separate systems—one oriented toward performance improvement and the growth of the employee, and the other one oriented toward a more global assessment of the employee for future planning purposes involving judgments not shared with him or her except in general terms.

A second dilemma arises around the identification of the employee's "development needs" and how that information is linked to other development activities. If the development needs are stated in relation to the planning system, the employee may never get the feedback of what his needs may have been perceived to be, and, worse, no one may implement any program to deal with those needs if the planning system is not well linked with line management.

Two further problems arise from this potential lack of linkage. One, if individuals do not get good feedback around developmental needs, they remain uninvolved in their own development and potentially become complacent. We pay lip service to the statement that only the individual can develop himself or herself, but then deprive the individual of the very information that would make sensible self-development possible. Two, the development needs as stated for the various employees in the organization may have nothing to do with the organization's needs for certain kinds of human resources in the future. All too often, complete lack of linkage between the strategic or business planning function and the human resource development function results in willy-nilly individual development based on today's needs and individual managers' notions of what will be needed in the future.

Organizational Rewards—Pay, Benefits, Perquisites, Promotion, and Recognition.
Books have been written about the problems and subtleties in linking organizational rewards to the other components of a HRPD system to ensure both short-run and long-run human effectiveness. For purposes of this short article, I wish to point out only one major issue: how to ensure that organizational rewards are linked both to the needs of the individual and to the needs of the organization for effective performance and development of potential. All too often the reward system is responsive neither to the individual employee nor to the organization, being driven more by criteria of elegance, consistency, and what other organizations are doing. If linkage is to be established, line managers must actively work with compensation experts to develop a joint philosophy and set of goals based on an understanding of what the organization is trying to reward and what employee needs actually are. As organizational careers become more varied and as social values surrounding work change, reward systems will probably have to become much more flexible both in time (people at different career stages may need different things) and by type of career (functional specialists may need different things than general managers).

Promotions and Other Job Changes. There is ample evidence that what keeps human growth and effectiveness going is continuing optimal challenge.[20] Such challenge can be provided for some members of the organization through promotion to more responsible jobs. For most members of the organization the promotion opportunities are limited, however, because the pyramid narrows at the top. An effective HRPD system will, therefore, concentrate on developing career paths, systems of job rotation, changing assignments, temporary assignments, and other lateral job moves that ensure continuing growth of all human resources.

One of the key characteristics of an optimally challenging job is that it both draws on the person's abilities and skills and that it has opportunities for "closure." The employee must be in the job long enough to get involved and to see the results of his or her efforts. Systems of rotation that move the person too rapidly either prevent initial involvement (as in the rotational training program), or prevent closure by transferring the person to a new job before the effects of his or her decisions can be assessed. I have heard many "fast track" executives complain that their self-confidence was low, because they could never really see the results of their efforts. Too often we move people too fast to fill slots and thereby undermine their development.

Organizational planning systems that generate slots to be filled must be coordinated with development planning systems that concern themselves with the optimal growth of the human resources. Sometimes it is better for the organization in the long run not to fill an empty slot in order to keep a manager in another job where he or she is just beginning to develop. One way of ensuring such linkage is to monitor these processes by means of a "development committee" composed of both line managers and personnel specialists. Here, the needs of the organization and the needs of the people can be balanced against each other in the context of the long-range goals of the organization.

Training and Development Opportunities.   Most organizations recognize that periods of formal training, sabbaticals, executive development programs outside of the company, and other educational activities are necessary in the total process of human growth and development. The important point about these activities is that they should be carefully linked both to the needs of the individual and to the needs of the organization. The individual should want to go to the program, because he or she can see how the educational activity fits into the total career. The organization should send the person because the training fits into some concept of future career development. It should not be undertaken simply as a generalized "good thing," or because other companies are doing it. As much as possible the training and educational activities should be tied to job/role planning. For example, many companies began to use university executive-development programs, because of an explicit recognition that future managers would require a broader perspective on various problems and that such "broadening" could best be achieved in the university programs.

Career Counseling, Joint Career Planning, Follow-up, and Evaluation.   Inasmuch as growth and development come from within the individual himself or herself, it is important that the organization provide some means for individual employees at all levels to become more proactive about their careers and some mechanisms for joint dialogue, counseling, and career planning.[21] This process should ideally be linked to performance appraisal, because it is in that context that the boss can review with the subordinate the future potential, development needs, strengths, weaknesses, career options, etc. The boss is often not trained in counseling, but does possess some of the key information the employee needs to initiate career planning. More formal counseling could then be supplied by the personnel development staff or outside the organization altogether.

The important point to recognize is that employees cannot manage their own growth development without information on how their own needs, talents, values, and plans mesh with the opportunity structure of the organization. Even though the organization may have only imperfect, uncertain information about the future, the individual is better off knowing that than making erroneous assumptions about the future based on no information at all. It is true that the organization cannot make commitments, nor should it unless required to by legislation or contract. But the sharing of information, if properly done, is not the same as making commitments or setting up false expectations.

If the organization can open up the communication channel between employees, their bosses, and whoever is managing the human resource system, the groundwork is laid for realistic individual-development planning. Whatever is decided about training, next steps, special assignments, rotation, etc., should be jointly decided by the individual and the appropriate organizational resource (probably the supervisor and someone from personnel specializing in career development). Each step must fit into the employee's life plan and must be tied into organizational needs. The organization should be neither a humanistic charity nor an indoctrination center. Instead, it should be a vehicle for meeting both the needs of society and of individuals.

Whatever is decided should not merely be written down but executed. If there are implementation problems, the development plan should be renegotiated. Whatever developmental actions are taken, it is essential that they be followed up and evaluated both by the person and by the organization to determine what, if anything, was achieved. It is shocking to discover how many companies invest in major activities such as university executive-development programs and never determine for themselves how effective those programs were, or what was accomplished in them. In some instances, they make no plans to talk to the individual before or after the program, so that it is not even possible to determine what the activity meant to the participant, or what might be an appropriate next assignment for him or her following the program.

I can summarize the above analysis best by emphasizing the two places where I feel there is the most fragmentation and violation of growth assumptions. First, too many of the activities occur without the involvement of the person who is "being developed" and therefore may well end being self-defeating. This is particularly true of job assignments and performance appraisal where too little involvement and feedback occur. Second, too much of the human resource system functions as a personnel *selection* system unconnected to either the needs of the organization or the needs of the individual. All too often it is only a system for short-run replacement of people in standard type jobs. The key planning functions are not linked in solidly and hence do not influence the system to the degree they should.

Planning for and Managing Disengagement

The planning and management processes reviewed below are counterparts of ones that have already been discussed but are focused on different problems: the late career, loss of motivation, obsolescence, and ultimately retirement. Organizations must recognize that there are various options available to deal with this range of problems beyond the obvious ones of either terminating the employee or engaging in elaborate measures to "remotivate" people who may have lost work involvement.[22]

Continuing Education and Retraining.   These activities have their greatest potential if the employee is motivated and if there is some clear connection between what is to be learned and what the employee's current or future job assignments require in the way of skills. More and more organizations are finding out that it is better to provide challenging work first and only then the training to perform that work once the employee sees the need for it. Obviously for this linkage to work well continuous dialogue is needed between employees and their managers. For those employees who have leveled off, have lost work involvement, but are still doing high quality work, other solutions are applicable.

Job Redesign, Job Enrichment, and Job Rotation.   This section is an extension of the arguments made earlier on job changes in general applied to the particular problems of leveled-off employees. In some recent research, it has been suggested that job enrichment and other efforts to redesign work to increase motivation and performance may work only during the first few years on a job.[23] Beyond that the employee becomes "unresponsive" to the job characteristics themselves and pays more attention to surrounding factors such as the nature of supervision, relationships with coworkers, pay, and other extrinsic characteristics. In other words, before organizations attempt to "cure" leveled-off employees by remotivating them through job redesign or rotation, they should examine whether those employees are still in a responsive mode or not. On the other hand, one can argue that there is nothing wrong with less motivated, less involved employees so long as the quality of what they are doing meets the organizational standards.[24]

Alternative Patterns of Work and Rewards.   Because of the changing needs and values of employees in recent decades, more and more organizations have begun to experiment with alternative work patterns, such as flexible working hours, part-time work, sabbaticals or other longer periods of time off, several people filling one job, dual employment of spouses with more extensive childcare programs, etc. Some are experimenting also with flexible reward systems in which employees can choose between a raise, time off, special retirement, medical or insurance benefits, and other efforts to make multiple career ladders a viable reality. These programs apply to employees at all career stages, but are especially relevant to people in mid-and late-career stages whose perceptions of their career and life goals may be undergoing important changes.

None of those innovations should be attempted without first clearly establishing a HRPD system that takes care of the organization's needs as well as the needs of employees and links them to each other. There can be little growth and development for employees at any level in a sick and stagnant organization. It is in the best interests of both the individual and the organization to have a healthy organization that can provide opportunities for growth.

Retirement Planning and Counseling.   As part of any effective HRPD system, there must be a clear planning function that forecasts who will retire and that feeds this information into both the replacement staffing system and the counseling functions, so that the employees who will be retiring can be prepared for this often traumatic career stage. Employees need counseling not only with the mechanical and financial aspects of retirement, but also to prepare them psychologically for the time when they will no longer have a clear organizational base or job as part of their identity. For some people it may make sense to spread the period of retirement over a number of years by using part-time work or special assignments to help both the individual and the organization to get benefits from this period.

The counseling function here probably involves special skills and must be provided by specialists. However, the line manager continues to play a key role as a provider of job challenge, feedback, and information about what is ahead for any given employee. Seminars for line managers on how to handle the special problems of preretirement employees would probably be of great value as part of their managerial training.

Planning for and Managing Replacement and Restaffing

With this step the HRPD cycle closes back upon itself. This function must be concerned with such issues as:

1. Updating the human resource inventory as retirements or terminations occur.
2. Instituting special programs of orientation or training for new incumbents to specific jobs as those jobs open up.
3. Managing the information system on what jobs are available and determining how to match this information to the human resources available in order to determine whether to replace from within the organization or to go outside with a new recruiting program.
4. Continuously reanalyzing jobs to ensure that the new incumbent is properly prepared for what the job now requires and will require in the future.

How these processes are managed links to the other parts of the system through the implicit messages that are sent to employees. For example, a company that decides to post publicly all of its unfilled jobs is clearly sending a message that it expects internal recruitment and supports self-development activities. A company that manages restaffing in a very secret manner may well get across a message that employees might as well be complacent and passive about their careers, because they cannot influence them anyway.

Summary and Conclusions

I have tried to argue in this article that human resource planning and development is becoming an increasingly important function in organizations, that this function consists of multiple components, and that these components must be managed *both* by line managers and staff specialists. I have tried to show that the various planning activities are closely linked to the actual processes of supervision, job assignment, training, etc., and that those processes must be designed to match the needs of the organization with the needs of the employees throughout their evolving careers, whether or not those careers involve hierarchical promotions. I have also argued that the various components are linked to each other and must be seen as a total system if it is to be effective. The total system must be managed as a system to ensure coordination between the planning functions and the implementation functions.

I hope it is clear from what has been said above that an effective human resource planning and development system is integral to the functioning of the organization and must, therefore, be a central concern of line management. Many of the activities require specialist help, but the accountabilities must rest squarely with line supervisors and top management. It is they who control the opportunities and the rewards. It is the job-assignment system and the feedback that employees get that is the ultimate raw material for growth and development. Whoever designs and manages the system, it will not help the organization to become more effective unless that system is *owned* by line management.

8

What Does "Product Quality" Really Mean?

David A. Garvin

In this article, the author reviews and synthesizes the varying definitions of product quality arising from philosophy, economics, marketing, and operations management. He then goes on to build an eight-dimensional framework to elaborate on these definitions. Using this framework, he addresses the empirical relationships between quality and variables such as price, advertising, market share, cost, and profitability. *SMR*.

Product quality is rapidly becoming an important competitive issue. The superior reliability of many Japanese products has sparked considerable soul-searching among American managers.[1] In addition, several surveys have voiced consumers' dissatisfaction with the existing levels of quality and service of the products they buy.[2] In a recent study of the business units of major North American companies, managers ranked "producing to high quality standards" as their chief current concern.[3]

Despite the interest of managers, the academic literature on quality has not been reviewed extensively. The problem is one of coverage: scholars in four disciplines—philosophy, economics, marketing, and operations management—have considered the subject, but each group has viewed it from a different vantage point. Philosophy has focused on definitional issues; economics, on profit maximization and market equilibrium; marketing, on the determinants of buying behavior and customer satisfaction; and operations management, on engineering practices and manufacturing control. The result has been a host of competing perspectives, each based on a different analytical framework and each employing its own terminology.

From *Sloan Management Review*, Fall 1984, Vol. 26, No. 1. Reprinted with permission.

At the same time, a number of common themes are apparent. All of them have important management implications. On the conceptual front, each discipline has wrestled with the following questions: Is quality objective or subjective? Is it timeless or socially determined? Empirically, interest has focused on the correlates of quality. What, for example, is the connection between quality and price? Between quality and advertising? Between quality and cost? Between quality and market share? More generally, do quality improvements lead to higher or lower profits?

Five Approaches to Defining Quality

Five major approaches to the definition of quality can be identified: (1) the transcendent approach of philosophy; (2) the product-based approach of economics; (3) the user-based approach of economics, marketing, and operations management; and (4) the manufacturing-based and (5) value-based approaches of operations management. Table 8.1 presents representative examples of each approach.

1. The Transcendent Approach

According to the transcendent view, quality is synonymous with "innate excellence."[4] It is both absolute and universally recognizable, a mark of uncompromising standards and high achievement. Nevertheless, proponents of this view claim that quality cannot be defined precisely; rather, it is a simple, unanalyzable property that we learn to recognize only through experience. This definition borrows heavily from Plato's discussion of beauty.[5] In the *Symposium,* he argues that beauty is one of the "platonic forms," and, therefore, a term that cannot be defined. Like other such terms that philosophers consider to be "logically primitive," beauty (and perhaps quality as well) can be understood only after one is exposed to a succession of objects that display its characteristics.

2. The Product-based Approach

Product-based definitions are quite different; they view quality as a precise and measurable variable. According to this view, differences in quality reflect differences in the quantity of some ingredient or attribute possessed by a product.[6] For example, high-quality ice cream has a high butterfat content, just as fine rugs have a large number of knots per square inch. This approach lends a vertical or hierarchical dimension to quality, for goods can be

Table 8.1 Five Definitions of Quality

I. Transcendent Definition

"Quality is neither mind nor matter, but a third entity independent of the two. . . . Even though Quality cannot be defined, you know what it is." (R. M. Pirsig, *Zen and the Art of Motorcycle Maintenance,* pp. 185, 213.)

". . . a condition of excellence implying fine quality as distinct from poor quality. . . . Quality is achieving or reaching for the highest standard as against being satisfied with the sloppy or fraudulent." (B. W. Tuchman, "The Decline of Quality," *New York Times Magazine,* November 2, 1980, p. 38.)

II. Product-based Definition

"Differences in quality amount to differences in the quantity of some desired ingredient or attribute." (L. Abbott, *Quality and Competition,* pp. 126–127.)

"Quality refers to the amounts of the unpriced attributes contained in each unit of the priced attribute." (K. B. Leffler, "Ambiguous Changes in Product Quality," *American Economic Review,* December 1982, p. 956.)

III. User-based Definition

"Quality consists of the capacity to satisfy wants . . . ." (C. D. Edwards, "The Meaning of Quality," *Quality Progress,* October 1968, p. 37.)

"Quality is the degree to which a specific product satisfies the wants of a specific consumer." (H. L. Gilmore, "Product Conformance Cost," *Quality Progress,* June 1974, p. 16.)

"Quality is any aspect of a product, including the services included in the contract of sales, which influences the demand curve." (R. Dorfman and P. O. Steiner, "Optimal Advertising and Optimal Quality," *American Economic Review,* December 1954, p. 831.)

"In the final analysis of the marketplace, the quality of a product depends on how well it fits patterns of consumer preferences." (A. A. Kuenn and R. L. Day, "Strategy of Product Quality," *Harvard Business Review,* November–December 1962, p. 101.)

"Quality consists of the extent to which a specimen [a product-brand/model-seller combination] possesses the service characteristics you desire." (E. S. Maynes, "The Concept and Measurement of Product Quality," in *Household Production and Consumption,* p. 542.)

"Quality is fitness for use." (J. M. Juran, ed., *Quality Control Handbook,* p. 2.)

IV. Manufacturing-based Definition

"Quality [means] conformance to requirements." (P. B. Crosby, *Quality Is Free,* p. 15.)

"Quality is the degree to which a specific product conforms to a design or specification." (Gilmore, June 1974, p. 16.)

V. Value-based Definition

"Quality is the degree of excellence at an acceptable price and the control of variability at an acceptable cost." (R. A. Broh, *Managing Quality for Higher Profits,* 1982, p. 3.)

"Quality means best for certain customer conditions. These conditions are (a) the actual use and (b) the selling price of the product." (A. V. Feigenbaum, *Total Quality Control,* p. 1.)

ranked according to the amount of the desired attribute that they possess. However, an unambiguous ranking is possible only if the attributes in question are considered preferable by virtually all buyers.[7]

Product-based definitions of quality first appeared in the economics literature, where they were quickly incorporated into theoretical models. In fact, the early economic research on quality focused almost exclusively on durability, simply because it was so easily translated into the above framework.[8] Since durable goods provide a stream of services over time, increased durability implies a longer stream of services—in effect, more of the good. Quality differences could, therefore, be treated as differences in quantity, considerably simplifying the mathematics.

There are two obvious corollaries to this approach. First, higher quality can only be obtained at higher cost. Because quality reflects the quantity of attributes that a product contains, and because attributes are considered to be costly to produce, higher quality goods will be more expensive. Second, quality is viewed as an inherent characteristic of goods, rather than as something ascribed to them. Because quality reflects the presence or absence of measurable product attributes, it can be assessed objectively, and is based on more than preferences alone.

3. The User-based Approach

User-based definitions start from the opposite premise, i.e., that quality "lies in the eyes of the beholder." Individual consumers are assumed to have different wants or needs, and those goods that best satisfy their preferences are those that they regard as having the highest quality.[9] This is an idiosyncratic and personal view of quality, and one that is highly subjective. In the marketing literature, it has led to the notion of "ideal points": precise combinations of product attributes that provide the greatest satisfaction to a specified consumer;[10] in the economics literature, to the view that quality differences are captured by shifts in a product's demand curve;[11] and in the operations-management literature, to the concept of "fitness for use."[12] Each of these concepts, however, faces two problems. The first is practical: how to aggregate widely varying individual preferences so that they lead to meaningful definitions of quality at the market level. The second is more fundamental: how to distinguish those product attributes that connote quality from those that simply maximize consumer satisfaction.

The aggregation problem is usually resolved by assuming that high-quality products are those that best meet the needs of a majority of consumers. A consensus of views is implied, with virtually all users agreeing on the desirability of certain product attributes. Unfortunately, this approach ignores the different weights that individuals normally attach to quality characteristics, and the difficulty of devising an unbiased statistical procedure for aggregating such widely varying preferences.[13] For the most part, these problems have been ignored by theorists. Economists, for example, have typically specified models in which the market demand curve responds to quality changes without explaining how that curve, which represents the summation of individual preferences, was derived in the first place.[14]

A more basic problem with the user-based approach is its equation of quality with maximum satisfaction. While the two are related, they are by no means identical. A product that maximizes satisfaction is certainly *preferable* to one that meets fewer needs, but is it necessarily *better* as well? The implied equivalence often breaks down in practice. A consumer may enjoy a particular brand because of its unusual taste or features, yet may still regard some other brand as being of higher quality. In the latter assessment, the product's objective characteristics are also being considered.

Even perfectly objective characteristics, however, are open to varying interpretations. Today, durability is regarded as an important element of quality. Long-lived products are generally preferred to those that wear out more quickly. This was not always true: until the late nineteenth century, durable goods were primarily possessions of the poor, for only wealthy individuals could afford delicate products that required frequent replacement or repair.[15] The result was a long-standing association between durability and inferior quality, a view that changed only with the mass production of luxury items made possible by the Industrial Revolution.

4. The Manufacturing-based Approach

User-based definitions of quality incorporate subjective elements, for they are rooted in consumer preferences: the determinants of demand. In contrast, manufacturing-based definitions focus on the supply side of the equation, and are primarily concerned with engineering and manufacturing practice. Virtually all manufacturing-based definitions identify quality as "conformance to requirements."[16] Once a design or a specification has been established, any deviation implies a reduction in quality. Excellence is equated with meeting specifications, and with "making it right the first time." In these terms, a well-made Mercedes is a high-quality automobile, as is a well-made Chevette.

While this approach recognizes the consumer's interest in quality—a product that deviates from specifications is likely to be poorly made and unreliable, providing less satisfaction than one that is properly constructed—its primary focus is internal. Quality is defined in a manner that simplifies engineering and production control. On the design side, this has led to an emphasis on reliability engineering,[17] and on the manufacturing side, to an emphasis on statistical quality control.[18] Both techniques are designed to weed out deviations early: the former, by analyzing a product's basic components, identifying possible failure modes, and then proposing alternative designs to enhance reliability; the latter, by employing statistical techniques to discover when a production process is performing outside acceptable limits.

Each of these techniques is focused on the same end: cost reduction. According to the manufacturing-based approach, improvements in quality (which are equivalent to reductions in the number of deviations) lead to lower costs, for preventing defects is viewed as less expensive than repairing or reworking them.[19] Firms are, therefore, assumed to be performing suboptimally: Were they only to increase their expenditures on prevention and inspection—testing prototypes more carefully, or weeding out a larger number of defective components before they become part of fully assembled units—they would find their rework, scrap, and warranty expenses falling by an even greater amount.[20]

5. The Value-based Approach

Value-based definitions take this idea one step further. They actually define quality in terms of costs and prices. According to this view, a quality product is one that provides performance at an acceptable price or conformance at an acceptable cost.[21] Under this approach, a $500 running shoe, no matter how well constructed, could not be a quality product, for it would find few buyers.

A recent survey of consumer perceptions of quality in twenty-eight product categories suggests that the value-based view is becoming more prevalent.[22] While ingredients and materials were seen as the key quality indicators in such categories as food, clothing, personal care, and beauty products—reflecting a product-based approach to the subject—the study's overall conclusion was that "quality is increasingly apt to be discussed and perceived in relationship to price."

The difficulty in employing this approach lies in its blending of two related but distinct concepts. Quality, which is a measure of excellence, is being equated with value, which is a measure of worth. The result is a hybrid—"affordable excellence"—that lacks well-defined limits and is difficult to apply in practice.

The Implications of Multiple Definitions

Most existing definitions of quality fall into one of the categories listed above. The coexistence of these differing approaches has several important implications. First, it helps to explain the often competing views of quality held by members of the marketing and manufacturing departments. Marketing people typically take a user-based or product-based approach to the subject; for them, higher quality means better performance, enhanced features, and other improvements that increase cost. Because they see the customer as the arbiter of quality, they view what happens in the factory as much less important than what happens in the field.

Manufacturing people normally take a different approach. For them, quality means conformance to specifications and an emphasis on "doing it right the first time." Because they associate poor quality with high levels of rework and scrap, manufacturing people usually expect quality improvements to result in cost reductions.

The Potential for Conflict.   These two views are obviously in conflict and can cause serious breakdowns in communications. Remedial efforts may become paralyzed if the coexistence of these competing perspectives is not openly acknowledged. For example, a large division of a major consumer-goods company recently reviewed its quality-management practices. The firm was especially interested in assessing its new-product introduction process, for new products were regarded as the key to competitive success. Two divergent views emerged. One group felt that the process had been quite successful: New products appeared regularly, customer complaints were few, and defective items had not been shipped to the trade in any large number. Another group felt that the process had to be revamped, because quality was so poor: New product releases were frequently delayed while designs were reconfigured to adapt to manufacturing requirements, and material and labor variances of several hundred thousand dollars had been incurred because of unanticipated expenditures on rework and scrap. Because of these disagreements, the project quickly stalled. Further progress requires the recognition that one group is employing a user-based definition of quality, while the other is employing a manufacturing-based approach. Only then are the two groups likely to agree on the nature of the problems they face.

The Need for Different Definitions.   Despite the potential for conflict, companies need to cultivate such differing perspectives, for they are essential to the successful introduction of high-quality products. Reliance on a single definition of quality is a frequent source of problems. For example, a Japanese paper manufacturer recently discovered that its newsprint rolls failed to satisfy customers even though they met the Japanese Industrial Standard. Conformance was excellent, reflecting a manufacturing-based approach to quality, but acceptance was poor. Other rolls of newsprint, however, generated no customer complaints even though they failed to meet the standard.[23] A leading U.S. manufacturer of room air conditioners faced the opposite problem. Its products were well received by customers and highly rated by *Consumer Reports*. Reject, scrap, and warranty costs were so high, however, that large losses were incurred. While the product's design matched customers' needs, the failure to follow through with tight conformance in manufacturing cost the company dearly.

These examples suggest the need to actively shift one's approach to quality as products move from design to market. The characteristics that connote quality must first be identified through market research (a user-based approach to quality); these characteristics must then be translated into identifiable product attributes (a product-based approach to quality); and the manufacturing process must then be organized to ensure that products are made precisely to these specifications (a manufacturing-based approach to quality). A process that ignores any one of these steps will not result in a quality product. All three views are necessary and must be consciously cultivated.

Nevertheless, each of the major approaches to quality shares a common problem. Each is vague and imprecise when it comes to describing the basic elements of product quality. Relatively few analysts, with the exceptions of Juran[24] and Maynes,[25] have shown an interest in these details. The oversight is unfortunate, for much can be learned by treating quality in a less homogeneous fashion.

Eight Dimensions of Quality

Eight dimensions can be identified as a framework for thinking about the basic elements of product quality:

1. Performance.
2. Features.
3. Reliability.
4. Conformance.
5. Durability.
6. Serviceability.
7. Aesthetics.
8. Perceived Quality.

Each is self-contained and distinct, for a product can be ranked high on one dimension while being low on another.

1. Performance

Performance refers to the primary operating characteristics of a product. For an automobile, these would be acceleration, handling, cruising speed, and comfort; for a television set, they would include sound and picture clarity, color, and ability to receive distant stations.

This dimension of quality combines elements of both the product- and user-based approaches. Measurable product attributes are involved, and brands can usually be ranked objectively on at least one dimension of performance. The connection between performance and quality, however, is more ambiguous. Whether performance differences are perceived as quality differences normally depends on individual preferences. Users typically have a wide range of interests and needs; each is likely to equate quality with high performance in his or her area of immediate interest. The connection between performance and quality is also affected by semantics. Among the words that describe product performance are terms that are frequently associated with quality as well as terms that fail to carry the association. For example, a 100-watt light bulb provides greater candlepower (performance) than a 60-watt bulb, yet few consumers would regard this difference as a measure of quality. The products simply belong to different performance classes. The smoothness and quietness of an automobile's ride, however, is typically viewed as a direct reflection of its quality. Quietness is therefore a performance dimension that readily translates into quality, while candlepower is not. These differences appear to reflect the conventions of the English language as much as they do personal preferences.

There is a clear analogy here to Lancaster's theory of consumer demand.[26] The theory is based on two propositions:[27]

All goods possess objective characteristics relevant to the choices which people make among different collections of goods. The relationship between . . . a good . . . and the characteristics which it possesses is essentially a technical relationship, depending on the objective characteristics of the good. . . .

Individuals differ in their *reaction* to different characteristics, rather than in their assessments of the characteristics. . . . It is these *characteristics* in which consumers are interested . . . the various characteristics can be viewed . . . as each helping to satisfy some kind of "want."

In these terms, the performance of a product would correspond to its objective characteristics, while the relationship between performance and quality would reflect individual reactions.

2. Features

The same approach can be applied to product features, a second dimension of quality. Features are the "bells and whistles" of products, those secondary characteristics that supplement the product's basic functioning. Examples include free drinks on a plane flight, permanent press as well as cotton cycles on a washing machine, and automatic tuners on a color television set. In many cases, the line separating primary product characteristics (performance) from secondary characteristics (features) is difficult to draw. Features, like product performance, involve objective and measurable attributes; their translation into quality differences is equally affected by individual preferences. The distinction between the two is primarily one of centrality or degree of importance to the user.

3. Reliability

Reliability is a third dimension of quality. It reflects the probability of a product's failing within a specified period of time. Among the most common measures of reliability are the mean time to first failure (MTFF), the mean time between failures (MTBF), and the failure rate per unit time.[28] Because these measures require a product to be in use for some period, they are more relevant to durable goods than they are to products and services that are consumed instantly. Japanese manufacturers typically pay great attention to this dimension of quality, and they have used it to gain a competitive edge in the automotive, consumer electronics, semiconductor, and copying machine industries.

4. Conformance

A related dimension of quality is conformance, or the degree to which a product's design and operating characteristics match preestablished standards. Both internal and external elements are involved. Within the factory, conformance is commonly measured by the incidence of defects: the proportion of all units that fail to meet specifications, and so require rework or repair. In the field, data on conformance are often difficult to obtain, and proxies are frequently used. Two common measures are the incidence of service calls for a product and the frequency of repairs under warranty. These measures, while suggestive, neglect other deviations from standard, such as misspelled labels or shoddy construction, that do not lead to service or repair. More comprehensive measures of conformance are required if these items are to be counted.

Both reliability and conformance are closely tied to the manufacturing-based approach to quality. Improvements in both measures are normally viewed as translating directly into quality gains because defects and field failures are regarded as undesirable by virtually all consumers. They are, therefore, relatively objective measures of quality, and are less likely to reflect individual preferences than are rankings based on performance or features.

5. Durability

Durability, a measure of product life, has both economic and technical dimensions. Technically, durability can be defined as the amount of use one gets from a product before it physically deteriorates. A light bulb provides the perfect example: After so many hours of use, the filament burns up and the bulb must be replaced. Repair is impossible. Economists call such products "one-hoss shays," and have used them extensively in modeling the production and consumption of capital goods.[29]

Durability becomes more difficult to interpret when repair is possible. Then the concept takes on an added dimension, for product life will vary with changing economic conditions. Durability becomes the amount of use one gets from a product before it breaks down and replacement is regarded as preferable to continued repair. Consumers are faced with a series of choices: Each time a product fails, they must weigh the expected cost, in both dollars and personal inconvenience, of future repairs against the investment and operating expenses of a newer, more reliable model. In these circumstances, a product's life is determined by repair costs, personal valuations of time and inconvenience, losses due to downtime, relative prices, and other economic variables, as much as it is by the quality of components or materials.

This approach to durability has two important implications. First, it suggests that durability and reliability are closely linked. A product that fails frequently is likely to be scrapped earlier than one that is more reliable; repair costs will be correspondingly higher, and the purchase of a new model will look that much more desirable. Second, this approach suggests that durability figures should be interpreted with care. An increase in product life may not be due to technical improvements or to the use of longer-lived materials; the underlying economic environment may simply have changed. For example, the expected life of an automobile has risen steadily over the last decade, and now averages fourteen years.[30] Older automobiles are held for longer periods and have become a greater percentage of all cars in use.[31] Among the factors thought to be responsible for these changes are rising gasoline prices and a weak economy, which have reduced the average number of miles driven per year, and federal regulations governing gas mileage, which have resulted in a reduction in the size of new models and an increase in the attractiveness to many consumers of retaining older cars. In this case, environmental changes have been responsible for much of the reported increase in durability.

6. Serviceability

A sixth dimension of quality is serviceability, or the speed, courtesy, and competence of repair. Consumers are concerned not only about a product breaking down, but also about the elapsed time before service is restored, the timeliness with which service appointments are kept, the nature of their dealings with service personnel, and the frequency with which service calls or repairs fail to resolve outstanding problems. Some of these variables can be measured quite objectively; others reflect differing personal standards of what constitutes acceptable service. For example, a recent study of consumer satisfaction with professional services found the major complaints to be that "the service was provided in a careless, unprofessional manner" and that "I feel I was treated as an object rather than as an individual."[32] These comments clearly reflect subjective views of what constitutes acceptable professional behavior. Other aspects of service can be assessed more objectively. Responsiveness is typically measured by the mean time to repair (MTTR), while technical competence is reflected in the incidence of multiple service calls required to correct a single problem. Because most consumers equate more rapid repair and reduced downtime with higher quality, these elements of serviceability are less subject to personal interpretation than are those involving evaluations of courtesy or standards of professional behavior. A number of companies have begun emphasizing this dimension of quality. Caterpillar Tractor's promise that it will deliver repair parts anywhere in the world within forty-eight hours and Mercedes' guarantee of twenty-four-hour (overnight) service in California and Arizona show that even top-of-the-line producers believe that this approach has value.

7. Aesthetics

The final two dimensions of quality are the most subjective. Both aesthetics and perceived quality are closely related to the user-based approach. Aesthetics—how a product looks, feels, sounds, tastes, or smells—is clearly a matter of personal judgment and a reflection of individual preferences. In fact, the marketing concept of "ideal points"—those combinations of product attributes that best match the preferences of a specified consumer—was originally developed to capture just this dimension of quality.[33]

8. Perceived Quality

Perceptions of quality can be as subjective as assessments of aesthetics. Because consumers do not always possess complete information about a product's attributes, they must frequently rely on indirect measures when comparing brands.[34] In these circumstances, products will be evaluated less on their objective characteristics than on their images, advertising, or brand names. These forces even affect scholarly judgments. When professors around the country were asked to rank the departments in their fields by quality, their rankings were only partially explained by such objective measures as the number of articles published in leading journals by members of the department. Both reputation—the historical strength of the department—and affiliation—the quality of the university to which a department was attached—were equally important in explaining the rankings.[35]

Together, the eight major dimensions of quality cover a broad range of concepts. Several of the dimensions involve measurable product attributes; others reflect individual preferences. Some are objective and timeless, while others shift with changing fashions. Some are inherent characteristics of goods, while others are ascribed characteristics.

The diversity of these concepts helps to explain the differences among the five traditional approaches to quality. Each of the approaches focuses implicitly on a different dimension of quality: the product-based approach focuses on performance, features, and durability; the user-based approach focuses on aesthetics and perceived quality; and the manufacturing-based approach focuses on conformance and reliability. Conflicts among the five approaches are inevitable because each defines quality from a different point of view. Once the concept is unbundled, however, and each dimension is considered separately, the sources of disagreement become clear.

The Strategic Importance of Quality Dimensions

A recognition of these eight dimensions is also important for strategic purposes. A firm that chooses to compete on the basis of quality can do so in several ways; it need not pursue all eight dimensions at once. Instead, a segmentation strategy can be followed, with a few dimensions singled out for special attention. For example, Japanese manufacturers have traditionally entered U.S. markets by emphasizing the reliability and conformance of their products, while downplaying the other dimensions of quality. The superior "fits and finishes" and low repair rates of Japanese automobiles are well known; what are less frequently recognized are their poor safety records (performance) and low corrosion resistance (durability). Despite these drawbacks, Japanese automobiles have come to symbolize the very best in quality for many American consumers.

This example suggests that firms can successfully pursue a relatively narrow quality niche. In fact, they may have no other choice, if competitors have already established broad reputations for excellence. In these circumstances, new entrants may be able to secure a defensible position only if they focus on an as yet untapped dimension of quality.

This pattern clearly fits the piano industry. For many years, Steinway & Sons has been the quality leader; its instruments are known for their even voicing (the evenness of character and timbre of each of the eighty-eight notes on the keyboard), the sweetness of their registers (the roundness and softness of tone throughout the piano's entire range), the duration of their tone, their long lives, and their finely polished woodwork.[36] Each piano is handcrafted, and each is unique in sound and style. Despite these advantages, Steinway has recently been challenged by Yamaha, a Japanese manufacturer that has developed a strong reputation for quality in a relatively short time. Yamaha has done so by emphasizing reliability and conformance, two dimensions of quality that are low on Steinway's list, rather than artistry and uniqueness. In fact, one of Yamaha's major selling points is that all of its pianos sound exactly the same. Both companies enjoy high profits, despite their widely varying approaches to quality.

This example suggests the importance of carefully targeting one's quality niche. The selection of a defensible niche, however, is only a first step. Operational requirements must also be met, for each dimension of quality imposes its own demands on the firm. High performance requires careful attention to design and a strong design staff; superior durability requires the use of long-lived or "derated" components and close cooperation between the engineering and purchasing departments; superior conformance requires attention to written specifications and precision in assembly; and exceptional serviceability requires a strong customer-service department and active field representatives. In each case, a different function enjoys the lead role, and different tasks are required for success. The managerial implications of this analysis should be obvious: After selecting the dimensions of quality on which it hopes to compete, a firm must tailor its organization and operations to meet these specific needs. Otherwise, the wrong departments may be elevated in status, or the wrong tasks pursued. Disaggregating the concept of quality allows companies to pinpoint these operating requirements as carefully as they target untapped markets.

Correlates of Quality

Managers are interested in quality primarily because of its marketing and financial implications. Many believe that a product's price, advertising, market share, costs, and profitability are connected in some way to product quality. The following section of the article explores the theory and evidence in each of these areas.

Quality and Price

The theoretical argument about the relationship between quality and price runs in both directions. On the one hand, quality and price are assumed to be positively correlated. If higher quality can be produced only at higher cost, and if costs and prices are, as economic theory suggests, positively related, then quality and price will move together.[37] This assumes, however, that consumers possess sufficient information to evaluate product quality. If they do not, they will rely on other cues when making that assessment, including comparative prices.[38] As Riesz points out, once managers observe this behavior, they may then respond by readjusting prices:

If managers believe that perceptions and perhaps consumer purchase decisions are positively correlated with price, they may set higher prices in order to imply higher product quality. Price, therefore, may become a means of differentiating a product. . . . Such pricing strategies . . . would likely result in a deterioration of the price-quality relationship within a product category.[39]

The theory, then, is equivocal. Quality and price may or may not be positively correlated, depending on the amount of information available to consumers. The empirical results are equally mixed. A number of studies have found a positive correlation between the two variables.[40] These studies, however, were based primarily on experimental evidence rather than on market data. When market data were used, the results differed by product category. Nondurables generally displayed a weak or negative correlation between price and quality (with quality measured by *Consumer Reports* rankings, which typically focus on product performance), while durables showed a significant positive correlation.[41] The findings for durables are broadly consistent with research on the purchase decision for major home appliances.

Westbrook *et al.* found that 86 percent of recent purchasers and 75 percent of prospective buyers felt that they had no difficulty judging the quality or reliability of competing brands.[42] A similar study, "The Buying Consumer: Room Air Conditioners," found that 85 percent of all buyers rated the product information available to them as adequate or more than adequate.[43] Where information of this kind is available, a positive correlation between price and quality is to be expected.

This relationship breaks down, however, in the more sophisticated experimental studies. Where multiple cues are present for inferring quality—brand name, store image, product features, or country of manufacture, in addition to price—the strong price-quality association of the earlier bivariate research weakens or disappears.[44] In these circumstances, quality assessment is guided less by price than by the other variables present.

Quality and Advertising

The theoretical argument for a positive association between quality and advertising was initially developed by Phillip Nelson.[45] A more formal modeling was later pursued by Richard Schmalensee.[46] Nelson first introduced the distinction between "search" and "experience" goods. The attributes of the former can be determined prior to purchase, while those of the latter can be learned only after the product has been purchased and used. The cut and fit of an article of clothing are examples of product characteristics that can be learned through search; the reliability and durability of a major home appliance are examples of traits that can be learned only through experience. Nelson then argued that for experience goods, higher levels of advertising would be associated with higher quality products. Schmalensee has summarized this argument succinctly:

High-quality brands will obtain more repeat purchases, *ceteris paribus,* than low-quality brands. Thus . . . sellers of high-quality brands will spend more to persuade consumers to try their wares, since *ceteris paribus* again, the present value of a trial purchase is larger. Nelson contends that this force causes better brands to advertise more in equilibrium as long as consumers respond to advertising at all; the level of advertising for experience goods is thus positively correlated with quality, regardless of what individual ads actually claim. Quality information is provided by the level of advertising, not the claims it makes.[47]

The evidence on this point is inconclusive. Analysts using both American and British data have found some evidence of a positive relationship between advertising and product quality (with quality again measured by *Consumer Reports* or *Consumers' Bulletin* rankings), but these results have been undercut by other studies. Rotfeld and Rotzoll, after reviewing the research on this topic, concluded that: "Advertised products are apparently of better quality than nonadvertised goods for some products, when rated by certain criteria, in some years. . . . But no broad generalizations can be made."[48]

Gilligan and Holmes, who expanded on the earlier studies by using a variety of different measures of both advertising expenditures and brand quality, reached a similar conclusion: "A heavily advertised product is just as likely to be poor quality as any other."[49] While these studies have involved both search and experience goods, the same conclusions apply if the analysis is limited to goods in the latter category. Nelson's claim that heavy advertising implies superior quality is, therefore, not supported by the available evidence. In fact, in a recent survey of consumer attitudes the majority of respondents felt that advertised products were no more likely to be dependable than were products without advertising.[50]

Quality and Market Share

The relationship between quality and market share is likely to depend on how quality is defined. If a high-quality product is one with superior performance or a large number of features, it will generally be more expensive, and will sell in smaller volume. But if quality is defined as fitness for use, superior aesthetics, or improved conformance, high quality need not be accompanied by premium prices. In that case, quality and market share are likely to be positively correlated.

Virtually all empirical work on this topic has employed the Profit Impact of Marketing Strategies (PIMS) data base.[51] All studies have, therefore, used the same, highly aggregated measure of quality. Each company in the PIMS survey was first asked the following questions: What was the percentage of sales of products or services from each business in each year which were superior to those of competitiors? What was the percentage of equivalent products? What was the percentage of inferior products? Quality indexes were then compiled for each firm by subtracting its percentage "inferior" from its percentage "superior."

Using these indexes, analysts have found a strong positive association between quality and market share. Those businesses in the PIMS study that improved in quality during the 1970s increased their market share five or six times faster than those that declined in quality, and three times as rapidly as those whose relative quality remained unchanged.[52] Cross-sectional studies using both bivariate[53] and multivariate methods[54] have confirmed the positive association between quality and market share.

Quality and Cost

Theoretical discussions of the relationship between quality and cost fall into three distinct categories. One group, following the product-based approach, argues that quality and direct cost are positively related. The implicit assumption here is that quality differences reflect variations in performance, features, durability, or other product attributes that require more expensive components or materials, additional labor hours in construction, or other commitments of tangible resources. This view dominates much American thinking on the subject. A second view, which draws on the operations-management literature, sees quality and cost as inversely related, because the costs of improving quality are thought to be less than the resulting savings in rework, scrap, and warranty expenses. According to this view, which is widely held among Japanese manufacturers and explains much of their dedication to the goal of "continuous improvement," quality is synonymous with the absence of defects, and the costs in question are quality costs.[55]

Quality costs are defined as any expenditure on manufacturing or service in excess of that which would have been incurred if the product had been built exactly right the first time.[56] In their most comprehensive form, these costs would include such hidden elements as the expense of carrying excess raw materials and work-in-process inventory to ensure that defective items do not shut down the production process, as well as the cost of owning and operating excess capacity in order to compensate for machine clogging and downtime. In practice, less inclusive measures are usually employed. Total quality costs typically include expenditures in the following four categories:[57] prevention (e.g., quality planning, worker training, and supplier education); appraisal (e.g., product inspection and testing); internal failures (e.g., rework and scrap); and external failures (e.g., warranty and product liability).

A number of analysts have extended this argument, claiming that improved conformance should eventually lead to a reduction in long-term manufacturing costs.[58] One justification for this claim has been the expected link between quality improvement and productivity gains. For example, simplified and easy-to-assemble designs should require fewer workers at the same time that they reduce defects. Investments in machinery and equipment should result in more consistent production as well as improvements in worker productivity. Quality improvements are also expected to lead to further savings, in the form of experience-based scale economies, through their impact on market share and (cumulative) production levels.[59]

While the evidence is limited, most empirical work suggests that superior conformance and total quality costs are inversely related. Garvin, for example, in a study of the room air conditioning industry, found that Japanese manufacturers, with defect and field failure rates between fifteen and seventy times lower than U.S. competitors, averaged total costs of quality that were 1.3 percent of sales.[60] The best American companies averaged rework, scrap, and warranty costs that alone were 2.8 percent of sales. At the U.S. firms with the poorest quality, these costs exceeded 5.8 percent of sales. Garvin also found that quality and productivity were positively related, even though firms employed similar technologies and showed few differences in capital intensity. In this industry, U.S. companies with the highest quality were five times as productive, when measured by units produced per man-hour of assembly-line direct labor, as companies with the poorest quality.

Several surveys have collected more comprehensive data on the costs of quality; these provide additional support for the above relationships. A 1977 survey, for example, found that companies with formal systems for assessing quality costs—which most analysts associate with superior quality management and low failure rates[61]—had lower total costs of quality than companies without such systems. Companies in the former group averaged quality costs that were 5.8 percent of sales; those in the latter, rework, scrap, and warranty costs that alone were 7.8 percent of sales.[62]

Moreover, the amount that companies are spending to prevent quality problems—and, therefore, to ensure lower failure rates—may very well be suboptimal. Gilmore found that at least one-quarter of the companies he surveyed were spending less than 5 percent of their quality costs on prevention; approximately one-half were spending less than 10 percent.[63] His conclusion was that greater expenditures on prevention would result in improved conformance and fewer defects; these, in turn, were likely to produce an overall reduction in the total costs of quality because of significant savings in rework, scrap, and warranty.

The PIMS data base has generally been used to examine the relationship between quality and direct cost. The results have varied considerably by industry. In one study, quality and direct cost were positively related for differentiated-product businesses but negatively related for homogeneous products.[64] In another study, the two were positively related in capital goods businesses but negatively related in components and supplies businesses.[65] However, the experience curve effect, with high quality leading to high market share, increases in cumulative production, and eventually, experience-based reductions in costs, were found in all types of businesses.[66]

The varying results of these studies may reflect differences in the definitions of quality used by firms in different industries. The PIMS quality index is highly aggregated; no distinction is made among performance, features, reliability, or the other dimensions of quality discussed earlier. As a result, different industries could be employing different definitions when assessing the quality of their products. This, in turn, would determine whether the relationship between quality and direct cost was positive or negative. For example, among homogeneous product businesses (e.g., chemicals), quality is often defined as "meeting specifications."[67] Such a conformance-based view of quality is likely to result in an inverse relationship between quality and direct cost. Among differentiated and capital-goods businesses, however, quality is likely to be equated with performance or features, suggesting a positive association between quality and direct cost. While these inferences are consistent with the PIMS findings, they require further research in order to be verified.

Quality and Profitability

Figure 8.1 shows two ways in which improved quality might lead to higher profitability. The first route is through the market: improvements in performance, features, or other dimensions of quality lead to increased sales and larger market shares, or alternatively, to less elastic demand and higher prices. If the cost of achieving these gains is outweighed by the increases in contribution received by the firm, higher profits will result.[68]

Quality improvements may also affect profitability through the cost side. Fewer defects or field failures result in lower manufacturing and service costs; as long as these gains exceed any increase in expenditures by the firm on defect prevention, profitability will improve.

Empirical studies using the PIMS data base confirm the strong positive association between quality and profitability.[69] High quality produces a higher return on investment (ROI) for any given market share: Among businesses with less than 12 percent of the market, for example, those with inferior product quality averaged an ROI of 4.5 percent, those with average product quality an ROI of 10.4 percent, and those with superior product quality an ROI of 17.4 percent.[70] Quality improvements, by increasing share, also lead to experience-based cost savings, and further gains in profitability.[71] The market-based link between quality and profitability is, therefore, well supported by the evidence. The second linkage described in Figure 8.1 is less firmly established. As an earlier discussion has shown, the relationship between quality and cost depends on how the terms are defined. Those studies that have equated quality with conformance, and cost with total quality cost, have found an inverse relationship between the two. They have not, however, carried the analysis a step further to find if profitability was similarly affected. Nor have the studies focusing on the connection

172

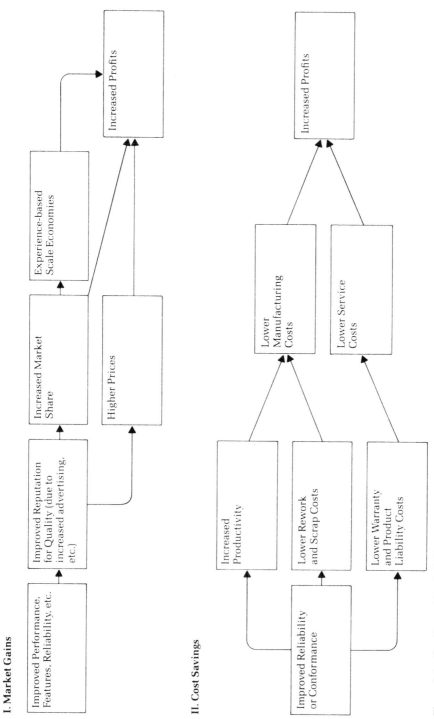

Figure 8.1 Quality and Profitability

between quality and direct cost taken into account differences in investment levels or capital costs, which would clearly affect the relationship between quality and ROI.

The empirical research on quality, then, has produced mixed results, with few clear directions for managers. The relationship between quality and such variables as price, advertising, and direct cost is both complex and difficult to predict. Few unambiguous results are found in the literature. Even where the expected relationships have emerged, further work is required because of the highly aggregated nature of the quality measures that have been employed. This is especially true of the studies relating quality to market share and profitability, for they have all employed the PIMS data base. These findings suggest a number of directions for future research.

Directions for Future Research

There is a clear need for more precise measures of product quality. Few studies have recognized the multiple dimensions of quality, and still fewer, the possibility that quality may have different meanings in different industries. Much of the empirical research on the correlates of quality needs to be replicated with these distinctions in mind. Similarly, analysts need to determine if the various dimensions of quality move together or separately, for otherwise, managers will be unable to position their companies to exploit particular quality niches.

These questions suggest two possible avenues of research. The first would focus on the determinants of consumer satisfaction, consumer perceptions of quality, and the relative importance of the various dimensions of quality in shaping buyer behavior. Andreasen, for example, has found that indexes of consumer satisfaction based on voiced complaints, objective measures of product nonperformance, satisfaction immediately after purchase, and satisfaction after initial problems have been resolved are not well correlated.[72] Each apparently measures a slightly different aspect of consumer satisfaction. Similar research is necessary to understand the precise connection between consumer satisfaction and the various dimensions of quality discussed in this article. As Takeuchi and Quelch point out, for many consumers "quality is more than [simply] making a good product."[73]

A second possible line of research would focus on manufacturing trade-offs. Traditionally, analysts have argued that manufacturing operations could be effective only if they pursued a limited set of objectives.[74] Low cost, high quality, rapid delivery, flexibility to volume changes, and flexibility to new product introductions were thought to be mutually incompatible.

Tradeoffs were unavoidable, and any one goal could be achieved only at the expense of others.

Japanese manufacturers, however, have succeeded in producing products that meet the twin objectives of high quality (conformance and reliability) and low cost. Their ability to do so has forced analysts to reconsider the concept of manufacturing tradeoffs, for many traditional assumptions no longer apply.[75] This area clearly warrants further research. Tradeoffs among the various dimensions of quality and between these dimensions and the objectives of cost, flexibility, and delivery must be better understood. Do the different dimensions of quality require different forms of expertise, or are firms likely to succeed on several dimensions at once? Durability, for example, often requires the use of sturdy and oversized components; does it also guarantee superior reliability, or is that more a reflection of how the assembly process is managed? More generally, which of the dimensions of quality are primarily a reflection of manufacturing skills, and which reflect design and engineering expertise? These questions must be answered if companies are to devise and execute effective strategies for competing on the basis of product or service quality.

Conclusion

Quality is a complex and multifaceted concept. It is also the source of great confusion: Managers—particularly those in different functions—frequently fail to communicate precisely what they mean by the term. The result is often endless debate, and an inability to show real progress on the quality front.

This article has identified several different perspectives on quality and has emphasized a number of critical dimensions. These distinctions are more than just theoretical niceties: They are the key to using quality as a competitive weapon. Managers must learn to think carefully about how their approach to quality changes as a product moves from design to market, and they must devise ways to cultivate these multiple perspectives. Attention must be focused on the separate dimensions of quality; markets must be closely examined for any untapped quality niches; and the organization must be tailored to support the desired focus. Once these approaches have been adopted, cost savings, market share gains, and profitability improvements can hardly be far behind.

9

Entrepreneurs, Champions, and Technological Innovation

Modesto A. Maidique

Successful radical innovation requires a special combination of entrepreneurial, managerial, and technological roles within a firm. As the firm grows and changes, these roles also change, and they tend to be performed by different people in different ways. The author draws conclusions from several cases of radical technological innovation to support these hypotheses. *SMR.*

There is plenty of reason to suppose that individual talents count for a good deal more than the firm as an organization.　　　　　　　　–Kenneth J. Arrow[1]

At all stages of development of the firm, highly enthusiastic and committed individuals who are willing to take risks play an important role in technological innovation. In the initial stages of the technological firm's development, these entrepreneurial individuals are the force that moves the firm forward. In later stages, they absorb the risks of radical innovation, that is, of those innovations that restructure the current business or create new businesses. As Ed Roberts has pointed out, "In the large firm as well as in the founding enterprise, the entrepreneur is the central figure in successful technological innovation."[2]

Successful innovation, however, requires a special combination of entrepreneurial, managerial, and technological roles. Furthermore, the characteristics of this network[3] of roles are a function of the stage of development of the firm. In this article, the theory of entrepreneurial roles—what we know about entrepreneurship and technological innovation—is combined with Scott's theory of corporate development to generate several hypotheses re-

From *Sloan Management Review*, Winter 1980, Vol. 21, No. 2. Reprinted with permission.

garding the evolution of entrepreneurial roles as the firm evolves from a small firm to a large, diversified firm.[4]

Three principal arguments are made: First, that the entrepreneurial role is essential for radical technological innovation, but that it manifests itself differently depending on the firm's stage of development. Second, that radical technological innovation, to be successful, requires top management participation in the entrepreneurial network. Third, that in addition to the independent entrepreneur and the product champion, an important intermediate entrepreneurial role is especially prominent in diversified firms—that is, the executive champion.[5]

Radical technological innovation, at any stage of development, can be viewed as requiring a recreation of the original entrepreneurial network—a merging of the roles the original entrepreneurial team performed: business definition, sponsorship, technical definition, and technical communication. As a business grows or becomes more diverse, the original entrepreneurial network becomes fragmented; these critical roles are decoupled, and a conservative bias is often introduced into subsequent innovations. Business definition becomes separated from technical definition by administrative systems, organizational hierarchy, and market and technological diversity. The business readjusts more slowly, or not at all, to technological discontinuities. Nonetheless, this decoupling is natural and necessary. It is impossible for the original entrepreneur to be closely tied to an increasingly large number of diverse innovations. He or she must, however, seek out and complete the network of entrepreneurship for that handful of radical innovations that will have significant impact on the future of the firm.

This article is organized into five sections. First, the literature on entrepreneurial roles and corporate development is briefly summarized. In the following three sections, the evolution of the network of entrepreneurial roles is examined by analyzing radical innovations in three different contexts: the small, the integrated, and the diversified technological firm.[6] In the last section some hypotheses are drawn from this analysis regarding the task of top management in the technology-based firm.

Entrepreneurship and Corporate Development: A Brief Review of the Literature

A rich literature exists on heroic, independent, technological entrepreneurs such as Thomas Watson, Jr., Henry Ford, and Edwin Land. During the last two decades, a new literature on entrepreneurship has also developed that emphasizes the role of individuals within the firm who exhibit entrepreneurial characteristics.

Entrepreneurs and Champions

The significance of the role of the entrepreneur has been recognized for at least two centuries. Schumpeter credits J. B. Say, an early nineteenth-century French economist, for being the first to recognize that the entrepreneur in a capitalist society is "the pivot on which everything turns."[7] According to Schumpeter, the entrepreneur

reforms or revolutionizes the pattern of production by exploiting an invention or, more generally, an untried technological possibility for producing a new commodity or producing an old one in a new way, by opening up a new source of supply of materials or a new outlet for products by reorganizing an industry. . . .[8]

On the other hand, the critical role that "champions" of technological change play within industrial organizations has been recognized only during the last two decades. In a seminal study of radical military innovations, Schon observed that certain committed individuals, *champions,* played the key role in successful innovations. Schon lists some fifteen major inventions of the twentieth century, such as the jet engine and the gyrocompass, in which individuals played a major role. In his studies, Schon found that "the new idea either finds a champion or *dies.*" To Schon, the "product champions" are critical, for

no ordinary involvement with a new idea provides the energy required to cope with the indifference and resistance that major technical change provokes. . . . Champions of new inventions . . . display persistence and courage of heroic quality.[9]

Schon's analysis led him to four basic conclusions:

1. At the outset, the new idea encounters sharp resistance.[10]
2. Overcoming this resistance requires vigorous promotion.
3. Proponents of the idea work primarily through the *informal* rather than the formal organization.
4. Typically, one person emerges as champion of the idea.

The product champion served as a catalyst for the development of a literature on internal entrepreneurial roles. In the decade following Schon's work, several new entrepreneurial (and related) roles and new names for old roles appeared in the innovation literature, such as "business innovators,"[11] "internal entrepreneurs,"[12] "sponsors,"[13] "change agents,"[14] "Maxwell demons or mutation selectors,"[15] "technical and manager champion,"[16] and "administrative entrepreneur."[17]

Collins and Moore[18] found very strong similarities between traditional or "independent" entrepreneurs and certain managers within the firm who operated like Schon's product champions: They called them "administrative entrepreneurs." Collins and Moore developed a psychological profile of the 150 independent and administrative entrepreneurs in their study and concluded that the "entrepreneurial personality, in short, is characterized by an unwillingness to submit to authority, an inability to work with it, and a consequent need to escape from it."[19] Some potential entrepreneurs find ways, at least temporarily, to satisfy their psychological needs by pursuing—sometimes in unorthodox ways—high-risk projects within the organization; others finally break away and create a new structure.

In two recent studies, Duchesneau[20] and Olsen[21] obtained statistical data on the presence of champions in the footwear and textile industries, respectively. Duchesneau interviewed senior managers in sixty-nine footwear firms and found that about two-thirds of them recognized the presence of "product champions" in their firms. In his study of twelve textile firms, Olsen found a "strong correlation" between early adoption of innovations and the existence of an identifiable champion. Olsen found identifiable champions in eight of the twelve firms in his study.[22]

SAPPHO

One of the first studies that attempted both to quantify the product-champion function and to break it down into subroles was the SAPPHO study.[23] In phase I of the SAPPHO project, twenty-nine pairs of successful and unsuccessful innovations were studied. Of the forty-three pairs of innovations in SAPPHO II, twenty-two were in the chemical industry and twenty-one in scientific instruments.[24] The forty-three pairs were compared along 122 dimensions, fifteen of which were found (on an aggregate basis) to have statistical significance higher than .1 percent (as determined by the binomial test). Another nine variables had statistical significance higher than 1 percent. The SAPPHO investigators used multivariate analysis to extract from these twenty-four variables five underlying areas of difference between successful and unsuccessful innovations:[25]

1. Strength of management and characteristics of managers.
2. Marketing performance.
3. Understanding of user needs.
4. Research and development (R&D) efficiency.
5. Communications.

To study the first of these factors—the role of key managers and technologists—the SAPPHO investigators defined four categories of key individuals:

1. *Technical innovator.* The individual who made the "major contribution on the technical side" to the development and/or design of the innovation.
2. *Business innovator.* The individual within the managerial structure who was responsible for the overall progress of the project.
3. *Product champion.* Any individual who made a decisive contribution to the innovation by "actively and enthusiastically promoting its progress through critical stages."
4. *Chief executive.* The "head of the executive structure" of the innovating organization, but not necessarily the managing director or chief executive officer.

The forty-three pairs of innovations were then tested to determine how, if at all, the presence of such key individuals explained the success of the innovation. The results for the five most significant parameters are summarized in Table 9.1. Surprisingly, the individual who emerged as the principal factor was *not* the product champion, but the "business innovator." In particular, the business innovator's power, respectability, status, and experience were important. However, the role of the product champion was also shown to discriminate significantly for success.

Thus, the SAPPHO study provides systematic evidence in favor of the champion hypothesis. The study also indicates that besides commitment and enthusiasm, the power and status of the sponsoring executive also play an important role in determining the success of an innovation. Often this latter

Table 9.1 Five Main Characteristics of Executives in Charge of Successful Innovations

Variable*	S	N[†]	F	%S[††]	Binomial Test[§]
1. The executive has more power.	20	19	4	75%	7.7×10^{-4}
2. The executive has more responsibility.	18	20	4	72%	1.3×10^{-3}
3. The executive has more diverse experience.	20	18	5	73%	2×10^{-3}
4. The executive has more enthusiasm.	14	27	2	71%	2×10^{-3}
5. The executive has higher status.	18	21	4	72%	2×10^{-3}

* S = variable discriminated for success; F = variable discriminated for failure; N = variable did not discriminate in either direction, or insufficient data were available to form the comparison.
†The N grouping presents a data-interpretation problem, since it's not clear how this group broke down between the "insufficient data" category or situations where the variable had a "neutral" effect or none at all.
††The %S was calculated by assuming that the N group was *equally* split between the insufficient data group and the neutral grouping. The "insufficient data" half was discarded and the remainder was split equally between the S and F groups. The "%S" was then calculated as a percentage of the new total S + F population.
§Calculated by SAPPHO group.

role is played by someone other than the "product champion"—that is (using the SAPPHO terminology), the "business innovator."

The significance of the SAPPHO data is made clearer by using Bower's model for the resource-allocation process.[26] He proposed a three-stage model for resource allocation in a large firm: Top management provides a business and structural *context* for decision making; within this context, middle management selects the projects that they support; higher level sponsorship, *impetus,* is required for successful completion of funding. At the root of the resource-allocation process are the specialists and lower level managers who give *definition* to the projects.

Using Bower's terms, the technical innovator provides technical *definition,* the business innovator provides *sponsorship* or *impetus,* and the chief executive provides business definition or *context.*[27] Viewed from this vantage point, the role of the product champion is to serve as a catalyst for increased sponsorship or impetus.

Similarly, the innovation process can also be viewed from the perspective of the key roles defined by Roberts. He expands the set of critical functions to include a technical-information role and a project-management role (see Tables 9.2 and 9.3 and Figure 9.1). The project manager anticipates the need for sponsorship by planning for the requirement of the innovation. The gatekeeper, a function characterized originally by Allen, acts as a clearing house for technical information for the technologists in the firm. In a subsequent paper, Roberts suggests that marketing and manufacturing gatekeepers, who can usually be identified, play important roles in the innovation process.[28]

Stages of Development of the Firm

While the literature on entrepreneurs and champions is primarily concerned with static behavior, a substantial literature exists on corporate development. However, this literature is concerned with overall description of the stages of corporate development, not with the specific issue of the entrepreneurial team. Nonetheless, the corporate-development literature does provide a framework for analyzing the development of entrepreneurial networks.

Galbraith proposed that the three stages of company evolution are small, medium, and large.[29] Chandler, on the other hand, suggested that the three basic stages are small, integrated, diversified. Scott, Salter, and others concur.[30]

Based on his study of the histories of about seventy large U.S. firms, Chandler proposed that, in most cases, firms follow a typical sequence of development.[31] After the initial entrepreneurial stage, the firm becomes

Table 9.2   Key Roles and Functions According to Different Investigators*

Function	Bower (1972)	Schwartz (1973)	SAPPHO (1974)	Kusiatin (1976)	Roberts† (1968, 1972, 1977, 1978)	This article††
Business, structure, and definition	Context	Context	Chief executive	——	——	Business definition, technological entrepreneur
Sponsorship	Impetus	Impetus	Business innovator, product champion	Manager champion, technical champion	Sponsor, product champion, project manager, internal entrepreneur	Executive champion, product champion, sponsorship, technological entrepreneur
Technical definition	Definition	Technical definition, factoring	Technical innovator	Technical champion	Creative scientist	Technical definition, technologist
Technical information	——	——	——	Technical champion	Gatekeeper	——
Market information	——	——	——	——	Market gatekeeper	——

* Roles and definitions vary from researcher to researcher and are only roughly comparable.
** See also Rhoades, Roberts, and Fusfeld (1978).
†See definitions in Table 9.3.

vertically integrated and managed by a centralized functional organization. Normally, this stage is followed by diversification, which is managed by a decentralized divisional organization.

This basic idea was further developed and extended by Scott, while he was working with Christensen and McArthur. A set of propositions delineating the various stages of corporate development resulted from a cooperative effort by Scott and Salter (see Table 9.4).[32]

Wrigley further elaborated on the three original stages and proposed three subclasses of diversified businesses: dominant business diversified, related business diversified, and unrelated business diversified.[33] Scott's classes, as modified by Wrigley, include the following:

Small (or entrepreneurial): single product or single product line company, with little formal structure, controlled by owner-manager.

Integrated: single-product line firm with vertically integrated manufacturing and specialized functional organizations. Owner-manager retains control of strategic decisions. Most operating decisions are delegated through policy.

Table 9.3 Definitions of Key Roles

Technological entrepreneur	The organizer of a technological venture who exercises control of the venture (typically by owning a substantial percentage of the equity) and assumes the risks of the business. Usually he is the chief executive officer.
Product champion	A member of an organization who creates, defines, or adopts an idea for a new technological innovation and who is willing to risk his or her position and prestige to make possible the innovation's successful implementation.
Executive champion	An executive in a technological firm who has direct or indirect influence over the resource allocation process and who uses this power to channel resources to a new technological innovation, thereby absorbing most, but usually not all, the risk of the project.
Technical definition	The basic performance requirements and associated specifications that characterize a proposal for a new technological innovation.
Sponsorship	The actions by which executives channel resources to innovative projects that they have chosen to support.
Business definition	A description of the business within which a firm chooses to compete and of the overall administrative practices that the firm will follow in that business.

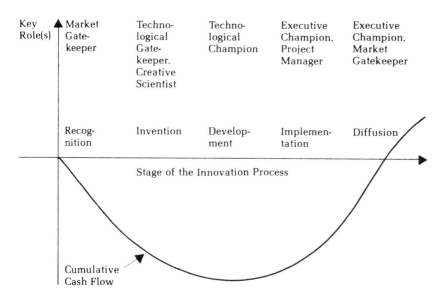

Key Role(s)	Market Gate-keeper	Techno-logical Gate-keeper, Creative Scientist	Techno-logical Champion	Executive Champion, Project Manager	Executive Champion, Market Gatekeeper
	Recognition	Invention	Development	Implementation	Diffusion

Stage of the Innovation Process

Cumulative Cash Flow

Figure 9.1

182

Table 9.4 The Three Stages of Organizational Development

Company characteristics	Stage I: Small	Stage II: Integrated	Stage III: Diversified
Product line	Single product or single line	Single product line	Multiple product lines
Distribution	One channel or set of channels	One set of channels	Multiple channels
Organization structure	Little or no formal structure; "one-man show"	Specialization based on function	Specialization based on product-market relationships
R&D organization	Not institutionalized; guided by owner-manager	Increasingly institutionalized search for product or process improvements	Institutionalized search for *new* products as well as for improvements
Performance measurement	By personal contact and subjective criteria	Increasingly impersonal, using technical and/or cost criteria	Increasingly impersonal, using *market* criteria (return on investment and market share)
Rewards	Unsystematic and often paternalistic	Increasingly systematic, with emphasis on stability and service	Increasingly systematic, with variability related to performance
Control system	Personal control of both strategic and operating decisions	Personal control of strategic decisions, with increasing delegation of operating decisions through policy	Delegation of product-market decisions within existing businesses, with indirect control based on analysis of "results"
Strategic choices	Needs of owner versus needs of company	Degree of integration; market-share objective; breadth of product line	Entry and exit from industries; allocation of resources by industry; rate of growth

Diversified: multiproduct firm with formalized managerial systems that are evaluated by objective criteria, such as rate of growth and returns on investment. Product-market decisions within existing businesses are delegated. Within the diversified group, there are three subcategories:

1. *Dominant business firms* that derive 70–95 percent of their sales from a single business[34] or a vertically integrated chain of businesses (e.g., General Motors, IBM, Xerox, U.S. Steel).
2. *Related business firms* that diversify into related areas where no single business accounts for more than 70 percent of sales (e.g., Du Pont, Eastman Kodak, General Electric).
3. *Unrelated business firms* that have diversified without necessarily relating new business to old, and where no single business accounts for as much

as 70 percent of sales (e.g., Litton, North American, Rockwell, and Textron).

Abernathy and Utterback have studied the process of corporate evolution using the "productive unit."[35] An economist might call the productive unit a simple firm: Abernathy and Utterback use the term to describe a related line of products, the manufacturing process, and the overhead structure required to develop, make, and market the products. Their work has significantly extended the literature on corporate evolution, but their focus has been on the evolution of the process segment rather than on managerial characteristics.

Abernathy and Utterback visualized newly created manufacturing processes as initially having some slack: Procedures are not fixed, and job design and material flow are informal and flexible. In short, the process is fluid. At the other extreme, once the process has been "perfected" by accumulation of experience, jobs become standardized, manual procedures are automated, and rigid specifications are instituted. The process becomes, in Abernathy and Utterback's term, specific. A transition phase joins these two external conditions.

In this model (Figure 9.2), product and process innovation proceed at different rates. Product innovation is highest in the fluid phase and declines monotonically through the transition and specific phases, as the slack is managed out. Process innovation appears slowly and rises as the accumulated flow of products through the processing stages increases the opportunity—and managerial pressures—to formalize the process and reduce costs.

A product or family of products emerges from the initial crops of new products and attains wide market acceptance and high volume. These products, called "dominant designs," make it possible to increase the rate at which the manufacturing process becomes systematized. As standardization increases, process innovation declines (see Figure 9.2).

Although we might expect some major transformations in managerial relationships as a process follows the path described above, Abernathy and Utterback do not discuss these transformations. Yet, in an earlier article, Abernathy and Townsend acknowledged (following Bright) that "management has a critical role in causing the process to evolve and in readying it for technological innovation."[36] These transformations in managerial relationships were not studied in the subsequent article, which used the extensive Myers and Marquis[37] data base (567 innovations, 120 firms, 5 industries), partly because the data base did not contain data on managerial issues.[38] Thus, regarding the evolution of managerial relationships in innovations,

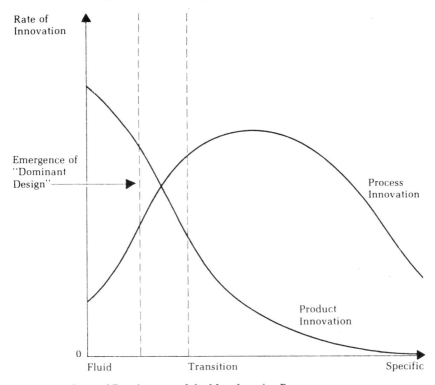

Figure 9.2 Stage of Development of the Manufacturing Process

Abernathy and Utterback do not go beyond referring to the broad "organic" and "mechanistic" descriptions of organizational relationships suggested by Burns and Stalker.[39]

In the next three sections, we use the three major corporate evolution contexts defined by Scott to examine entrepreneurial roles in radical innovations. We start with the small, or entrepreneurial, techological firm.

Stage I: The Small Technological Firm

The technological entrepreneur, in addition to defining the firm's business, plays (and enjoys playing) the dual role of sponsor and definition agent. Technological entrepreneurs often intervene (sometimes excessively) in the definition phase of innovations.

At Redactron Office Automation, a start-up firm specializing in automatic-editing components, founder and President Evelyn Berezin[40] explained her part in the defining of her company's first product:

When we reached the stage of spelling out detailed specifications, it became apparent that the engineers simply hated to commit things to writing. So I wrote out all the detailed specifications myself, usually dictating them while I was commuting back and forth to the plant. That's how the system got designed.[41]

And it wasn't by whim that Berezin decided on the specifications. Prior to the definition phase, she had spent weeks in the field observing people who used IBM automatic-editing equipment. Berezin considered closeness to the market imperative:

If you don't go there yourself but rely instead on what other people tell you, the information is likely to be distorted or the impressions incomplete. When you're designing a new product, you simply cannot afford to have layers of people between you and the eventual product users.[42]

Clearly, Berezin believed that the power and vision of the CEO should be brought into intimate contact with both technical experts and customers.

A similar pattern becomes evident from studying Henry Kloss, the founder of Advent Corporation. For Kloss, a classic technological entrepreneur, Advent was his third technology venture. He was a founder of Acoustic Research (AR). From there, he moved on to start KLH (both AR and KLH make high-quality consumer audio products). One of Kloss's principal reasons for starting Advent was his desire to retain control: He sold his shares of AR "under duress, and his share of KLH Corporation with mixed feelings."

Like Berezin, Kloss was familiar with the market and the most advanced technologies. He directed Video Beam, Advent's large-screen television project, from start to finish. According to Kloss, "I am responsible for the concept of the product and the initial demonstration that the idea is feasible. . . ." He delineated personal contributions, such as

choosing the optimal size of tubes; deciding the critical tolerances in the final product, making tradeoff choices between costs and qualities; working with consultants in the tube-making business and making the best judgment out of their recommendations as to production processes, specifications and material tolerances. . . .[43]

Kloss laid out the manufacturing and assembly plant when the time came to make the product. He was at the time the chief executive officer of Advent, which then had annual sales of $16 million.

The Kloss-Berezin phenomenon can occur in other countries. Efraim "Efi" Arazi, an Israeli electrical engineer educated at MIT, founded Sci-Tex in 1968. The company makes electro-optical systems, and it now has annual sales of over $10 million. Sci-Tex had an appointed administrator of R&D, but "Efi felt that would not preclude him from being involved, from continuing to participate very actively in the problem-solution process which had become his own lifeblood."[44]

In all three cases (Advent, Redactron, and Sci-Tex), the entrepreneur helped define new products while retaining control as CEO. For the entrepreneur sees the company as a giant erector set and retains the right to play with any of the pieces. For Kloss, the ideal situation would be that of Edwin Land, chairman and technical director of billion-dollar Polaroid. Land reputedly has access to any level of R&D while functioning as CEO.

Stage II: The Integrated Firm

Thus what the entrepreneur created passed inexorably beyond the scope of his authority. . . . What the entrepreneur created, only a group of men sharing specialized information could ultimately operate.[45]

If the entrepreneur succeeds, he or she creates a dilemma. Growth means more products, more people, more managers—a transition from a small to an integrated firm. Continued growth requires changes in the entrepreneur's role. Technological progress and organizational complexity act as dual forces on the entrepreneur to cause him or her to give up technical definition and sponsorship of most new projects.

Robert Noyce, the coinventor of the integrated circuit and cofounder and chairman of Intel, puts it this way:

Maybe you can do good technical work for ten years, if you work hard at it, but after that the younger guys are better prepared. It's a question of technical obsolescence, if you will.[46]

Like Noyce, Ken Olsen, chairman of Digital Equipment Corporation (DEC), has moved away from technical definition, though he, like Henry Kloss, is reputedly a "shirt-sleeved engineering type."[47] After a recession, Olsen explained in an interview: "I let the engineers do the designing; my concern was to keep the team together."[48] Olsen is vitally concerned with maintaining open communications to ensure that the best proposals come to his attention. He meets regularly with an engineering committee comprised of about twenty engineers from all levels of DEC. Olsen sets the agenda and periodically disbands and reconstitutes the committee to maintain a fresh flow of ideas. He sees his role as that of a catalyst, or a "devil's advocate": He expects that the best solutions to technical problems will be developed by his technicians.

Often Olsen's role is that of a sponsor. One DEC manager had been championing a project whose approval had become mired in red tape. Olsen sat in on a meeting in which this man's difficulties emerged. Olsen asked about the project and wondered out loud why such a promising idea was finding such little support. The manager describes what followed: "Suddenly the barriers to my project came down. What normally might have taken a year or more to complete became a six-month project."[49] Sponsorship had replaced technical definition.

Such sponsorship of product champions is critically important for continued innovation. Schwartz studied innovation in two major technology-based firms (one was DEC) and concluded that middle managers served as integrators between technical specialists and top management.[50] The middle managers decided which proposals would be submitted for approval, negotiated terms of support for a proposal, and selected the criteria for program evaluation. According to Schwartz, these functions "tended to add a conservative bias to proposals. As a result, the innovations studied were incremental rather than radical."[51] The technological or product champion seeks to break through these barriers, but his or her attempts meet with little success without adequate sponsorship.

The development of the float-glass process at Pilkington Brothers, an integrated British glass manufacturer, is a classic case of technological championing. A few years after joining the firm, Alistair Pilkington, a distant relative of the founding family, conceived a radically new way of making plate glass one evening while he was washing the family dishes. That evening was the beginning of a risky crusade to develop the float-glass process, during which, according to Pilkington, "chaps were literally taken off on stretchers from heat exhaustion, yet [they] came back for more."[52]

Developing this process was a big financial gamble for Pilkington Brothers. After the fundamentals of the process had been proved in the lab, over 100,000 tons of unsalable glass costing $3.6 million were produced in the pilot plant. Month after month, Alistair Pilkington faced the firm's directors with a new request for $280,000 of operating funds and with promises of progress on the project. For a company with net profits of about $400,000 per month, this was a major risk; yet Pilkington continued to get approval until salable glass was finally produced in 1958. Alistair Pilkington succeeded by persisting in his role as technological champion, despite continued setbacks and high risks.[53] His credit, however, must clearly be shared with Harry Pilkington, the entrepreneurial chairman of the board, who absorbed the risks of young Alistair's innovation and who made it possible for the company later to reap $250 million in licensing fees from its competitors. The Pilkington story is often given as a classic example of the product champion. In fact, it is a classic example of the entrepreneur and the champion working in unison—the simplest entrepreneurial network. The champion proposes, the entrepreneur disposes.

Both at DEC and at Pilkington Brothers, the entrepreneur's role evolved from technical definition to sponsorship. But the entrepreneur was still the primary impetus for new projects, especially large ones. Other people, like the young engineering manager at DEC and Alistair Pilkington, had assumed the role of technical definition and had become technological champions for their projects. Olsen and the senior Pilkington found it easy to continue to act as sponsors for key projects in their firms. This was possible partly because the technologies of their integrated, single product line firms could be grasped by top management more easily than could the technologies of a diversified firm.

Stage III: The Diversified Firm

Diversified firms that have a dominant business (one that accounts for over 70 percent of sales) operate that business as if they were integrated, single product line firms. Such dominant businesses are usually controlled by top management through a functional structure, while the remainder of the businesses are managed through product divisions.[54] In these firms, the relationship between entrepreneurs and champions in the dominant business resembles that which we found in integrated, single product line firms like DEC and Pilkington. The entrepreneur gives up definition of products in the dominant business, but he keeps tight reins on sponsorship, particularly for major products. IBM in the late 1960s is a case in point.

Outsiders see IBM as a reflection of its products—a model of orderliness and rationality. To many, IBM is the epitome of the modern corporation: technologically powerful and highly innovative, but predictable and smoothly managed. Yet in 1964, after months of chaotic infighting, Tom Watson, Jr. (then IBM's CEO), made the extraordinarily risky decision to commit IBM to a revolutionary new line of computers, the System 360. The program's projected cost, $5 billion, exceeded the total assets (or, for that matter, the annual sales) of IBM that year. The System 360 was revolutionary in three major ways:

1. It depended heavily on microcircuitry (technology now commonplace, but then in its infancy).
2. The series was comprised of six basic computers designed so that users could scale up from one machine to another without having to rewrite existing programs.
3. The six models (30, 40, 50, 60, 62, 70) were to be made available simultaneously.

Bob Evans, the line manager who acted as technological champion for the new computers, explained: "We called this project 'you bet your company.' "[55]

According to one IBM executive, Watson had grown up with the IBM computer business and therefore "was able to use the informal organization to obtain the knowledge necessary to make the right decisions."[56] Watson once invited Fred Brooks, who at that time was the 360 project-design manager, and other technical experts to his ski lodge in Vermont for a detailed discussion of the critical programming-compatability issues. Watson also relied on T. Vincent Learson, a group executive whom he had tapped in 1954, to head IBM's entry into computers. Learson, a "tough and forceful personality," was "impatient with staff reports and committees," and he tended to "operate outside the conventional chain of command."[57] Learson was known to go directly to lower level management when he needed information.

The decision to go ahead with the 360 system shook IBM to its core. Sweeping organizational changes were instituted (three reorganizations over a six-year period), technically oriented executives diluted some of the traditional power of the marketing staff, IBM World Trade stopped trying to develop its own computers. IBM shifted from being simply an assembler of computer components to making its own components. In the process it became for a time the world's largest manufacturer of integrated circuits.

The success of IBM's System 360 is now legendary. It became the dominant design in business computers, and Learson was promoted to president of IBM shortly after its introduction. But in 1966 it was far from clear that Watson's gamble would be successful, and IBM's management agreed that "no meaningful figure could be put on the gamble." But a decade later it was clear that Watson had bet his company—and won.

Like Harry Pilkington and Ken Olsen, Watson and Learson communicated directly with the technical experts, and they relied on informal information networks to supplement the data they were able to obtain directly. Middle managers, like Brooks, Evans, and Alistair Pilkington, championed the new products. But top management made the major resource-allocation decisions, and they had the insight to make winning decisions, because they were dealing with single product line businesses, with which they had grown up.

When diversified firms enter fields with which the dominant entrepreneur is not intimately familiar, the process changes. Now a new kind of champion emerges, bridging the gap between the entrepreneur and the technological champion. Within the scope of their authority and responsibility, these "executive champions" are modeled after the independent entrepreneurs discussed above. Sometimes, they are simply the original independent entrepreneur in a new corporate context, in which their power is circumscribed. In other cases, they grow out of the roots of the existing corporate culture.

In 1975, for example, Redactron, facing financial difficulties, agreed to merge with the Burroughs Corporation. Though Evelyn Berezin kept her title of president of Redactron, she became a Burroughs employee in 1976. In an interview shortly after joining Burroughs, she explained her philosophy of management:

> In a small company the real cost is not in the operating expenses, or in buying some new pieces of gear, or hiring a new person—it's time. Reducing your development or commercialization time is worth virtually whatever you have to pay.

Redactron and three other companies in the Burroughs structure operated as relatively autonomous businesses within Burroughs, which was then a $2 billion corporation with 50,000 employees and fifty plants. At Burroughs, Berezin's role had changed considerably, partly as a result of her continued quest to gain precious time. Now she was far more concerned with resource allocation than with product definition. She explained her new role:

> Burroughs's product management is involved in the resource-allocation process, thus I am constantly involved in funding decisions. I have told my managers "you go do it, I'll get the funds." But there are limitations: For instance, I don't have authority to increase the engineering budget, but I can determine how programs are carried out. Secondly, all raises go through Detroit. I can't unilaterally increase people's salaries, but my people know that I will champion them.

Berezin cited a specific example:

> We had developed a new peripheral device which was very sophisticated yet inexpensive. It was a new technology. It was, in a word, "gorgeous." Yet corporate engineering said no, they were working on something else and this project could not be supported. The tooling that was required was on the order or $50,000 and had to be approved by corporate. My capital budget, however, had been approved at the beginning of the year, and I could only approve new items below $5,000.
>
> What did I do? I took the device to top management. What happened? The project was approved. I had to fight for four months, but I won the fight. In a good large company, if you fight—long enough—you win.

Evelyn Berezin, similarly to Tom Watson, Jr., was sponsoring a member of her organization who had proposed a promising new project. The key difference was that the circumscription of her authority required that she seek higher level sponsorship to implement the project. Berezin was an "executive champion" several times removed from the detailed technical definition, but without the entrepreneurial clout to be the ultimate sponsor. Thus, in this example, we find a new kind of champion—more senior in the managerial structure than the technological champion, who, in fact, is often a sponsor for the latter within the limits of his or her responsibility.

In 1974 just after Ronald Peterson had returned to Grumman Aerospace from a year as a Sloan Fellow at MIT, he was tapped by the president of Grumman to head an exploratory group on advanced energy systems. His immediate concern was with resource allocation, and in particular, with the authority that would go with his new position. Peterson, who had done his MIT thesis on innovation, felt that unless he reported directly to chief executive Joseph G. Gavin, Jr., the probability of success for his project would be reduced. "I've learned enough about new ventures," explained Peterson, "to know they don't work unless they get top level attention." Soon after, Peterson became manager of the Energy Program Department, and he reported directly to Gavin.[58]

After studying the alternatives open to Grumman, Peterson decided not to follow in the footsteps of aerospace firms bidding on proposals for esoteric new technologies, such as giant wind machines, oceanic platforms, and orbiting power stations.[59] Peterson decided instead to shun government proposals and to concentrate first on low-technology solar hot-water and space-heating installations. He knew that, in order to achieve his goals, he needed the freedom to operate the business differently and independently from the traditional management style of the parent firm.

In 1977 when Joseph G. Gavin, Jr., was appointed president of the Grumman Corporation, parent company of Grumman Aerospace, he appointed Peterson general manager of the Grumman Advanced Energy Systems Division. "I've been fortunate that Gavin has had a long-term interest in energy and since the beginning has played the sponsor role on this project." Peterson explained why the new division was established:

One of the main reasons for establishing this division was not to be hampered with aerospace procedures, salaries, and infrastructure. . . .
    In this position I have a lot of authority. . . . I can sign for anything up to a million dollars on the annual plan without any counter signature. I have the power to raise salaries and hire and fire people. In effect, I am the president of a virtually independent corporation.[60]

Peterson had become, within the limits approved by Gavin, an executive champion who was willing and able to risk Grumman's resources on projects proposed by technological champions in his organization.

Conclusion: Evolution of the Entrepreneurial Network

The relatively small number of cases and industries studied, the incompleteness of some of the secondary data, and the complexity of the processes examined limit us to hypothesis generation. But the data suggest a framework to explain how the relationship between the network of entrepreneurial roles and radical innovation changes with stage of process development and increasing organizational complexity. The proposed framework is illustrated in Figure 9.3.

The small firm is easiest to analyze. Here, there is usually one business unit and one source of managerial sponsorship for technological projects: the entrepreneur. However, as in Efi Arazi's case, problem solving is part of the technological entrepreneur's lifeblood. Thus, most technological entrepreneurs continue to hold on to most, or all, of the reins of product definition, often until it is too late: Henry Kloss neglected financial and other duties of corporate management until he eventually lost control of his firm. Involvement in product definition without upsetting the firm's organizational hierarchy is not difficult for entrepreneurs in small firms. Most of the technical people are generally old colleagues of the entrepreneur or were hired directly by him or her. But even the most capable entrepreneur has limits. One of the most brilliant entrepreneurs I've met thought himself impervious to these limitations when he moved into his plant, cot and all. Within a few months, after a divorce and a nervous breakdown, he too realized that he had a limit.

Unless the entrepreneur recognizes that at some point—two or three projects for some, perhaps a dozen for others—he or she must retreat from the product-definition role, the firm is likely to fail. Berezin, as is evident from our second encounter with her, had begun such a transition.

The integrated technology firm, such as DEC and Pilkington Brothers, illustrates the entrepreneur's transition from the definition role. In these

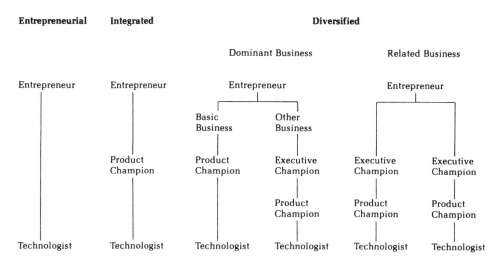

Figure 9.3 The Evolution of the Entrepreneurial Network

firms, the CEO was technically knowledgeable and still played a pivotal role in the innovation process—for radical innovations. Harry Pilkington and Ken Olsen did not define the new products, but they used their technical expertise and their organization's informal channels to gather information from their technical people. Although Pilkington and Olsen were managing firms several times smaller than Watson's IBM, all three chief executive officers viewed providing impetus to at least the radical technical innovations as a key part of their role. Nonetheless, there is a limit to how many projects a chief executive can sponsor. Olsen, for instance, could afford to be very visible in his firm's resource-allocation process. Watson, as CEO of a $4 billion firm, could be involved only in those projects that might reshape the entire future of his firm—like the System 360. Similarly to the small company entrepreneurs, Watson and Olsen had excellent informal information networks that made available to them vitally important data for their decision making without destroying the firm's organizational structure. And that is precisely what they did: they made the major technological decisions and absorbed risks. Sponsorship replaced definition.

Increasing organizational complexity requires that others also sponsor innovations. The CEO, or the overall top management team, should be the sponsor for radical changes in large organizations; yet many other important projects also need sponsors.[61] Ronald Peterson argued that Joseph G. Gavin, Jr., had been the "sponsor" for his energy group. It was clear, however, that by the time Grumman Advanced Energy Systems had become a division, Peterson, not Gavin, had become the sponsor for most new projects. Gavin primarily helped to set overall business direction. In short, Peterson and Berezin functioned as executive champions who, *within their business units,* behaved similarly to Olsen, Watson, and Pilkington, Sr.

The inherent disorder produced by direct interaction of the central sources of sponsorship with the defining or proposing agents is a unifying thread in all the cases studied. By promoting informality in communications, interacting with first-line technical people, reviewing proposals outside of the "conservative bias" of middle management, and finally *deciding,* the entrepreneurial heads of the executive structures studied helped to perpetuate the fluidness, slack, and disorder that Abernathy and Utterback found in the highly innovative initial stages of process development.

In a study of the evolution of the structure of the firm,[62] Abernathy and Utterback suggest that the "normal" direction of transition in a business unit, and more generally, in a firm, is toward a more rigid process that implies more product homogeneity, increased automation, and more bureaucratic management. In this phase, both product and process innovation begin to approach zero (see Figure 9.2).

However, Abernathy and Utterback do not propose that the "normal" direction of process and organizational evolution is inexorable. They leave the door open for reversals. Utterback has argued that major innovation, usually originating outside the existing industry, is the key catalyst for a reversal. New ventures—larger firms entering a new business—are credited with the lion's share of the innovations that create important threats for the present competitors.[63] In a later article, Abernathy and Utterback concluded that government sponsorship, through either purchases or direct regulation, can also have a major impact on innovation in an industry.[64] The recent downsizing of automobiles is a case in point.

Some firms, however, do revolutionize themselves from within. We argue here that when this happens it is the consequence of entrepreneurial sponsorship. This lever for change is not often used. Established firms generally respond to technological invasions by perfecting their present technology. The history of the fountain-pen, steam-locomotive, and razor-blade industries and their response to ballpoint pens, diesel locomotives, and electric razors are illustrative examples.[65]

When the sources of sponsorship are buffered, major changes either do not come about, or, alternatively, occur through a spinoff. Soon after the System 360 had been introduced at IBM, Gene Amdahl, a brilliant designer who had been part of its creation, proposed a new generation of computers based on advanced integrated circuits. After failing to get sponsorship for his proposals, Amdahl quit IBM in frustration and set out to develop his own computer in 1971. The result was the Amdahl 470, introduced in 1975, that was 1.4 to 1.8 times faster than the IBM 370/168 while costing 8 to 12 percent less. Amdahl's sales, four years after the introduction of the 470, were running at an annualized rate of over $400 million.[66] Although IBM later introduced a system with comparable performance, the attitude toward technological champions seems to have changed significantly since the Watson days. Frank Cary, IBM's present chairman, says, "From now on, change will be evolutionary rather than revolutionary."[67]

In summary, managing radical technological change is a fundamental element of top management's task in the technology-based firm. To succeed in coping with new waves of technology, the chief executive must, in Ted Levitt's words, "attack the problem of change."[68] He or she should develop an environment where risk taking by executive champions and product champions will lead to new ventures and products. Most important, if the top manager is to thwart the drift toward rigidity and organizational inertia that usually accompanies success, he or she must be personally involved in the entrepreneurial networks that lead to radical technological change, for only the chief executive can make decisions, provide the resources, and absorb the risks necessary for such change.

10

Information Technology:
A New Competitive Weapon

Gregory L. Parsons

In recent years information technology has dramatically altered the structure of markets in a number of industries. Although many managers understand the potential impact of information systems on their firm's competitive position, others fail to consider strategy implications when selecting a system. This article presents a multilevel framework for assessing the competitive impact of information technology on a firm, and provides a guide for integrating information systems with a firm's strategy. *SMR*.

Significant advances in the related technologies of computers, telecommunications, data-access and storage devices, graphics equipment, and software have created a wide spectrum of new opportunities for managers. The speed, cost, size, and capabilities of the new information technology (IT) continue to improve rapidly, and there appear to be unlimited applications that could be "computer enhanced." However, in spite of the new wealth of technological advances, the ability of most businesses to assimilate and apply IT lags far behind the available opportunities. Although many authors have noted the shortfall over the years, the effect of the 1980s on this "strategic gap" is much more critical.[1] Senior executives increasingly feel that their businesses should receive more benefit from technology investment, but few are able to articulate the impact IT has or should have on their businesses.

In a recent study, three senior executives not directly involved in the technology were asked to assess the impact of IT on their businesses; their responses were quite different. A divisional president of a large industrial corporation described the effect of IT:

From *Sloan Management Review*, Fall 1983, Vol. 25, No. 1. Reprinted with permission.

I think information technology contributes at least 3 percent of our bottom-line profit margins. Operationally, we couldn't get through the week without the system support, and in the marketplace, I don't think we could hold our market share without the technology. But this is mainly a gut feeling. I can't back up these estimates with numbers or specific reasons.

The chief strategist for a major U.S. bank said:

The technology is our top strategic concern, not because it outweighs everything else, but because we are unsure what to do with it. Although we have a strategy for the marketplace, the technology issues seem to be eluding us. On the one hand, it's important, everybody agrees on that, but then we end up doing projects based on a series of piecemeal technical decisions. We can't seem to grasp the bigger picture.

The chief financial officer of a large consumer goods manufacturing company explained his view of IT:

We've really cleaned up our data-processing act since the mid-1970s. The systems run well and now we're mainly fine-tuning. I expect we'll be doing primarily maintenance programming in the foreseeable future. I feel that we've gotten most of the benefits from the technology currently available. As the cost comes down, more projects will be financially justified and then we'll do them.

From these remarks and the comments of many other senior executives questioned about IT, two issues are clear. First, the importance of IT varies widely from firm to firm. In some firms, IT is a top-level strategic concern; in others, it is basically perceived as an administrative convenience. Second, there is no commonly accepted guideline or framework for measuring the importance of IT to a business. Most planning approaches for this technology do not take into account its strategic relevance.[2] Although executives have a "feeling" about IT's importance, few could explain why it is as important as they believe it to be. Even fewer could articulate how important it should be for the future.

Clearly, IT is having a significant impact on many firms, and it is now or will become a strategic concern for many firms over the next five years. It has been estimated that in those five years more than $1 trillion will be spent on IT investments. Such technical improvements as telecommunications, personal computers, computer-assisted manufacturing, and computer-aided design are just a few of the recent developments that have made IT an increasingly important component of the products, services, and operations of many firms.

This article presents a three-level framework to help senior managers assess the current and potential impact of IT on their businesses (see Table 10.1). This framework was developed from the results of a two-year study of more than a dozen companies. It is based on a recognition and analysis of

Table 10.1   The Three-Level Impact of IT

Industry Level

IT changes an industry's:
  Products and services
  Markets
  Production economics

Firm Level

IT affects key competitive forces:
  Buyers
  Suppliers
  Substitution
  New entrants
  Rivalry

Strategy Level

IT affects a firm's strategy:
  Low-cost leadership
  Product differentiation
  Concentration on market or product niche

the competitive environment and strategies of business, and focuses on the opportunities for firms to use IT to improve their competitive positions. In order for IT to become a viable competitive weapon, senior management must understand how IT may impact the competitive environment and strategy of the business. Such an understanding will enable managers to direct IT resources to the firm's most important targets.

The Impact of IT at the Industry Level

At the global level, IT changes the fundamental nature of the industry in which the firm competes. When IT changes an industry, it may impact the nature of the industry's products and services, the industry's markets, and/or the industry's economics of production.

Products and Services.   In some industries, IT may change the very nature of the industry's products and services, substantially altering the product life cycle and significantly increasing the speed of distribution. For example, because of advances in IT, the products and services of the publishing industry are undergoing significant changes. As the industry moves from a paper product to an electronically based one, the time and space constraints for product development and distribution are shortened. Authors and news sources are preparing electronic manuscripts and text, which are sent to publishers on floppy discs or directly from computer to computer. Electronic manuscripts are edited on word processors, typesetting is computerized, and graphics are generated by computers. Promotional materials are distributed by telecommunications, and readers can buy the product from the publisher's electronic data base. The time lag between an idea for a new product and its mass distribution could be virtually eliminated. Small publishers who can adopt the technology have substantially reduced the product-development cycle, gaining a significant advantage over larger competitors.

Markets.   IT can significantly change the markets of some industries. For example, financial companies will face a market of computer-literate consumers and businesses that will demand electronically based products and services. IT has already created a new product line called cash-management systems, which are offered by large banks. As IT erases traditional geographic market limitations, financial-services companies must now compete in a global market. The emerging technology for automatic-teller machines (ATMs), home banking, and electronic-funds transfer is making more sophisticated financial products and services possible and increasing the overall demand for them.

Production Economics.   IT developments may change the basic economics of production in some industries. In the distribution industry, IT is dividing businesses into two categories: those that have computerized warehousing and inventory control, and those that have manual operations. Businesses with computerized capabilities have the ability to serve a national market and are breaking the industry pattern of regional distribution. Such national distributors also enjoy other advantages, such as economies of scale in marketing, software, and hardware. Because of control problems and high costs, businesses with manual operations are limited to local markets by their technological position. IT will also affect the production economics in some industries by changing the industry's historical tradeoff between standardization and flexibility. Some equipment-manufacturing plants have already used IT to achieve unit costs that remain essentially constant, whether one unit or one million units are produced. This new potential will effectively remove many of the traditional competitive advantages in these industries. IT will reduce historical economies of scale in some areas while extending them in others. Because of the monitoring, controlling, and coordinating potential of IT, larger and more efficient facilities can be built that will capture new economies of scale by utilizing machinery, space, energy, and specialized labor more efficiently.

There are critical implications for firms that compete in industries in which IT is changing the nature of the business. Traditional rules of competition will change, new economies of scale will evolve, and entry barriers will erode in one area and spring up in others. There will be new competitors, new products and services, new distribution channels, and different levels of demand and elasticity. Product life cycles will be shortened, and the value-added stream of the industry will be redistributed.

Before management can consider the long-run impact IT will have within their firm, they must understand how IT is changing the industry. This is entirely consistent with most views of corporate strategy, which begin with an understanding of the external environment of the firm.[3] At the industry level the impact of IT ranges from major (e.g., in the banking industry) to minor (e.g., in the aluminum industry). To effectively link IT to the strategic needs of the firm, management must anticipate the impact of IT at the industry level *before* it occurs, so that strategies can be developed to position the firm appropriately in the new industry setting. For example, given the current rate of development in telecommunications and office technology, video conferencing may become a major substitute for some business air travel in less than ten years; this would significantly affect the airline industry's business-travel market. Today's CEO and strategist must address a crucial question: What impact will IT have on our industry over the next five to ten years in terms of products and services, markets, and production economies?

The Impact of IT at the Firm Level

At the firm level, the impact of IT is determined by the specific competitive forces facing the firm. Porter described five competitive forces that form the industry structure and the competitive "arena" for each firm in the industry.[4] These five forces are the buyers, the suppliers, the substitutes, the new entrants, and the rivals within a particular industry. Each firm in every industry faces these five generic forces; the specific manifestations of these forces determine a firm's profitability and range of potentially successful strategies. This framework for competition provides a useful vocabulary for defining the key issues facing a firm today and in the future. By using this framework, management can learn how IT changes an industry structure through the competitive forces that shape that industry.

Competitive Forces

As IT affects the products, services, or operations of a business, it may change the relationship between an industry and its suppliers. For example, the use of sophisticated quality-control systems by the auto industry is forcing steel producers to become much more quality conscious. This is even addressed in contracts, and it will change the mix of suppliers. As industries become much more dependent upon IT, the IT supplier will become an important force for a firm to consider when planning strategy. For example, it will be interesting to see how firms react when they realize that a major cost of their operations is dependent upon IBM's pricing strategy.

It will also change the level of sophistication of some industries' suppliers. Suppliers of funds to financial institutions are increasingly more sophisticated (and consequently more powerful), because IT allows them to monitor and redeploy investments with astonishing ease. Competitively, firms in industries in which IT is impacting the supplier relationship must be concerned with how this change will affect a supplier's power in dealing with the industry.

IT will also affect the buyer relationships of industries as new products, services, and distribution channels evolve. Buyers in the banking industry can now choose products and services from a variety of channels. The buyer/industry relationship has been fundamentally changed by ATMs, point-of-sale terminals (POSs), and electronic home banking. IT has also altered the product mix of industries as firms have packaged information around a basic service. For example, a large distribution company has enhanced its service by offering retail customers computer-generated inventory-management reports on a fee-for-service basis.

IT also impacts the rate of substitution in some industries. For example, a large overnight carrier has recognized that electronic mail may substantially substitute for paper-based communications and is developing an electronic-based business. IT will speed up the life cycle of many products by shortening the development process through computer-aided design (CAD) and computer-aided engineering (CAE). Firms that succeed by duplicating products at low cost will respond to product innovators much more rapidly and accelerate the substitution process.

IT affects the rate of new entry into industries by negating existing entry barriers or creating new ones. For example, in the banking industry, IT-based access to banking services has seriously eroded the traditional entry barriers enjoyed by many branch offices. In the distribution industry, IT has created new entry barriers by requiring investment in extensive computer and telecommunication networks that are used to control costs in large-scale multilocation distribution facilities. In effect, IT has created a new scale-economy barrier that the new entrant must overcome in order to price competitively and still be profitable.

Finally, IT changes industry structure by affecting the rivalry bases among intraindustry competitors. By introducing a new competitive weapon into various settings, IT sparks outbreaks of firm warfare. Recently, American and United Airlines have used their reservation systems to competitive advantage by listing their own flights ahead of competitors' flights (termed "systems bias") and by negatively promoting competitors' flights. Certain securities brokerage firms have exploited IT to introduce a radical form of cost competition through the telecommunication and computer-based discount brokerage. In the banking industry, leading banks see smaller competitors joining forces through shared ATM networks. Clearly, IT will contribute significantly to rivalry in many industries in a number of as yet unknown ways.

Because the competitive forces of buyers, suppliers, substitution, new entrants, and rivalry can significantly impact a firm, managing IT is a vital element of a firm's strategy and part of its competitive domain. Although IT represents a challenge or threat to a firm's established ways of doing business, it also represents opportunities for gaining new competitive advantages. IT resources can be used as competitive weapons to improve a firm's position in its competitive environment.

Creating Competitive Advantages

Buying Power.   The buyer groups of an industry represent a force that, if strong, can reduce the profitability of an industry. For example, strong buyer power exists if customer groups are very concentrated or if they purchase large volumes relative to the industry's total sales. When a handful of buyers represent an industry's entire market, then the importance of each buyer to each selling competitor is so great that concessions are a way of life for the industry, and potential profits are reduced. Buyers also have significant power if the cost of changing suppliers or changing to a substitute product is low. The lack of "switching costs" between an industry and its buyers can result in reduced profitability.

There are two ways in which IT can be a strategic weapon for reducing buyer power. First, IT can introduce switching costs, making it more costly for a buyer to change suppliers. IT has greatly increased the ability of many firms to raise switching costs for buyers. For example, a large medical-supply company has provided on-line order entry terminals and inventory-management software for customers. As the customers' systems are integrated with the supplier's, it becomes much more difficult for customers to order from a competitor. If customers change suppliers, they incur testing and implementation costs and the cost of retraining personnel and developing new procedures. The more sophisticated the systems, the greater the switching costs and the less power buyers have to switch indiscriminately to a competitor.

Second, IT represents a strategic weapon for dealing with powerful buyers by providing the capability for firms to develop buyer-information systems that determine the profit potential of various buyer groups. All industries have certain customers who are extremely expensive to service relative to the average customer. In addition, some firms are particularly well suited to service some customer groups but not others. However, it is usually very difficult for a manager to determine the overall attractiveness of a current or potential market segment to the business. For example, because of the insurance industry's historical tradition of providing full service to all business customers, there has been no attempt to match products to customer segments in order to maximize profit. Consequently, although they have a wealth of data, most insurance companies have poor information to answer such crucial questions as: How much does it cost to service a particular market segment? How should our customer portfolio be pared to fit our particular capabilities? To address these critical issues, a large insurance firm is building an extensive claims data base to go beyond actuarial calculations in an attempt to determine which potential markets will be most profitable. As the overall cost of servicing insurance customers increases significantly due to deregulation and competition, buyer selection is a key issue, and the strategic application of IT resources will provide a competitive advantage.

Supplier Power.   Strong supplier groups may reduce much of an industry's potential profits. The suppliers of an industry include the sources for raw materials, machinery, capital, and labor. Suppliers will be powerful if they are very concentrated or if the buyer faces very high costs to obtain information, to shop, or to negotiate.

IT represents a strategic opportunity for a firm when it can be used to mitigate the factors driving the power of suppliers, thus improving the firm's competitive position. For example, IT can be used as a viable alternative for high-priced labor. Recent developments in robotics and computer-aided manufacturing not only reduce the cost of labor outright, but they also reduce labor's power to demand industry profits. A manufacturing company recently installed a real-time labor-efficiency management system that is tied directly to the wage-incentive system specified in the union contract. The owner of the business feels that this system has provided a significant advantage in dealing with his labor force.

IT can also be used to avoid high switching costs. One of the major problems facing the banking industry is its inability to strategically manage its largest single cost—the cost of money. The sources of funds for a bank include customer deposits, money markets, certificates of deposit, and others. The interaction of various interest rates for these sources creates a complex problem for bank management, especially during times of extreme interest-rate volatility. The lack of comprehensive information systems to monitor and evaluate a bank's current and future money position represents a severe strategic disadvantage in dealing with the major supplier—the financial markets. IT is a critical tool to help the banking industry respond more effectively to fluctuations in these markets. Currently, the lack of strategic IT severely limits the ability of many banks to quickly gather, process, and decide on optimal funds sourcing.

Because of historical and economic conditions, many industries are subject to intense supplier power. Although some of this power is uncontrollable, the strategic application of IT often represents a potential competitive advantage.[5]

Substitution.   The existence of cost-effective substitutes for a product (e.g., margarine for butter) may limit potential profitability in an industry. In some instances, a substitute product can virtually eliminate an industry; this happened when the silicon-chip-based calculator replaced the electromechanical adding machine. An industry must recognize that both existing and potential substitutes will affect the overall demand for products and the profitability that will result from serving the remaining demand. This reduced profitability results from price competition with substitutes, the cost of advertising against substitutes, and product innovation directed at substitutes. However, substitution also represents an opportunity for an industry or a firm within an industry to increase its own market by offering its products as substitutes to another industry's buyers.

IT becomes a potential strategic factor in dealing with the competitive force of substitution when it affects the buyer's decision to substitute or not. This decision is affected by altering the relative price-performance comparison with the substitute, by lowering cost or improving the perceived performance, and by increasing or decreasing the range of functions performed by a product.

One example of substitution based on IT involved a large brokerage firm that developed a new financial product to support a range of product features through a sophisticated information system. Although the product features existed separately in other products, the combination of features and easy customer use made this product an effective substitute for many existing products in spite of the price premium. This product has been extremely successful and now has a host of imitators.

New Entrants.   For existing competitors, new entrants present a concern because they will extract some of the industry's profits. For example, increased competition can be touched off by new entrants who use price-cutting tactics to gain market penetration; this occurred when the Japanese entered the U.S. automobile industry market. Unless industry demand grows fast enough to accommodate the number of new entrants, average profitability will decline. New entrants are especially devastating when they do not have the same objectives or constraints as existing industry participants.

Entry barriers are the major structural components of an industry that slow or exclude new entrants. Although entry barriers take many forms, sizes, and shapes, they all create a more favorable situation for an existing industry participant than for a potential entrant. This better situation may be based on costs, reputation, service, technology, or some other characteristic important to success in the industry. Entry deterrents are tactics or processes that an industry or a firm can employ to make a potential entrant reconsider his entry.

Deep price cutting during a new entrant's test marketing can act as a deterrent by emphasizing the industry incumbent's relative cost advantage over the potential entrant. It can also confuse the test market results.

Entry barriers and deterrents are key aspects of an industry's continued success. Without continual maintenance of the barriers, new entrants will sneak into the industry, usually in the most profitable segments of the market. A firm's strategy must also take into account entry barriers because a new entrant will often target a vulnerable competitor. Industry leaders are particularly responsible for maintaining entry barriers and creating deterrents. A firm that contemplates entering a new industry must consider the entry barriers to be overcome and any potential retaliatory action by the violated industry. There are a number of ways to penetrate a new industry, including undertaking joint ventures and acquisitions, focusing on a nonthreatening industry niche, or developing new technology that circumvents historical barriers.

IT can be used as a strategic element to deal with new entrants, both offensively and defensively. For example, a major insurance company has continually led the industry by building and maintaining a large on-line telecommunications network to its agents. As new, increasingly sophisticated insurance products are rapidly introduced, this network will continue to grow as an entry barrier. Agents must now have much more on-line support, training, and promotional backup, and this network provides that support. Without such support, a new entrant will not be an effective competitor. Another example involves a large financial-service company that has built a reputation of quality service and that offers the greatest geographical coverage of any competitor. The company's quality of service and ability to serve a worldwide customer base are built upon IT capabilities, which represent a capital barrier and which support a reputation barrier.

IT will also be used by industrial firms trying to achieve new manufacturing economies of scale relative to competitors, new entrants, and substitutes. The potential of these firms to gain scale economies using IT will depend upon the possibility of going beyond stand-alone applications (which have been the predominant industrial use of IT). To develop new scale economies, IT must be viewed as an organizing concept to use when redesigning the manufacturing process. New economies of scale will be achieved only by identifying the strategic impact of IT and deploying IT resources to achieve the desired competitive effect.

Rivalry.   Industry rivalry can vary from very intense "guerilla warfare" to a very relaxed "country club" approach. Very intense rivalry depletes the industry of some potential profits, because actions detrimental to the entire industry may occur as competitors struggle to the death for an advantage. The airline industry provides a good example of this. Because of intense rivalry, airline companies are price cutting far below their real costs. Although one competitor may eventually win, the entire industry is losing.

Dealing with competitors strategically does not always mean destroying them. To operate effectively over time, most industries require a group of good competitors. Having proper competitors allows a firm to earn more profits, develop more new markets, and create better entry barriers than it could alone. For a firm to cope strategically with the competitive force of rivalry, management must identify when to compete, when to cooperate, and how to do so effectively.

IT presents major opportunities for companies to affect the degree of firm rivalry and the methods used to deal with it. Firms can improve both their own competitive position and the entire industry by utilizing IT-supported data, IT distribution channels, and potential IT links within the industry. In the banking industry, IT represents a tremendous strategic opportunity for individual firms to deal with increasingly intense rivalry. For example, smaller rival banks may share a common group of ATMs against a market share leader. In the airline industry, shared reservation systems are a way to improve overall service to the consumer. In the railroad industry, standardized data and communications networks between firms offer a way to improve railroad transportation service. Other examples of cooperative IT use by rivals include computer-to-computer connections, joint IT ventures, and shared software.

Since IT presents a virtually unlimited opportunity to structure the relationship between a firm and its competitors, it should be a vital component of any strategy for dealing with rivals. The key, of course, is to know which IT relationships should be cooperative and which should be competitive.

The five forces of buyer power, supplier power, substitution, new entrants, and rivalry shape the competitive environment for each firm in an industry. These forces vary in the manner and degree to which they will impact each firm in the industry. As part of its strategic analysis, each firm must identify the specific competitive forces and underlying economics that determine the strength and stability of those forces. The importance of IT as a competitive resource can then be estimated by isolating where IT can be used to alter a competitive balance or parry a competitive thrust. Although this may sometimes happen by accident, the analysis presented here provides a method of identifying the most likely opportunities, and it should, therefore, improve a firm's luck.

The Impact of IT on Strategy

The industry setting not only determines the average profitability of a firm, but it also forms the competitive environment within which a firm's strategy must operate. Successful firms in an industry position themselves relative to industry forces by effectively implementing one or more generic strategies:

- Overall cost leadership on an industry-wide basis.
- Differentiation of products and services on an industry-wide basis.
- Concentration on a particular market or product niche.

Each of these strategies provides a general framework within which a firm sets functional policies and procedures and performs activities that implement that strategy. If a firm executes one of these strategies successfully, it will enjoy an advantage relative to industry forces that will yield higher than average returns.

IT can impact the ability of firms to execute a particular generic strategy. For example, a large financial-service company holds its cost-leadership position in the industry because of a sophisticated application of IT that substantially reduces the cost of transmitting and processing transactions. A manufacturing firm has distinguished its products by achieving levels of quality control and precision that competitors cannot match. The key to its advantage is a quality-control information system and the heavy use of computerized machine tools, which provide much greater accuracy while tripling productivity.

IT can contribute to a generic strategy in a variety of ways, because the successful execution of such a strategy requires the broad support of all functional areas in a firm. This is a unique characteristic of IT and distinguishes IT from other technologies that may impact a manufacturing process or product characteristics, but not other functional areas in a firm. IT is utilized for experimentation support in research laboratories, for computer-aided design and engineering in engineering departments, and for production control in factories. IT is also used for market analysis and distribution support in marketing departments, as a sales tool in the field, for office recordkeeping, and for planning in executive offices. In the long term, nearly all functions of all firms can be computer enhanced to some degree. The strategic issue is: Given scarce resources of time, money, and staff, which applications are most important to automate?

Supporting Strategies with IT

Clearly, a firm should use IT to support, reinforce, or enlarge its business strategy.[6] In general, firms pursuing an overall cost-leadership strategy should use IT to reduce costs either by improving the productivity of labor or by improving the utilization of other resources, such as machinery and inventory. Firms following a differentiation strategy should use IT either to add unique features directly to the product or service or to contribute to quality, service, or image through the functional areas. Although a firm may benefit from an IT application that is not consistent with its competitive strategy, it will enjoy much greater strategic benefits from an IT application that is consistent with and supportive of its competitive strategy. Understanding a firm's strategy is critical to the selection of appropriate automation projects, because applications that contribute to a cost-leadership strategy are very different from applications that contribute to a differentiation strategy. "Cost leadership requires aggressive construction of efficient scale facilities, vigorous pursuit of cost reduction from experience, tight cost and overhead control, avoidance of marginal customer accounts, and cost minimization in areas like R&D, service, sales force, advertising, and so on."[7]

When a firm pursues a cost-leadership strategy, IT must create or support opportunities in these same areas. IT applications can substantially reduce costs in the functional areas of engineering, design, and manufacturing and can reduce waste significantly, improve productivity, and identify marginal customers. The firm that vigorously pursues a cost-leadership strategy should identify and execute IT projects that support and advance such a strategy.

Conversely, a strategy to achieve a differentiated position in an industry has a very different set of requirements. The differentiation strategy requires a perceived uniqueness in design, brand image, technology, product features, customer service, dealer networks, or some other category. Usually, firms pursuing a differentiation strategy are most successful when they establish uniqueness in several categories. A distribution company specializing in periodicals differentiated itself in service reliability, responsiveness to customer needs, and additional product features primarily through its computer systems. Among nationwide periodical distributors, this firm is perceived as the most sophisticated and highest quality firm in the industry.

IT can support a differentiation strategy in a variety of ways. IT can contribute to superior customer service by providing historical customer profiles and by increasing the availability of spare parts with a dealer-inventory system. IT can contribute to high quality through the use of quality-control systems and through the use of computer-aided manufacturing systems that provide flexibility and improved responsiveness to customer needs. IT can create better product designs, satisfying both manufacturing and marketplace requirements. In some instances, IT can also provide access to markets that would otherwise be too remote to service.

Table 10.2 shows how IT applications must be specifically chosen to support the generic strategy of a firm. Applications supporting a low-cost generic strategy are designed to take advantage of existing and emerging IT to achieve a low-cost position in an industry. By examining Table 10.2, we can see that applications supporting a low-cost strategy are substantially different from applications supporting a differentiation strategy. The strategic success of IT projects within a firm depends upon how well they support the firm's competitive strategy. In one instance, a firm following low-cost strategy gained little strategic benefit from a computer system that offered many options and much flexibility, but that was very expensive to operate. Over time, the overall cost-leadership strategy of the firm continued to narrow the product line and to streamline operations, requiring the functional areas to standardize and limit options. The large, expensive, multioption system, which was still being developed, ran counter to the firm's strategy. As a result, the system was only partially used and parts of it were never implemented. Now company operations executives feel that using the system makes it difficult for them to meet their functional objectives as dictated by the cost-leadership strategy. They want to scrap the system and buy their own package, which will run on a minicomputer.

In other firms, IT developments were linked to a specific strategy, and users were very enthusiastic about implementing the systems. They felt the systems were valuable in helping them carry out assignments within the

Table 10.2 IT Applications That Support Generic Strategies of Firms

	Generic Strategies	
	Low Cost	**Product Differentiation**
Product Design and Development	Product engineering systems Project control systems	R&D data bases Professional work stations Electronic mail CAD Custom engineering systems Integrated systems for manufacturing
Operations	Process engineering systems Process control systems Labor control systems Inventory management systems Procurement systems Quality monitoring systems	CAM Quality assurance systems Systems for suppliers Quality monitoring systems
Marketing	Streamlined distribution systems Centralized control systems Econometric modeling systems	Sophisticated marketing systems Market data bases Graphic display systems Telemarketing systems Competition analysis systems Modeling systems Service-oriented distribution systems
Sales	Sales control systems Advertising monitoring systems Systems to consolidate sales function Strict incentive/monitoring systems	Differential pricing systems Office/Field communications Customer/Sales support systems Dealer support systems Customer order entry systems
Administration	Cost control systems Quantitative planning and budgeting systems Office automation for staff reduction	Office automation to integrate functions Environment scanning and nonquantitative planning systems Teleconferencing systems

overall strategy. System designers must realize that the strategic benefit of a system will be realized only if there is a commitment to and acceptance of the system by multiple functions and levels within the organization. Effective strategy requires coordination of many interfacing functions; management must consider such factors as supporting subsystems, personnel, and compensation in order to ensure that an IT system will contribute significantly to a strategy. For example, highly sophisticated, IT-enhanced tools for selling insurance will not be effective if salespeople are not hired, trained, and motivated to use the systems.

Although it is clear that IT applications should be consistent with a firm's strategy, little attempt is made in many firms to understand how it will impact the firm's strategic position in the industry or how it might support a business strategy. For example, a number of major U.S. banks have recently removed their top information-systems executives. Although a variety of explanations were given for these management changes, the underlying reason was that IT was not being managed in a manner consistent with the strategic needs of the banks. The problem, of course, was not that these executives could not develop IT that was consistent with the bank's strategy. The problem was and continues to be that neither the bank executives nor the information-systems executives understand how IT affects their business. Neither group can articulate how computer hardware and software should support or extend the bank's ability to make money.

Conclusion

This article has presented a conceptual framework to help the senior executive answer the critical question: Is IT a competitive weapon in my business? For years technical experts have expressed concern over whether a firm's computer systems met its needs. Unfortunately, these experts did not understand the needs of a business from a competitive viewpoint, and they did not perceive IT to be in the competitive domain of a business. In spite of this general lack of strategic direction, firms in many industries are using IT to their competitive advantage. As technology continues to evolve rapidly and becomes a major factor in more industries, firms must begin to manage information technology strategically. The framework presented here describes the first steps management should take to link IT to a firm's competitive environment and strategy by analyzing the impact of it at the industry, firm, and strategy levels.

By understanding *when, where,* and *how* IT will impact a firm, management can develop an explicit IT strategy that makes the necessary tradeoffs and directs resources to take advantage of opportunities and to mitigate threats. Without such an understanding, firms will continue to ride a speeding technological roller coaster, spending more money and acquiring new hardware without sound business justification.

11

Strategic Management in Multinational Companies

Yves L. Doz

The evolution of multinational companies (MNCs) over the last decade has been characterized by a growing conflict between the requirements for economic survival and success (the economic imperative) and the adjustments made necessary by the demands of host governments (the political imperative). Faced with the conflict between the economic and political imperatives within a business, MNCs can respond in several ways. This article, based on intensive field research of the management processes in about a dozen MNCs, analyzes *strategies* and *administrative processes* used by MNCs to reconcile the conflicting economic and political imperatives. *SMR*.

The evolution of multinational companies (MNCs) over the last decade has been characterized by a growing conflict between the requirements for economic survival and success (the *economic* imperative) and the adjustments made necessary by the demands of host governments (the *political* imperative). The lowering of trade barriers and the substantial economies of scale still available in many industries combined with vigorous competition from low-cost exporters push the MNCs toward the integration and rationalization of their activities among various countries.[1] Yet, the very international interdependence created by freer trade and MNC rationalization make individual countries more vulnerable to external factors and their traditional domestic economic policies less effective.[2] As a result, most governments turn more and more to specific sectorial policies implemented through direct negotiations with the companies involved and through incentives tailored to them.[3] Both the economic and political imperatives thus take on increasing importance in the management of the multinationals.

From *Sloan Management Review*, Winter 1980, Vol. 21, No. 2. Reprinted with permission.

This article, based on intensive field research of the management processes in about a dozen MNCs, analyzes strategies and administrative processes used by MNCs to reconcile the conflicting economic and political imperatives. Findings are presented in four sections. First, MNC strategies to respond to the dual imperatives are described and contrasted. Second, conditions under which MNCs are likely to find one or another strategy most suitable for individual businesses are reviewed. Third, the interaction between strategies and the nature of internal management processes is analyzed. Fourth, implications for the management of interdependencies between businesses in diversified multinationals are outlined. In the conclusion, means to increase the overall managerial capability of the company are explored.

Multinational Strategies

Faced with the conflict between the economic and political imperatives within a business, MNCs can respond in several ways. Some companies clearly respond first to the economic imperatives, and follow a worldwide (or regional)[4] business strategy where the activities in various countries are integrated and centrally managed. Other companies forgo the economic benefits of integration and let their subsidiaries adjust to the demands of their host government (as if they were national companies), thus clearly giving the upper hand to the political imperative. Finally, some companies try to leave their strategy unclear and reap benefits from economic integration and political responsiveness, in turn, or find compromises between the two. These three strategies are described in this section.

Worldwide Integration Strategy

Some companies choose to respond to the economic imperative and improve their international competitiveness. For companies that already have extensive manufacturing operations in several countries, the most attractive solution is to integrate and rationalize their activities among these countries. Individual plants are to provide only part of the product range (but for sales in all subsidiaries), thereby achieving greater economies of scale.[5] Plants can also be specialized by stages in the production process, and they can be located in various countries according to the cost and availability of production factors for each stage (energy, labor, raw materials, skills).[6] Texas Instruments' location of labor-intensive semiconductor finishing activities in Southeast Asia, or Ford's and GM's Europe-wide manufacturing rationalization, as well as their investments in Spain, illustrate the integration strategy.

Extensive transshipments of components and finished products between subsidiaries located in different countries result from such a strategy. Integration also involves the development of products acceptable on a worldwide basis. The "world car" concept pushed by GM, Ford, and Japanese exporters is an example of this approach. The driving principle of this integration strategy is the reduction of unit costs and the capture of large sales volumes; in industries where economies of scale are significant and not fully exploited within the size of national markets, it can bring sizable productivity advantages. For instance, Ford's unit direct manufacturing costs in Europe were estimated to be well below those of national competitors supplying a comparable car range. In industries where dynamic economies of scale are very strong (such as semiconductors), the cost-level differences between such leaders as Texas Instruments and smaller national firms were significant. Similarly, IBM was believed to have costs significantly lower than its competitors.[7]

Where integration brought substantial cost advantages over competitors, the integrated firms could allocate part of the benefits from their higher internal efficiency to incur "good citizenship" costs in the host countries, and still remain competitive with nonintegrated firms. Some companies had a policy of full employment, balanced internal trade among countries, and performance of R&D in various countries. Such a policy may lead to less than optimal decisions, in a short-term financial sense, as it has some opportunity costs (for instance, the location of new plants and research centers in countries where a company sells more than it buys, instead of in low-wage or low-manufacturing-cost countries). However, such a policy may also be the key to host countries' long-term acceptance of companies as leading worldwide corporations.

The benefits of integration not only enable the MNC to be better tolerated, thanks to its ability to incur higher good citizenship costs, but integration itself can be seen as making expropriation less likely in developing countries.[8] Integration provides more bargaining power to MNCs for ongoing operations and also makes extreme solutions to conflicts with host governments (such as expropriation) into outcomes where both the host country and the MNC stand to lose.

A well-articulated worldwide integration strategy also simplifies the management of international operations by providing a point of view on the environment, a framework to identify key sources of uncertainties, and a purpose in dealing with them. The worldwide integration strategy can guide managers in adopting a *proactive* stance. The simplicity of the driving principle of the integration strategy also makes a consistent, detailed strategic planning process possible, as it provides a unifying focus to the various parts of the organization. This process both guides the implementation of strategy and provides for its refinement and evolution over time.

National Responsiveness Strategy

Some companies forgo the potential benefits of integration and give much more leeway to their subsidiaries to respond to the political imperative by having them behave almost as if they were national companies. Yet, the affiliation of subsidiaries to a multinational company can bring them four distinct advantages over purely national competitors. These advantages are:

1. The pooling of financial risks.
2. The spreading of research and development costs over a larger sales volume (than that of local competitors) without the difficulties involved in licensing transactions.
3. The coordination of export marketing to increase overall success in export markets.
4. The transfer of specific skills between subsidiaries (e.g., process technology or merchandising methods).

In this approach, each subsidiary remains free to pursue an autonomous economic or political strategy nationally as its management sees fit, given the situation of the national industry. In industries where the government plays a key role (nuclear engineering and electrical power, for instance), national strategies are primarily political. In industries where other local factors are important sources of differentiation (e.g., food processing), but where government plays a less prominent role, strategies are economic.[9]

In a nationally responsive MNC, the resources, know-how, or services of the headquarters (or of other subsidiaries) are called upon only when the subsidiary management finds them helpful. Little central influence is exercised on the subsidiaries. The nationally responsive MNC, as a whole, has no strategy, except in a limited sense (Brown Boveri's technical excellence, for instance), and the strategy is usually not binding: Subsidiaries follow it only when they see it in their own interest. Manufacturing is usually done on a local-for-local basis, with few intersubsidiary transfers. Coordination of R&D and avoidance of duplications are often difficult, particularly when host governments insist upon R&D being carried on locally on specific projects for which government support is available (new telecommunication technologies or microelectronics, for instance).

Administrative Coordination Strategy

Rejecting both clear-cut strategic solutions to the conflict between the economic and political imperatives offered by worldwide integration and national responsiveness, MNCs can choose to live with the conflict and look for structural and administrative adjustments instead of strategic solutions. Such adjustments are aimed at providing some of the benefits of both worldwide (or regional) integration and national responsiveness.

The strategy (literally) is to have no set strategy, but to let each strategic decision be made on its own merits and to challenge prior commitments. Individual decisions thus do not fit into the logic of clear goals, the reasonableness of which is tested against a comprehensive analysis of the environment and an assessment of the organization's capabilities. Strategy is not the search for an overall optimal fit, but a series of limited adjustments made in response to specific developments, without an attempt to integrate these adjustments into a consistent comprehensive strategy.[10]

The need for such adjustments emerges when new uncertainties are identified. These uncertainties can offer opportunities (e.g., the possibility to invest in a new country) or threats (e.g., the development of new technologies by competitors), or lend themselves to conflicting interpretation (the willingness of a government to grant R&D subsidies, but with some local production requirements). Instead of taking a stable proactive stance vis-à-vis the environment and relying on the chosen strategy to provide a framework within which to deal with sources of uncertainties and to make specific decisions as the need arises, companies using administrative coordination absorb uncertainties and try to resolve conflicts internally each time new uncertainties question prior allocations of strategic resources. In short, strategy becomes unclear, shifting with the perceived importance of changes in the economic or political environment, and it may become dissolved into a set of incremental decisions with a pattern which may make sense only after the fact. Administrative coordination does not allow strategic planning. We are farther from the "timed sequence of conditional moves" representing the usual goal of strategic planning and much closer to public administration, where issues get shaped, defined, attended to, and resolved one at a time in a "muddling through" process that never gives analytical consideration to the full implications of a step.[11]

By adopting such an internally flexible and negotiable posture, administratively coordinated companies make themselves more accessible to government influence, and become Janus-faced. On certain issues and at certain points in time, a view consistent with worldwide rationalization will prevail, in other cases national responsiveness will prevail, and in many cases some uneasy blend of the two will result. Some of the central control of the subsidiaries (so critical in multinational integration) is abandoned, making it easier for them to cooperate with powerful partners such as government agencies or national companies on specific projects. Because commitments of resources are not all made consistently over time, and as the company is not likely to be very rationalized (given the role accorded to host governments' demands), excess resources are not likely to allow for large costs of good citizenship. In short, compared with multinational integration, administrative coordination trades off internal efficiency for external flexibility. Whereas multinational integration seeks to provide the organization with enough economic power for success, administrative coordination seeks to provide the flexibility needed for a constantly adjusted coalignment of the firm with the more powerful factors in the environment and with the most critical sources of uncertainty.[12] Acceptability to host governments derives from flexibility.

The Three Strategies Compared

Both the worldwide (or regional) integration strategy and the national responsiveness strategy correspond to clear tradeoffs between the economic and the political imperatives. Integration demonstrates a clear preference for the economic imperative; the MNC attempts to fully exploit integration's potential for economic performance and shows willingness to incur large citizenship costs in exchange for being allowed to be very different from national companies. Conversely, national responsiveness minimizes the difference between the MNC and national companies, and thus minimizes the acceptability problems. It expresses a clear sensitivity to the political imperative, at the expense of economic performance. The economic advantages of multinationality are confined to a few domains: financial risks, amortization of R&D costs, export marketing, and skill transfers among the subsidiaries.

Administrative coordination, because it aims at a constantly fluctuating balance between the imperatives, is an ambiguous form of management. There is a constant tension within the organization between the drive for economic success based on clear economic strategy, and the need to consider major uncertainties springing from the political imperative. The following comment, made by a senior manager in an administratively coordinated MNC, illustrates the tension:

In the long run we risk becoming a collection of inefficient, government-subsidized national companies unable to compete on the world market. Yet, if we rationalize our operations, we lose our preferential access to government R&D contracts and subsidies. So we try to develop an overall strategic plan that makes some competitive sense, and then bargain for each part of it with individual governments, trying to sell them on particular programs that contribute to the plan as a whole. Often we have to revise or abandon parts of our plan for lack of government support.

Markets, Competition, Technology, and Strategy

In thinking about which type of strategy may suit a particular MNC or an individual business within a diversified MNC, it is important to consider the markets being served, the competition being faced, and the technology being used by the firm. The argument will focus on products and industries for which multinational integration pressures are significant, leaving aside products for which national taste differences (food), high bulk to value-added ratio (furniture), dependence on perishable products (food), small optimal size (garments and leather goods), or other such factors usually make rationalization unattractive or unfeasible.

Market Structure and Competition

The range of possible multinational strategies depends upon the structure of the world market in terms of customers and barriers to trade. First, for some products (such as electrical power systems or telecommunications equipment), the technology and economies of production would very strongly suggest global rationalization, but political imperatives are so strong as to prevent it. The international trade volumes, either captive within MNCs or in toto, for telecommunications equipment and power systems are extremely low.[13] In developed countries theoretically committed to free trade, restrictions come through monopoly market power of government-controlled entities—Post, Telegraph, Telephone (PTT), for instance—or through complex legislation and regulation that create artificial market differentiation. EEC regulations on trucks, officially designed for safety and road degradation reasons, effectively create barriers to entry for importers. In a similar way, inspection regulations for equipment (including the parts and components) purchased by state agencies in many European countries, effectively make it difficult to incorporate imported components into end products sold to the state.

In developing countries, market-access restrictions are more straightforward. Under such conditions of restricted trade and controlled market access, worldwide strategic integration is obviously difficult. Often, the very nature of the goods, their strategic importance, as well as characteristics such as bulky, massive equipment produced in small volumes for a few large customers, reinforce the desire on the part of governments to control suppliers closely.[14]

Second, at another extreme, there are some goods that are traded quite freely, whose sales do not depend on location of manufacture or nationality of the manufacturer, and for which economies of scale beyond the size of national markets are significant. In such industries the only viable strategy is worldwide (or regional) integration. This is the strategy followed by all volume car manufacturers in Europe, led by Ford and General Motors but also including such national champions as Fiat, Renault, or Volkswagen. Smaller companies are adopting a specialization strategy by moving out of the price-sensitive volume market and serving the world market from a single location (BMW, Daimler Benz).

Third, and most interesting, are businesses (such as computers or semiconductors) whose markets are partly government-controlled and partly internationally competitive. In such businesses the market is split between customers who select their suppliers on economic grounds and customers that are state-owned or state-influenced and evidence strong preference for some control over their suppliers. Products such as computers or integrated circuits are of sufficient strategic and economic importance for host governments to try to have some control over their technology and their production.[15] In such industries governments try to restrict the strategic freedom of all multinationals and show great willingness to reward flexibility. Honeywell, for instance, was liberally rewarded for agreeing to create a joint venture between its French subsidiary and Compagnie Internationale pour l'Informatique, the ailing leader of the French computer industry. In addition to favored access to the French state-controlled markets, the joint venture received substantial grants and research contracts.

In these industries where both the economic and political imperatives are critical, multinationals face the most difficult choice between various possible strategies. Some companies may choose to integrate their operations multinationally, and some may choose to decentralize their operations to better match the demands of individual governments and benefit from their support and assistance. Still others may not make a clear strategic commitment and may instead resort to administrative coordination.

Yet, this choice is likely to look significantly different to various MNCs according to their competitive posture within their industry. In broad terms, firms with the largest overall shares of the world market are likely to find integration more desirable. There are several reasons for this choice.

Benefits of Integration. First, still assuming that there are unexploited economies of scale, large firms can achieve lower costs through integration than can smaller firms. The company with the largest overall share of the world market can become the low-cost producer in an industry by integrating its operations, thus making life difficult for smaller competitors. Conversely, smaller firms (with significant market shares in only a few countries) can remain cost competitive, so long as larger competitors do not move to regional or worldwide integration. Firms that integrate across boundaries in a market that is partly price competitive and partly government-controlled, can expect to gain a larger share of the price-competitive market and confine smaller competitors to segments protected by governments that value flexibility and control more than lower prices.[16]

Influence.   Second, one can hypothesize that larger firms can have more influence on their environment than smaller ones, and thus find it more suitable to centralize strategic decision making and ignore some of the uncertainty and variety in the environment.[17] In particular, larger firms can take a tougher stance vis-à-vis individual governments when needed and woo them with higher costs of good citizenship. How much integrated firms may be willing to give to host governments as costs of citizenship to maintain strategic integration may vary substantially. A leading integrated firm in a partly government-controlled market with no comparable direct competitor (IBM, for instance) may be willing to provide a lot to host countries in order to maintain its integration. Conversely, when keen worldwide competition takes place among integrated companies of comparable strength (e.g., Texas Instruments, Motorola, and Fairchild), the economic imperative becomes much more demanding for each of them, and none may be willing to be accommodating for fear that the others would not match such behavior. In short, the following proposition can be made: The more one integrated firm is submitted to direct competition from other integrated companies, the less it will be willing to provide host governments, except in exchange for profitable nonmatchable moves.

The implications of this proposition in terms of public policy toward industry structure are significant. At the regional or worldwide level it raises the issue of whether to encourage competition, or to favor the emergence of a single integrated leading MNC and then bargain with that company on the sharing of revenues. Similarly, a significant industrial policy issue at the national level is whether to encourage competition, or to provide a single multinational with the opportunity for a profitable nonmatchable move.[18]

Conversely, smaller firms (such as Honeywell in comparison with IBM) could draw only lesser benefits from rationalization and would have to be extremely flexible in dealing with the uncertainties represented by host governments. Thus, smaller firms are likely to find administrative coordination more suitable and will enlist host governments' support and subsidies to compete against leading MNCs. Market-access protection, financial assistance, or both can be the only way for these smaller firms—multinational or not—to keep a semblance of competitiveness. In the same way that firms in competitive markets can differentiate their products (or even their strategy) to avoid competing head on against larger firms, firms in these markets under partial government control differentiate their strategy by trading off central control over their strategy for government protection. The willingness of governments to trade off economic efficiency for some amount of political control, as well as the importance of short-term social issues (chiefly employment protection), make such strategic differentiation possible.[19]

For smaller MNCs such differentiation usually involves forgoing integration and letting host governments gain a say in strategic decisions affecting the various subsidiaries. Yet, because the MNC still attempts to maintain some competitiveness in market segments not protected by governments, it is likely to find administrative coordination—despite the ambiguity and managerial difficulty it involves—the lesser evil.

Finally, national companies can attempt to achieve some economies of scale through interfirm agreements for the joint manufacture of particular components (car engines) or product lines (Airbus A300). Over time, national companies can move to develop a globally integrated system. A case in point is Volkswagen, whose U.S.-assembled "Rabbits" incorporate parts from Brazil, Germany, and Mexico. Where free trade prevails among developed countries, as in the automobile industry, this may be the only suitable strategy for national companies.

In summary, one can hypothesize a relationship between the extent of government control over (and limits to) international trade in an industry, the relative international market share of a firm active in that industry, and the type of strategy it adopts. In industries where free trade prevails, all competitors are expected to have to follow a worldwide (or regional) integration strategy. In industries in which governments take a keen interest, but where they control the markets only partly, and where formal free trade prevails (computers, for instance), all three strategies are likely to coexist within an industry. Finally, in industries where the political imperatives prevail and whose markets are mostly state-controlled, all competitors can be expected to adopt a national responsiveness strategy.

Data supporting the relationship summarized above are presented graphically in Figure 11.1. It shows the results of the in-depth study of six industries where the economic and the political imperatives strongly conflict. However, one word of caution is necessary here: The patterns shown represent only the *preferred* strategy of a company. Most companies will have

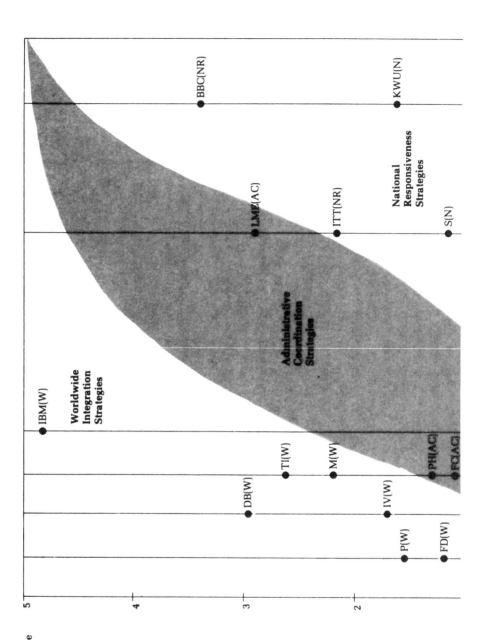

Relative market share
(8 firms included) of
MNCs in Western
Europe

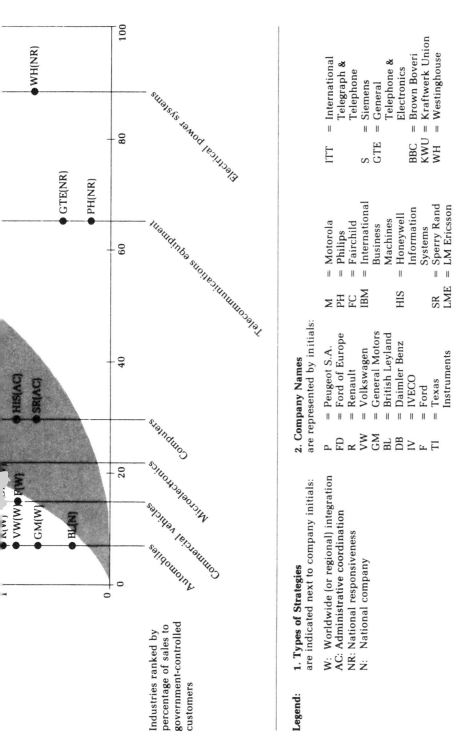

Industries ranked by
percentage of sales to
government-controlled
customers

Legend:

1. Types of Strategies
are indicated next to company initials:

W: Worldwide (or regional) integration
AC: Administrative coordination
NR: National responsiveness
N: National company

2. Company Names
are represented by initials:

P	= Peugeot S.A.	M	= Motorola
FD	= Ford of Europe	PH	= Philips
R	= Renault	FC	= Fairchild
VW	= Volkswagen	IBM	= International
GM	= General Motors		Business
BL	= British Leyland		Machines
DB	= Daimler Benz	HIS	= Honeywell
IV	= IVECO		Information
F	= Ford		Systems
TI	= Texas	SR	= Sperry Rand
	Instruments	LME	= LM Ericsson

ITT	= International	
	Telegraph &	
	Telephone	
S	= Siemens	
GTE	= General	
	Telephone &	
	Electronics	
BBC	= Brown Boveri	
KWU	= Kraftwerk Union	
WH	= Westinghouse	

Figure 11.1 Customers, Market Shares, and Multinational Strategies

deviant subsidiaries, because within a given industry trade restrictions vary among countries. The figure was built from data in Western Europe and assumes that, in a given industry, trade restrictions are about the same for all countries. That may be approximately true within Western Europe, but is obviously false in other regions. For instance, Ford's European operations achieve integration at the regional level; Ford's other international subsidiaries are much more nationally responsive and often isolated by tough local restrictions (for instance, in Latin America). In passing, it may be hypothesized that companies with substantial operations in numerous countries (within the same industry) break them up into regional management units when they face wide differences in the conditions of trade among the regions. Obviously, the value added of products with respect to their weight or bulk also plays a role in limiting worldwide integration in a few industries where the value added per unit of weight is very high, and economies of scale and/or factor cost differences among regions are substantial (e.g., microelectronics).

Technology

Technology is usually seen as an important variable in the interface between MNCs and host governments. The introduction by MNCs of many innovative high-technology products and the high market shares they still enjoy in their sales create much tension with host governments. Major industries, such as computers, microelectronics, or aerospace, remain dominated by U.S. multinationals. In tensions between economic and political imperatives within an industry, technology then plays a key role. MNCs that control the technology of specific industries have more power in bargaining with governments and also create technology barriers to competition from national firms. Often the minimal scale requirements increase so rapidly in high technology industries as to make it almost impossible for national firms to catch up.[20]

Technology, Trade, and Strategic Integration. Higher technology products are likely to correspond to freer trade. First, there is ample evidence that MNCs most often introduce their innovations in their home markets first.[21] So long as the new technology is not adopted by many countries, freer trade is likely to prevail for newer products than for older ones. Second, during the technology-diffusion process within the MNC, the need to transfer the new technology quickly to subsidiaries creates pressures to increase coordination among them. Companies thus find it more desirable and easier to integrate regionally or to tilt their administrative coordination toward more integration. In terms of the graphics of Figure 11.1, a new higher technology can be represented by a move to the left. The move can affect a given industry as a whole if the technology is available to all MNCs but not to any national company, or more likely the move can be firm-specific.

In the study of the telecommunications industry, both moves were found. First, the shift to electronic switching and digital coding led the industry as a whole to be characterized by freer trade and by the opening of markets to new suppliers, as the various national PTTs were deciding upon their first orders for new equipment in the 1970s. Second, within the industry, LM Ericsson has always tried to be "one step ahead" of its competitors in technology, and to run its operations in a more integrated way than its competition. Conversely, ITT has most often been a technology follower, but let its subsidiaries be quite responsive to the demands of their host governments. It can be hypothesized that, within an industry where the political imperatives are significant, higher technology firms (relative to their competitors) strive for integration, and can achieve some measure of it, and lower technology firms (relative to their competitors) strive for national responsiveness.

Technology, Scale, and Government Intervention. It is also important to recognize that technological evolution can increase the minimal efficient scale of an industry and call to question the viability of national responsiveness. Even where restricted trade prevails, as the efficient scale increases in a high-technology industry, pressures grow for domestic mergers and rationalization. Where multinational and national firms compete, the multinationals are unlikely to be the winners in a merger drive. Government interest is likely to prompt mergers into the "national champion," rather than to let the national industry be entirely controlled from outside. A national responsiveness strategy, i.e., a rather autonomous national subsidiary, makes such mergers into a national champion easier for the government to implement.

The examples of the French electrical power industry and telecommunications equipment in France and Great Britain tend to confirm the above analysis. In the case of electrical power systems, the transition from fossil fuel boilers to nuclear steam supply not only led to higher minimal efficient scale in the manufacture of turbogenerators, but also increased the interests of host governments in the industry. Two distinct effects were thus combined: minimal size increase and governments' greater interest in the technology itself.[22]

The Influence of Technology.   This leaves us with less than a full understanding of the role of technology in the interface between MNCs and host governments in developed countries. On the one hand, for a given industry, a move to higher technology and new products can permit a firm (or all firms in an industry if they have access to the new technology) to be more multinationally integrated and centrally managed than it would otherwise be. There is some unclear causal relationship here, as integration is made possible by higher technology but is also required to facilitate technology transfer within the MNC.[23] On the other hand, it seems that very high technologies become extremely important in developed countries and prompt governments to try to narrowly control their development and use. Also, the move to higher technology often results in larger minimal efficient scale. This scale can be used by integrated multinationals to defend their market shares and attack smaller or less integrated firms, e.g., in microelectronics. In industries where trade is restricted, the government's usual responses are mergers into a "national champion" first, and development of multinational government-sponsored programs second.

In both cases multinationals do not stand to benefit. This was clearly the case in electrical power systems. Telecommunications equipment was more ambiguous. Some countries were moving toward national consolidation (Brazil, France, the UK), and in others new electronic technology was resulting in more open markets (Australia, South Africa, Spain, and several small European countries). Electronic technologies obviously increased the importance of the industry, yet provided opportunities to more integrated firms (e.g., LM Ericsson) or national firms with a distinctive technology (e.g., CIT Alcatel). When technology increases both the pressures to integrate within the industry and the interest governments take in the industry, either integration within MNCs across boundaries or integration within a country through government-directed mergers can prevail.

Managerial Implications

In practice, it is important to an MNC, or to executives running individual businesses in diversified multinationals, to recognize those changes in market openness, industry structure, and technology of an industry that foreshadow a need to change the overall strategy. Two simple examples are illuminating. Until the mid-1970s, General Motors ran its international operations as a collection of nationally responsive autonomous subsidiaries. With the globalization of the industry and the rationalization and integration of key competitors (mainly Ford), this posture became untenable. The strongest of the subsidiaries, Adam Opel in Germany, was able to hold its own in Europe, competing as a national company. But other subsidiaries, particularly Vauxhall in the UK, were severely hurt. In 1975, General Motors started to bring the various subsidiaries together more closely through a series of administrative changes. By 1978, these moves resulted in an administrative-coordination approach where numerous contradictions and ambiguities emerged. GM Overseas Operations' top management considered such administrative coordination as a transitional stage toward global integration. Many GMOO managers, however, felt that contradictions between the lingering desire for national subsidiaries' responsiveness and the emerging worldwide integration needs would not be easily resolved. In any case, the company had missed several precious years and had to struggle hard to remain competitive in Europe.

Conversely, in the late 1960s, Westinghouse was looking for acquisitions in the European electrical-power industry. It hoped to expand its business in Europe quickly, thanks to its light-water nuclear-reactor technology, which was emerging as a clear technological winner over indigenous European technologies. To "better" manage its European operations, Westinghouse moved to a worldwide product-group structure, aiming at multinational integration. At the same time, as we have seen, the increased minimal scale of the industry, the strategic importance of nuclear-related technologies, and the failure of Europe's own efforts in commercial reactors all combined to increase government sensitivity to the industry. The discrepancy between the national responsiveness demanded by governments and what Westinghouse appeared willing to provide resulted in tensions in Belgium, France, and Germany, a substantial scale-down of Westinghouse's European expansion plans, and a shift in its strategy. In 1975, a former president of Westinghouse's Power Group commented: "Our basic policy (for nuclear engineering and power plant sales) is to do it in whatever way a country would require." Yet, Westinghouse had probably lost the one opportunity to become an enduring factor in the European power-system industry.

Choice of Strategy and Management Process

We have seen that both worldwide (or regional) integration and national responsiveness lead to relatively straightforward management processes that are grounded in a clear strategy and a clear-cut delineation of headquarters' and subsidiaries' roles and responsibilities. Yet, the relative managerial simplicity both these strategies offer has an opportunity cost: It makes specific adjustment to the varying demands of governments difficult, and it may prevent the company from entering certain businesses or certain countries.

Such limitations make administrative coordination attractive as a way to increase the MNC's flexibility in finding balances between the economic and the political imperatives that match more closely the specific conditions of a given business in a given country. It is important to recognize that both worldwide integration and national responsiveness almost represent ideal polar opposites. Some MNCs are likely not to wish (or be able) to exercise a clear choice, and thus find themselves improvising compromises through some process of administrative coordination.

In particular, when the political imperative is significant, its very nature makes clear-cut analytical choices impossible. Contrary to the economic imperative, information on the political imperative is most often indirect and not controllable centrally. When a subsidiary manager claims that his plans rest on the word of local intermediaries or on his relationships with national government officials, it is difficult, at best, for managers at headquarters to determine the soundness of his assumptions. The fact that the government's public logic is often quite different from the reality of the situation and from actual policy-making processes makes it even more difficult for corporate or regional managers to understand the situation. As a result, top management's inability to reach an analytical choice on decisions involving the political imperative leads to adaptive coalitional decision making in which the firm internalizes tensions and uncertainties and tries to incorporate them into its decision-making process.

Decision Processes and Administrative Coordination

On any particular strategic decision, the company is trying to reach a satisfactory compromise given past decisions and past commitments of resources. Decisions cannot be left to either the subsidiary or the regional (or global) headquarters levels. They have to be reached by some group that collectively captures contradictions in the environment, internalizes them, and resolves them through contention, coalition, and consensus. Individual managers, representing different interests within the company and approaching questions from different points of view, are left to take sides on decisions according to how they perceive problems and how they prefer to deal with sources of uncertainty. In short, the question of deciding "what is right" becomes linked to that of "who is right" and "whose views are favored." Top management, instead of providing the inspiration for a strategic design and managing its implementation, shifts to a new role of deciding how to make decisions: who should be represented, with which voice, on which decisions. Top management can also provide some limits: Would such decisions represent too wide a departure from the usual to be accepted? Choices on how to reach decisions can still be guided by a sense of which decisions, or which classes of decisions, should be made with integration as a priority, and which should be made with responsiveness as a priority. The way to convey such a sense of priority is not to decide in substance on specific decisions (except when irreconcilable conflicts occur) but to act on the way in which decisions are made, to influence the making and undoing of specific coalitions, or to help the shift of coalitions among decisions.

Managing Dependencies

How can top management achieve such influence? Primarily by keeping control of dependencies between subunits competing for power and by regulating the game they pursue. Strategic and operational dependencies can be used to determine who, in the long run, has power over which class of decisions or what functions. For instance, the subsidiaries can be made dependent on the corporate headquarters or on domestic product divisions for key components or for process technology. Conversely, the domestic divisions can be dependent on subsidiaries for export sales. A central difficulty of this approach is the divisiveness introduced within the company by managing dependencies through arm's-length power relationships. Top management also has to develop some integrative forces (for instance, through training, career paths, and compensation) to balance these divisive forces and preserve some sense of corporate identity and loyalty.

Over the long run, successful administrative coordination hinges on the maintenance of a balance between divisive and integrative forces that reflects a structure of dependencies among subunits. Careful control of the dependencies between national subsidiary managers, and product unit managers through the use of functional managers and administrative managers, was found to provide top management tools for maintaining such a balance.

Functional Managers. The substantive expertise of functional managers is needed by supporters of multinational integration as well as by supporters of national responsiveness. Managers preferring multinational integration still depend upon functional managers and "the field" (in various countries) to achieve such integration. Conversely, national managers depend on support from functional and administrative headquarters staff and product divisions, even though they try to pursue national responsiveness strategies. Because the power of functional managers is based on needed expertise, they may preserve a relatively uncommitted posture between multinational integration and national responsiveness.

Yet functional managers, over time, can develop a functional logic that is aligned to either national responsiveness or worldwide integration. Manufacturing staffs, for instance, can develop a logic that calls for integration and rationalization or for flexible local plants serving separate national markets. Within each function, of course, further distinctions can develop. For instance, rationalized component plants and local-for-local end-product plants can be favored, or distribution channels can be perceived as very different, whereas similar advertising can be used. By influencing corporate functional managers directly in the development of their preference for integration or responsiveness, and by then bringing them to throw their weight to particular issues and not to others, top management can develop a repertoire of intervention methods for making particular decisions.

Administrative Managers.   Administrative procedures and the managers in charge of them can also be used by top management to maintain the tension between integration and responsiveness. To begin with, the formal structure usually provides a dominant orientation. Even when this structure is a matrix, it is usually complemented by fairly elaborate administrative procedures and guidelines that provide a dominant orientation by defining who is responsible for what and whether it is a primary or a secondary responsibility. Various devices, such as committees and task forces that cut across the formal structure, can be used to bring about changes in perception or to reach actual decisions. Planning processes can also be designed, so that integration and responsiveness are considered. For instance, a contention process can exist between subsidiaries and product divisions (e.g., LM Ericsson). Interestingly, IBM had such a system very formalized and well developed among its regions and product groups, and between them and corporate functional staffs. Measurement systems can be set so that managers will see it as their duty to call to top management's attention "excessive" integration, autonomy, or responsiveness (e.g., GTE[24] or GM). Personal reward and punishment systems may be designed to reinforce tensions or ease them according to the measurement criteria and yardsticks used. Management of career paths can also be used to provide multiple views and facilitate coordination.

Administrative staff managers, and the way they design and run their administrative systems, provide top management with the same type of leverage as functional managers. One can expect the controller to strive for uniformity of accounting practices and comparability of results worldwide, opposing differentiation between subsidiaries. Personnel management, on the other hand, can either favor uniformity of pay scales and benefits worldwide, or leave this decision to subsidiaries. The way in which the administrative function develops its own operating paradigm[25] can be managed so that its specific procedures support responsiveness or integration.

Dangers of Administrative Coordination

Even with the potential offered by functional and administrative managers for managing administrative coordination effectively, certain drawbacks are inescapable. In particular, administrative coordination may lead to strategic paralysis, fragmentation, or bureaucratization.

Strategic Paralysis.   The willingness to respond to environmental changes when the environment is intrinsically ambiguous and contradictory is likely to lead to strategic paralysis. Students of ambiguous situations where several environments are relevant to decisions have stressed the danger of paralysis created by giving relatively equal power to managers most sensitive to different aspects of the environment.[26] Not using a stable pattern of resource commitment over time, according to spelled-out goals, may lead to considerable waste and overall failure. It is fascinating to see that, in an environment where IBM is a strong leader, the agreements on the merger between C2I and Honeywell Bull in France spelled out a substantive strategy to avoid the risk of strategic paralysis. On the other hand, one could draw numerous examples of strategic paralysis from very refined, stable administrative coordination processes.[27]

Strategic Fragmentation.   Administrative coordination involves the use of dependencies and the management of power. In the absence of a strategic design, the management groups' loyalty must be maintained, lest managers' frustrations lead to increasingly disjointed and partial decisions and to fragmentation. Cultural identity is often a means to circumvent these divisive forces. For instance, all top managers at LM Ericsson come from the same Stockholm telecommunications engineering school; the whole top management of Philips remains Dutch and has gone through the same formative experiences. Similarly, strong cultural identity facilitates the foreign expansion of Japanese companies.

Bureaucratization.   Managers faced with uncertain situations and power relationships may be tempted to reduce their perceived uncertainties. By developing bureaucratic procedure to cope with uncertainties, managers will gain power for themselves. Bureaucratic procedure also creates uncertainties for other members of the organization.[28] This leads to bureaucratization and lack of sensitivity to the outside environment. More time is spent on infighting than on external action.

Even assuming that administrative coordination does not lead to strategic paralysis, fragmentation, or bureaucracy, it remains an expensive way to run a business. The internal management process, with its multiple negotiations and complex coalitional processes, consumes much managerial energy and time, and can slow down decision processes considerably. It can also lead to "horse trading" and more suboptimal decisions than would be warranted by the situation at hand.

Should administrative coordination be avoided wherever possible, then? The answer is probably yes, but with the qualifications developed in the first part of this article. When free trade prevails and competitors follow a world-wide integration strategy, a clear choice should be made between committing enough resources to a business and divestment. In industries where governments evince interest, administrative coordination seems, at best, to be a way for the weaker, smaller international companies to stay in certain industries (Honeywell in data processing, Philips in integrated circuits). In industries where trade is restricted, the alternative is between national responsiveness and administrative coordination. For technology leaders within their industry, administrative coordination makes sense, as it can possibly provide for easier technology transfer, and host governments can accept such coordination as a price for receiving the technology.

Strategy in the Diversified Multinational[29]

So long as the several businesses of the multinational rely on the same strategy, the overall corporate management task is not greatly complicated by business diversity. Texas Instruments uses one extreme posture which applies the same semiconductor business logic and global integration framework across the board to all of its businesses.

Another extreme would be a multinational conglomerate adopting a purely financial approach and letting each business develop its own business logic independently. Yet, in most cases, such simple solutions as that of Texas Instruments or the multinational conglomerate are not applicable: The various businesses of the diversified multinational straddle several adaptation patterns and are interdependent. This raises the issues of strategic and administrative differentiation among the businesses, and of managing the interdependencies among differentiated businesses.

Differentiation and Interdependencies

Difficulties develop when the various businesses of a multinational straddle several adaptation patterns; some are most suitably managed through global strategic integration, others through administrative coordination, and still others through national responsiveness. It usually happens that, because of a history of dominance in one business, one pattern is preferred and applied across the board. For instance, Brown Boveri was slow to recognize that its industrial businesses, particularly small motors and breakers, would be faced with worldwide competition following the EEC trade liberalization. When competition came, Brown Boveri was even slower to react, because the logic of the whole organization and the energy of top management were geared to success in the government-controlled, restricted-trade power-system and electrical-equipment businesses.

In a similar vein, after World War II, Philips had strong national organizations and weak worldwide product groups coordinating its activities. With freer trade (following the development of the EEC), moves were made to increase the power of product divisions and to foster integration in similar businesses between national organizations. This led to a balanced product-geography-function matrix that faced great difficulties in businesses where administrative coordination did not fit well. Businesses, such as TV picture tubes or standard semiconductors, did not achieve full integration at a regional (color TV) or global (semiconductors) level, and telecommunications equipment did not enjoy sufficient national autonomy to achieve responsiveness comparable to that of competitors.

An obvious response to the difficulties faced by Brown Boveri or Philips is to differentiate the management among product lines, letting each find the appropriate balance between the economic and the political imperatives.

Yet, extensive interdependencies among businesses usually make management differentiation difficult. Interdependencies are of several types. They can involve common technologies among several businesses. For instance, magnetic-tape technology at Philips served several product groups: data systems, instrumentation, medical products, professional recording, and audio consumer products. Interdependencies can also derive from vertical integration. The bulk of Philips' electronic-component production was transferred internally to be incorporated into Philips' end products; still Philips also wanted to compete on the open market for semiconductors. Interdependencies are also market related, with different products sold to the same customers. IBM's Data Processing Complex's and General Business Group's system offerings overlap at the lower end of medium systems and compete against each other for the same orders. Finally, when products are sold to government-controlled customers, interdependencies may become political. Brown Boveri was commonly told: "We are willing to import your power stations, but what about you creating an export-oriented motor plant in one of our depressed areas to generate employment and offset the trade deficit that importing your power stations would create?"

It is important to recognize the difference in nature between internal interdependencies (common technology, joint production, vertical integration) and external ones (same customers, host governments, and so forth). When interdependencies are internal, the choice of how to relate businesses (from pure arm's length to joint administration) can be made by management. When interdependencies are external, such choice is usually imposed by external agents. The terms under which to coordinate component and TV set production could be decided internally in Philips. However, the Belgian government's orders for Philips' computers were conditional upon the maintenance of Philips' employment levels in Belgium. The consumer-product groups, whose internal interdependencies with the computer group were negligible, but who had high-cost factories they wanted to close down in Belgium, suffered from the deal. Allegedly, this problem played some role in Philips' decision to withdraw from the mainframe computer business enitrely.

Managing Interdependencies

The central tradeoff in the examples presented above is that between strategic and administrative clarity for individual businesses (i.e., enabling clear choices to be made between worldwide integration and national responsiveness), and the complexity of managing interdependencies.

Developing some clarity usually involves selectivity in the management of interdependencies. It is important to recognize that, within a diversified multinational, the relative importance of various interdependencies may change over time as the "critical factors"[30] in the strategy of a business evolve. ITT was able to revise frequently the formal structure of its European operations to respond to changes in the relative importance of interdependencies. The basic method used by ITT was to organize itself into several product groups worldwide. Each of these was managed somewhat differently: The Automotive Group (auto parts and accessories) and the Microelectronics Group, for instance, were pursuing worldwide integration strongly, whereas the Telecommunications Equipment Group stuck to its national-responsiveness strategy. The Business Systems Group pursued regional integration in Europe. Individual businesses could be moved among these groups as warranted by changes in competition, technology, and government intervention. In the mid-1970s, ITT moved the line making private telephone-exchange-switching products from the Telecommunications Equipment Group to the Business Systems Group, where it joined other office equipment. The successful adaptation of electronic switching technology to private exchange and the penetration of the private exchange market by such aggressive, integrated firms as IBM had shifted the key dependency from technology (Telecommunications Equipment Group) to marketing (Business Systems Group). In a similar vein, when ITT adopted worldwide strategic integration for its microelectronics business, it spun off the telecommunication-related components to the Telecommunications Equipment Group. Also ITT decreased the interdependencies between microelectronics and telecommunications in order to achieve a clear strategy for each business.

The development of clarity for Brown Boveri and Philips was more difficult than for ITT. Because they were less widely diversified (most of their products were related), they could not reduce any interdependencies easily. Yet some of their businesses were subject to worldwide product standardization and price competition (for instance, radios at Philips and motors at BBC), and others were more affected by regional or national differences (power systems at BBC, hi-fi's at Philips). These different competitive conditions led to divergent strategic directions among businesses.

An approach to interbusiness coordination, being tried by several companies is the use of corporate functional staff in conjunction with planning committees. At Brown Boveri, corporate marketing staffs coordinate the activities of the various national subsidiaries product line by product line. Between various members of the corporate marketing staffs tradeoffs between businesses can be made, and the interdependencies can be managed. Assisting the corporate marketing staff in the strategic coordination of each business are several levels of committees. Some of these committees are functional and others are product-oriented. Functional committees coordinate certain types of interdependencies among technologies and markets of several product groups. Other committees formed by regrouping product division managers of the different subsidiaries are in charge of managing the regional integration/national responsiveness tradeoffs. Unfortunately, the committees often lack the consensus necessary for action, as each member adopts a parochial view.

Faced with similar problems, IBM gave operating units the right to take issue with the plans of other operating units ("nonconcurrence" in IBM's internal language) that would impact their activities adversely. Through this approach IBM has been able to force subunits to consider interdependencies in their planning and budgeting process and to reach a joint solution before their plans can be approved. Top management can also take the initiative of presenting key strategic issues that require coordination between subunits as "focus issues" to be dealt with explicitly in the planning process.[31] Other companies have also pulled key interdependencies of great strategic importance out of the regular structure: Brown Boveri, for instance, established a separate nuclear-policy committee with the task of managing all interdependencies relating to nuclear energy.

The management of interdependencies raises difficult issues. Because costs and benefits of interdependencies lend themselves to ambiguous conflicting interpretations, interdependencies provide a rich arena for power plays and coalition bargaining. While particular coalition configurations seem endless in their variety, they add to the task of strategic management. Furthermore, coalitions often involve external agents. For instance, individual managers can rely on their government to establish linkages among product groups. It is not uncommon for alliances to develop, at least tacitly, between host governments and subsidiaries to decrease the dependence of the subsidiary on headquarters and to develop "binding" commitments with the government.

Faced with such difficulties, MNC corporate management is likely to strive for administrative uniformity across businesses. Yet, unless all businesses can be successful with the same strategic logic, some degree of differentiation between businesses remains necessary. In short, uniformity is impossible when businesses straddle several adaptation patterns. Uniformity is possible on some aspects (financial reporting and measurement at ITT, for instance), provided that great leeway for differentiation is left to other aspects. Yet, to avoid cognitive overload at the corporate management level, there are strong pressures toward administrative uniformity, thus making the substance of decisions at the business-unit level accessible to the corporate level in a common format. Such administrative pressure for uniformity may prevent the appropriate strategic differentiation among businesses and the development of strategic clarity. These necessary strategic and administrative differentiations suggest that it is usually not possible to maintain a unitary corporate office dealing with the substance of decisions. Similarly, a diversified MNC needs (beyond the divisionalized form) a corporate office that only manages selected aspects of the operations and influences decision processes, while leaving room for differentiation among businesses—unless all follow the same worldwide integration strategy.

As a concluding note for this section, it may be hypothesized that the complex multinational structures, usually called matrix (or grid) and mixed types, represent an attempt by diversified MNCs to respond to the problems of combining the development of a strategy for each business with the need to manage interdependencies between businesses. Thus, they are not aberrant or transitory structural stages only. Matrix structures correspond to the corporate desire to manage interdependencies among businesses while allowing strategic integration to develop. Mixed structures correspond to a clear differentiation and separation between businesses that follow different adaptation patterns.

Conclusion—Combining Strategic Clarity and Administrative Coordination

The most difficult tradeoff for the diversified MNC is the one between clarity at the business level (multicountry integration or national responsiveness) and the benefits derived from operating and strategic interdependencies between businesses. The added complexity, compared to domestic diversified companies, of coping with broader environmental variety, makes the management of interdependencies less straightforward and more difficult.

Some simplification can be obtained by limiting and buffering interdependencies. For instance, at LM Ericsson, the national subsidiaries were dependent upon the center for components and technology, but the center could be severed from any subsidiary without great difficulty. Interdependencies between subsidiaries were negligible. Japanese companies usually adopted similar approaches to manage their joint ventures abroad. Philips was treating its semiconductor acquisition in the U.S., Signetics, differently from its European operations, leaving much strategic freedom to the company. So both operating and strategic interdependencies can be structured in such a way as to minimize the need for managing them. There is a tradeoff between the complexity of managing many interdependencies and the joint benefits they bring.

One way companies have tried to order tradeoffs is to manage simultaneously along several dimensions. For instance, as the Dow Chemical matrix was becoming unbalanced, the operating responsibilities moved toward area executives, thus providing regional integration across vertically interdependent businesses at the area level (Europe, Far East, etc.). Yet, a Corporate Product Department was created with veto power over strategic resource allocation and control over interdependencies between areas.[32] Administrative systems were used by Dow to provide autonomy for regional strategic integration, except for the planning and resource-allocation process that was used to check strategic integration and keep the autonomy of areas within bounds.

In an even more discriminating way, IBM's strategic planning process provided for functions, product lines, and areas (or countries) to be managed jointly in a cohesive process. At various stages during the process, inputs and control points were set up, so that both the need for integration in relevant units (which differed between functions, businesses, and areas of the world) and the administrative coordination needed between interdependent businesses were recognized, and conflicts were resolved through a contention process.

ITT was not only letting different businesses develop their own strategies, but was also using the various management levels differently. Regional headquarters controlled product and business strategies, but their weight, compared to that of national subsidiary managers, varied considerably from one business to another. The overall planning process was managed from worldwide product group headquarters in New York. Finally, measurement, control, and evaluation were corporate-level responsibilities.

More research is needed to conceptualize adequately the responses of these companies. However, the companies discussed all used very sophisticated methods for providing both strategic integration and administrative coordination according to the needs for strategic focus and operating or strategic interdependencies between subunits.

12

An Approach to
Strategic Control in MNCs

C. K. Prahalad

Yves L. Doz

This article considers the problems of maintaining strategic control over subsidiaries in a multinational firm. The authors argue that the nature of strategic control by the head office over its subsidiaries shifts with time. As resources such as capital, technology, and management become vested in the subsidiaries, head offices cannot continue to rely on control over these resources as a means of influencing subsidiary strategy. The authors outline a conceptual framework that defines *organizational context,* and they argue that it can be used as an alternate means of exerting influence. *SMR.*

The extent to which the head office (HO) of a multibusiness multinational corporation (MNC) can control the strategies of its overseas subsidiaries is emerging as an issue of considerable interest to a variety of publics.[1] Top managers in MNCs, which have a significant part of their assets, sales, and profits (often more than 50 percent) attributable to overseas operations, would like to be assured that the strategic direction of subsidiaries is controlled from the HO. However, given that subsidiary operations are increasing in size and scope, how can the HO control effectively? Politicians, especially those from developing countries, are worried about the degree to which decisions of the subsidiaries operating on their soil are controlled by the HO of the multinational corporation. Their overriding concern is the extent to which subsidiaries can be responsive to the developmental goals of host governments.

For the researcher, this situation raises the age-old issue of centralization versus decentralization in an extremely complex setting—complexities

From *Sloan Management Review,* Summer 1981, Vol. 22, No. 4. Reprinted with permission.

brought about by multiple cultural environments, differences in competitive structures, pressures of host governments, and the presence of joint-venture partners. The key research question is: What are the dynamics of strategic control of subsidiaries by the HO in MNCs?

The Changing Nature of Strategic Control Examined

In this article, we present the results of our research over the last five years on the changing nature of the strategic control process between the HO and subsidiaries. (See the Appendix for a description of the research design.) Our thesis is that as subsidiaries mature and become autonomous with respect to strategic resources such as technology, capital, management, and access to markets, the HO's ability to control the strategies of subsidiaries is significantly reduced.

The HO, faced with an inability to exert control over the subsidiaries on the basis of the subsidiaries' dependence on strategic resources, must find substitute mechanisms. Creating a sophisticated organizational context—a blend of organizational structure, information systems, measurement and reward systems, and career planning and a fostering of common organizational culture— can compensate for the erosion of HO's capacity to control subsidiaries. In this article we illustrate why the HOs of multinational corporations must constantly be aware of the shifting importance of resource dependency and organizational context in providing a total control capability.

The Concept of Strategic Control

Strategic control is the extent of influence that a head office has over a subsidiary concerning decisions that affect subsidiary strategy. Some typical decisions that reflect the strategy of a subsidiary are choice of technology, definition of product market, emphasis on different product lines, allocation of resources, expansion and diversification of subsidiary operations, and a willingness to participate in a global network of product flows among subsidiaries. Further, the HO is interested not only in influencing the strategic decisions of subsidiaries, but also in monitoring their progress toward fulfilling the strategic expectations.

The HO-Subsidiary Milieu

The HO's desire to exercise strategic control over subsidiaries has been supported by two developments over the last several decades. Major companies increasingly have derived a larger share of their sales and profits from overseas subsidiaries and have sent abroad a growing share of their assets. In addition to this surge in the importance of overseas activities, several MNCs also have found that in many of their businesses, subsidiaries' markets enjoy a higher growth potential than the U.S. market.

Impact of Global Competition.   The changing pattern of competition during the last decade has had another critical influence on the desire of HO groups to control subsidiary strategies. Several industries—autos, ball bearings, motorcycles, consumer electronics, chemicals, steel, tires, heavy electrical systems, earth-moving equipment, to name a few—are increasingly dominated by a small number of worldwide competitors.[2] This implies that an MNC must develop a global strategy in addition to several national strategies to be successful. It must transcend the boundaries of national markets in determining sourcing patterns, pricing strategies, product designs, technology level, and financing. HOs are, therefore, increasingly drawn into the activities of subsidiaries by the shifting nature of competition. The HO must not only coordinate the operations of subsidiaries but also must increasingly influence the direction of subsidiary strategies to conform to the needs of a global strategy. The pressures resulting from the increasing importance of overseas activities and the changing character of global competition—i.e., the economic imperatives that pressure the MNC to rationalize global operations—tend to trigger desires on the part of HO managers to centralize control.

Impact of Host Government Demands.   While the economic imperatives increase the tendency to centralize, host government demands (in both developing and developed countries) penalize centralization. Businesses in which an MNC is involved attract government attention and intervention for several reasons:

- They are important for national defense (e.g., jet engines).
- They represent an important infrastructure (e.g., railroads, telecommunications).
- They are key national industries that are threatened (e.g., the watch industry in Switzerland and the automobile industry in the United States).
- They are in industries in which it is difficult to gain access to key technologies (e.g., semiconductors, computers).

In some cases, effects on balance of payment and employment are key concerns of host governments. In some developing countries, all MNCs, irrespective of the nature of the business in which they are involved, attract attention (e.g., India, Mexico, Brazil). Whatever the motivations for government intervention in subsidiary strategy, the impact of this political imperative encourages the subsidiary to seek greater autonomy.[3]

Joint Ventures: Added Complexity.   In addition to the political imperative, many MNCs have had to contend with joint-venture partners. During the late 1960s and early 1970s, MNCs desiring greater coordination have found it difficult to continue to tolerate joint ventures.[4] However, joint ventures may become the only way to compete globally in several industries, such as telecommunication equipment, consumer electronics, and data-processing equipment. Joint-venture partners complicate the task of HO–subsidiary coordination.

The dynamics of HO control over subsidiary strategy are influenced not only by the conflicting demands of the economic and political imperatives of an MNC's operation but also by the changing nature of the HO–subsidiary relationship. For example:

1. As subsidiaries mature and grow in size, they can afford an adequate level of internal management talent and R&D investment.
2. As the industry matures, the technological advantage that the HO had over the subsidiary disappears.
3. Management know-how, as a distinct resource, is becoming widespread. Moreover, the management skills needed by subsidiaries operating in environments dissimilar to that of the parent—like a highly regulated environment (e.g., India, Nigeria), or a highly inflationary environment (e.g., Brazil), or a relatively low-technology environment (e.g., Indonesia)— may be unavailable at the HO.
4. Subsidiaries with large volume, adequate technology, and management capability may develop their own overseas activities. Typically, this involves marketing products outside the national boundaries of the subsidiary. Staff groups in the MNC's HO may attempt to coordinate exports from subsidiaries to third countries, but cases where subsidiaries either ignore or contest these attempts at coordination are common. In some cases, subsidiaries even invest in manufacturing facilities in third countries without subjecting themselves to the coordination of the HO groups.[5]
5. Under pressure from host governments, who may want to use MNC subsidiaries to further national developmental goals, subsidiaries may diversify into businesses unfamiliar to the HO (e.g., Union Carbide's move into shrimp fishing in India).

As a result of these trends, the HO must depend on mechanisms other than control over strategic resources—capital, technology, management, or access to markets—as a basis for strategic control. The essential strategic control dilemma in an MNC can be summarized as follows:

1. The HO cannot rely exclusively on the use of strategic resources as a basis of control, especially in situations where the subsidiaries are more or less self-sufficient in such resources. This forces MNCs to reexamine the process of control where the relationship between the HO and subsidiaries is not based on a one-way dependence. Yet, in order for the HO to develop a global strategy, it has to gain the cooperation of subsidiaries who may be autonomous in their strategic resource requirements. This creates the need to formulate the strategic control process in the context of reciprocal dependence between the HO and subsidiaries.
2. The strategic control process has inherent tensions imposed on it by the economic and political imperatives of a global business. This means that responsiveness and flexibility in strategy must coexist with desires for global rationalization.
3. Since the strategy must be responsive to environmental demands, it can lead to uncoordinated and fragmented resource commitments. However, in order to gain global competitive advantage, the MNC must be able to focus its resource commitments.
4. The strategic process must be more than just responsive to competitive pressures or host government demands in a reactive mode. It must support purposive, proactive changes in strategy.
5. Under competitive pressure or a profit crisis (a reactive situation), changes in strategy can be imposed. However, to implement proactive strategic changes, the HO and subsidiaries must perceive the legitimacy of these changes.

These five conditions, in our view, represent the key issues in the strategic control process for MNCs.

An Approach to Strategic Control

Dependence of a subsidiary on the HO for strategic resources allows the HO to control subsidiary strategy by controlling the flow of resources. However, the five dilemmas outlined above indicate that MNC managers should identify approaches other than the use of subsidiary "dependence" as the basis for strategic control.

In our research, we have found that MNCs in mature businesses increasingly have to depend on "subtle mechanisms" for influencing the strategic direction of their subsidiaries. We suggest that the alternative to substantive control, i.e., restricting the flow of strategic resources, is the creation of an organizational context. This would facilitate the relationship between the HO and subsidiaries in such a way that the HO can continue to influence and monitor subsidiary strategy.

The dynamics of the strategic control process as businesses mature may be illustrated schematically. (See Figure 12.1.) In addition to the maturity of business, the size, maturity, and quality of subsidiary management should be considered as well as the motivation of subsidiary managers to become independent of the HO with regard to strategic resources.

As illustrated in Figure 12.1, the ability of HO managers to use allocation of strategic resources as levers for control diminishes as the business and/or subsidiary matures. This declining role of substantive control is illustrated by the line SS1. On the other hand, for the HO to influence subsidiary strategy, a certain minimum level of control may be needed. This is represented by the line MM1. If the MNC depends only on substantive control mechanisms to influence subsidiary strategy, then, as businesses and/or subsidiaries mature, a control gap will develop. The HO will not be able to influence subsidiary strategy.

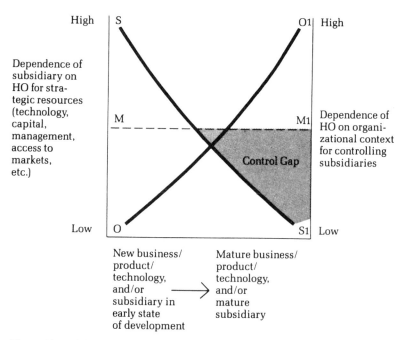

Figure 12.1   Schematic Representation of Shifts in Control Mechanisms in HO-Subsidiary Relationship

Recognizing Loss of Control. Most often, HO managers who depend solely on substantive control mechanisms do not recognize the erosion of their ability to control subsidiaries. Typically, they recognize their inability to control subsidiary strategies only when competitive pressures call for a coordinated action and HO managers find that they cannot orchestrate such action.

Organizational context can be used as an effective substitute for substantive control. While the need for (and desire to create) a substitute for substantive control is highest when the control capability is at S1, there is no justification in waiting for a crisis. Furthermore, as the ability to use substantive control diminishes, the dependence of HO managers on the alternative—organizational context—to influence strategy of subsidiaries increases as shown by line OO1. Ideally, a combination of substantive control mechanisms and organizational context should provide an adequate basis for HO managers to stay above line MM1—and to avoid the problems caused by control gap.

Creating an Appropriate Organizational Context

The task of creating an appropriate organizational context for strategic control is built on two sets of concepts. First, we develop the notion that an organization is an aggregation of four orientations—cognitive, strategic, power, and administrative. Second, we identify the type of organizational mechanisms that managers can use to manipulate these four orientations. We will demonstrate that an ability to manipulate the four orientations provides managers with the alternative to substantive control.

The Four Orientations

Hierarchical notions have dominated our thinking about organizations. As a firm's overseas activities evolve, the organizational form also evolves.[6] Typically, the firm begins with an autonomous subsidiary system that is followed by an international division structure. As the scope of its overseas activities increases, the firm adopts a global structure integrated by area, product, or matrix.

These are three ideal modes of categorizing organizational structures used by MNCs. In most businesses, the strategic tensions created by balancing the economic and political imperatives force the MNC managers to work with a variety of hybrid structures.[7] Some businesses are organized by product, others by area, yet others by matrix structures. In a "pure organizational form"—whether organized by area or product—the hierarchy dominates. The hierarchy determines:

1. The nature of information that managers collect and use, or their "world view" (in an area structure, information that is relevant to national portfolios of diverse businesses; while in a product structure, information that is relevant to business portfolios consisting of diverse countries).
2. The way managers decide to compete—on a local for local basis (area organization) or by global rationalization (product organization).
3. The people who have the power to commit strategic resources (area managers or product managers).
4. The basis for administrative procedures, such as career progression (across businesses in an area organization or within a business across area organizations).

In other words, in these pure organizational forms, if one knows "who the boss is," or if one understands the hierarchy, one can understand the organization—its capabilities and limitations.

Complex Strategies, Complex Structures

For a product organization to become sensitive to area needs (or vice versa), structural changes are needed.[8] However, few MNCs have the privilege of adopting the simple strategic postures that a pure "area" or "product" mode indicates. Complex strategic postures that balance multiple and often conflicting goals (economic versus political imperatives) require complex structures. Hierarchical concepts applied to such an organization are of little use in helping managers to understand or manipulate the organization.

In a complex organizational form that seeks to balance national and global priorities flexibly from decision to decision, several orientations need to be managed explicitly. We consider a complex organizational form as the means to manage the four orientations:

1. *Cognitive orientation,* or the perception of the "relevant environment" by individual managers within the organization. The relevant environment of a business is constructed of an understanding of the key competitors, the competitive structure, and the forces that are likely to mold the pattern of evolution of that business. We have to recognize that in a complex organization, different types of managers (area, product, and functional) and managers at different levels can have very different perceptions of the relevant environment. In other words, their cognitive orientations can be very different.
2. *Strategic orientation,* or the competitive posture and methods of competition that the various groups of managers are willing to adopt. If the various managers have different cognitive orientations, then they will

have different perceptions of an appropriate strategic orientation to cope with the threats or to exploit the opportunities inherent in their different world views.

3. *Power orientation,* or the locus of power among managers in the organization to commit resources—financial, technological, and managerial— to pursue a strategy.

4. *Administrative orientation,* or the orientation of support systems such as the accounting system and the personnel system. Accounting data, for example, may be consolidated along product lines or along national subsidiary lines.

In a pure hierarchical organization, the four orientations tend to be aligned with the hierarchy. For example, in a pure product organization, the cognitive orientation of managers (the perception of competitive threats and opportunities) tends to be global; the strategic orientation tends to favor a rationalized global strategy; the power to commit resources is vested with product managers; and the support systems, such as accounting and personnel (the administrative orientation), are built to support it. However, in a complex organization that may have a hybrid or matrix structure, all four orientations need not be aligned.

HO managers who operate in hybrid or matrix structures should recognize that to gain and retain strategic control, they should influence the four orientations. By suitably modifying the four orientations, the strategic direction can be altered. In our research, we find that strategic change can be initiated by altering any one of the four orientations.

However, in order for the change process to be completed, the power orientation must be changed. What emerge as key findings are that HO managers must be sensitive to the distribution of power, and that they must manage the loci of power.

HO managers in the hybrid or matrix structures can use a variety of administrative mechanisms to influence the four orientations. These mechanisms can be classified as:

1. *Data Management Mechanisms.* Included in this category are mechanisms that generate and regulate the flow of information within the organization. Accounting systems, planning and budgeting systems, and management information systems belong in this category.

2. *Manager Management Mechanisms.* Included in this category are power to assign managers to key positions, executive-compensation plans, management-development programs, career progression, performance evaluation, and socialization patterns.

3. *Conflict Resolution Mechanisms.* Since conflict and tension are inherent

in hybrid or matrix structures, mechanisms to resolve conflicts (such as task forces, planning committees, integrators, coordinating groups, and decision-responsibility assignments) are some of the important elements of a manager's tool kit.

Managers can use a variety of these mechanisms to exercise influence selectively and to change the four orientations in an organization.

Substantive Versus Organizational Context in Control

HO managers, in order to influence subsidiary strategy, should be sensitive to the use of both substantive controls, as well as to the use of organizational context as an approach to control. To retain substantive control, the HO managers must ensure that they continue to have strategic resource superiority over the subsidiaries—whether by technology, product design, marketing know-how, or capital. This does not mean that the subsidiaries should be kept weak. (Very strong subsidiaries can be very dependent.)

For example, IBM's major subsidiaries in the UK, Germany, France, and Japan are large and technologically capable. While they operate significant manufacturing and R&D facilities, IBM ensures that no non-U.S. subsidiary is self-sufficient in all key systems. Each subsidiary markets a total line of systems but can manufacture only some. As a result, all the subsidiaries are woven into a corporate network of product, resource, and competency flows that can be orchestrated by HO managers.[9]

On the other hand, the sophistication of managers in using the administrative tools to alter the four orientations can serve a similar end.

The Strategic Control Dilemma

The strategic control dilemma can now be redefined. We can classify MNCs and their various businesses. This is shown in Figure 12.2. The four categories of MNCs that results are:

1. *Fragmented*—where the possibilities of substantive control are low and the sophistication of HO managers in using organizational context is also low. In such a case, coordinating the strategies of subsidiaries or influencing subsidiary strategies are extremely difficult. In such situations, MNCs tend to move the subsidiary up to the status indicated in quadrants (B) or (D), give up attempts at coordination, or divest the subsidiary altogether.[10]

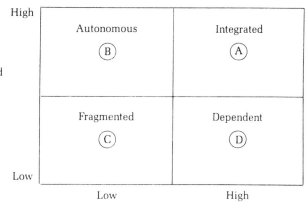

Figure 12.2   The Strategic Control Dilemma in MNCs

2. *Dependent*—where the sophistication of the organizational context is low, but the subsidiaries continue to be dependent on the HO for strategic resources. Typically, this situation exists in technology-intensive businesses (e.g., Westinghouse's nuclear-power business in Europe during the early 1970s) or where the subsidiaries are small. As the technology matures and as subsidiaries grow, the tendency for the control capability to drift toward quadrant (C), a fragmented state, cannot be ruled out.

3. *Autonomous*—where the subsidiaries are self-sufficient in strategic resources and their dependence on HO is low. However, the sophistication of managers in using organizational context is high. While the subsidiaries are autonomous, HO managers can still exercise significant influence over subsidiary strategy.

    For example, LM Ericsson, the Swedish telecommunications firm, has traditionally relied on a common corporate value system and patterns of socialization to influence subsidiary strategy.[11] MNCs in this category often attempt to move toward quadrant (A), the integrated state.

4. *Integrated*—where the MNC has built a high degree of substantive and organizational context control capability. IBM is an example.[12]

We have found, in our research, firms who were attempting to move from (C) to (D), (C) to (B), and (B) to (A), as well as those who were unfortunate enough to move from (D) to (C) and (B) to (C). The most interesting challenge to top management is the move from (C) to (B) or (D) and then to (A).

A crisis may provide opportunities for top managers to intervene and introduce systems that can help the transition process. However, when there is no apparent profit crisis, the task is considerably more difficult.

Conclusion

We have argued in this article that the ability of HOs to influence subsidiary strategy cannot be taken for granted. With the maturing of subsidiaries and with the eroding of HO control over strategic resources, alternative approaches to strategic control become necessary. We have suggested that sophistication in using organizational context can offset the erosion of strategic control capability at the HO.

We have classified MNCs and the nature of their strategic control capabilities (using substantive control and organizational context control as the two basic approaches) into the four categories—fragmented, autonomous, dependent, and integrated. This scheme provides us with a basis for diagnosing the state of the HO control over subsidiary strategy in a multinational corporation. It is also useful in deciding a desirable future state and a basic approach—be it substantive control or organizational context—to develop control.

Appendix

Research Methodology

The research project on which this article was based lasted a total of six years. In 1974, following the pilot study of a diversified materials and chemicals company, a small sample of companies that were in the process of shifting from subsidiary autonomy to headquarters control and centralized strategy making was studied in detail. These companies were LM Ericsson, Brown Boveri & Cie., General Telephone and Electronics, General Motors, Gamma (disguised European diversified MNC), Nippon (disguised Japanese multinational), Ford Motor Co., Corning Glass Works, IVECO, Alcan, and Massey Ferguson. Some of these companies were studied by doctoral students. The evolution of each company was documented through internal company documents and interviews with involved executives at headquarters and at subsidiaries. Interviews numbered between twenty and sixty per company. In some cases, such as GM, IVECO, or Corning, events were followed as they unfolded, since the researchers got involved before the shift was completed.

Detailed descriptions of the various evolutions were then written and checked with managers in the particular company for accuracy and completeness. Some of these descriptions have been published as cases; others will be as they are released by the companies.

From these descriptions were developed chronological protocols identifying the sequence and timing in the use of managerial mechanisms, their intent, and their results. In turn, the general propositions presented in this article are the researchers' conceptualization of the data offered by the protocols and the company descriptions.

Notes and References

Introduction

1. See A. C. Hax and N. S. Majluf, *Strategic Management: An Integrative Perspective* (Englewood Cliffs, NJ: Prentice-Hall, 1984).
2. For a brilliant analysis of the various models of decision making, see G. T. Allison, *Essence of Decision: Explaining the Cuban Missile Crisis* (Boston: Little, Brown, 1967).
3. H. I. Ansoff, *Implanting Strategic Management* (Englewood Cliffs, NJ: Prentice-Hall, 1984); A. C. Hax and N. S. Majluf (1984); P. Lorange, *Corporate Planning: An Executive Viewpoint* (Englewood Cliffs, NJ: Prentice-Hall, 1980); M. E. Porter, *Competitive Strategy: Techniques for Analyzing Industries and Competitors* (New York: Free Press, 1980); M. E. Porter, *Competitive Advantage: Creating and Sustaining Superior Performance* (New York: Free Press, 1985); and B. Yavitz and W. H. Newman, *Strategy in Action: The Execution, Politics, and Payoff of Business Planning* (New York: Free Press, 1982).
4. R. M. Cyert and J. G. March, *A Behavioral Theory of the Firm* (Englewood Cliffs, NJ: Prentice-Hall, 1963); C. E. Lindblom, "The Science of 'Muddling Through'," *Public Administration Review,* Spring 1959, pp. 79–88; H. A. Simon, *Administrative Behavior: A Study of Decision-Making Processes in Administrative Organization* (New York: Free Press, 1976); and H. E. Wrapp, "Good Managers Don't Make Policy Decisions," *Harvard Business Review,* September–October 1967, pp. 91–99.
5. The three articles in the series are J. B. Quinn, "Strategic Goals: Process and Politics," *Sloan Management Review,* Fall 1977, pp. 21–37; J. B. Quinn, "Strategic Change: 'Logical Incrementalism'," *Sloan Management Review,* Fall 1978, pp. 7–21; and J. B. Quinn, "Managing Strategic Change," *Sloan Management Review,* Summer 1980, pp. 3–17.
6. One of the most successful and popular of these is T. J. Peters and R. H. Waterman, Jr., *In Search of Excellence* (New York: Harper & Row, 1982).
7. M. A. Maidique and R. H. Hayes, "The Art of High-Technology Management," *Sloan Management Review,* Winter 1984, pp. 17–31.
8. For a good discussion of the leadership issue, see W. G. Bennis and B. Nanus, *Leaders: The Strategies for Taking Charge* (New York: Harper & Row, 1985); and Eliza G. Collins, ed. *Executive Success: Making It in Management* (New York: John Wiley, 1983). The latter is a collection of *Harvard Business Review* papers in the area of leadership.
9. N. M. Tichy and D. O. Ulrich, "The Leadership Challenge—A Call for the Transformational Leader," *Sloan Management Review,* Fall 1984, pp. 59–68.
10. S. M. Davis, *Managing Corporate Culture* (Cambridge, MA: Ballinger, 1984); T. E. Deal and A. A. Kennedy, *Corporate Cultures—The Rites and Rituals of Corporate Life* (Reading, MA: Addison-Wesley, 1982); and E. H. Schein, *Organizational Culture and Leadership* (San Francisco, CA: Jossey-Bass, 1985).
11. E. H. Schein, "Does Japanese Management Have a Message for American Managers?" *Sloan Management Review,* Fall 1981, pp. 55–68.
12. W. Ouchi, *Theory Z: How American Business Can Meet the Japanese Challenge* (Reading,

MA: Addison-Wesley, 1981); and R. T. Pascale and A. G. Athos, *The Art of Japanese Management: Applications for American Executives* (New York: Simon & Schuster, 1981).

13. E. H. Schein, "Coming to a New Awareness of Organizational Culture," *Sloan Management Review,* Winter 1984, pp. 3–16.

14. For a detailed discussion of the tasks required for an explicit articulation of the vision of the firm, see A. C. Hax and N. S. Majluf (1984), Chs. 4 and 12.

15. For an excellent discussion of horizontal strategy, see M. E. Porter (1985), Chs. 9, 10, 11, and 12.

16. E. B. Roberts and C. A. Berry, "Entering New Businesses: Selecting Strategies for Success," *Sloan Management Review,* Spring 1985, pp. 3–17.

17. A useful reference to the portfolio matrix literature is A. C. Hax and N. S. Majluf (1984), Chs. 7, 8, 9, and 10. See also P. Haspeslagh, "Portfolio Planning: Uses and Limitations," *Harvard Business Review,* Vol. 60, No. 1, 1982, pp. 58–73.

18. M. Beer, B. Spector, P. R. Lawrence, D. Q. Mills, and R. E. Walton, *Managing Human Assets* (New York: Free Press, 1984).

19. For additional references to human resource strategy see T. A. Barocci and T. A. Kochan, *Human Resource Management and Industrial Relations* (Boston, MA: Little, Brown, 1985); C. J. Fombrun, N. M. Tichy, and M. A. Devanna, *Strategic Resource Management* (New York: John Wiley, 1984); A. C. Hax, "A New Competitive Weapon: The Human Resource Strategy," *Training Development Journal,* May 1985, pp. 76–82; and W. Skinner, "Big Hat, No Cattle: Managing Human Resources," *Harvard Business Review,* Vol. 59, No. 5, pp. 106–114.

20. N. M. Tichy, C. J. Fombrun, and M. A. Devanna, "Strategic Human Resource Management," *Sloan Management Review,* Winter 1982, pp. 47–61.

21. E. H. Schein, "Increasing Organizational Effectiveness Through Better Resource Planning and Development," *Sloan Management Review,* Fall 1977, pp. 1–20.

22. E. H. Schein, *Career Dynamics* (Reading, MA: Addison-Wesley, 1978).

23. W. J. Abernathy, K. B. Clark, and A. M. Kantrow, *Industrial Renaissance—Producing a Competitive Future for America* (New York: Basic Books, 1983); E. S. Buffa, *Meeting the Competitive Challenge—A Manufacturing Strategy for U.S. Companies* (Homewood, IL: Richard D. Irwin, 1984); C. H. Fine and A. C. Hax, "Manufacturing Strategy: A Methodology and an Illustration," *Interfaces,* November–December 1985, pp. 28–46; R. H. Hayes and S. C. Wheelwright, *Restoring Our Competitive Edge: Competing through Manufacturing* (New York: John Wiley, 1984); A. M. Kantrow, ed., *Survival Strategies for American Industry* (New York: John Wiley, 1983); R. J. Schonberger, *Japanese Manufacturing Techniques* (New York: Free Press, 1982); and W. Skinner, *Manufacturing: The Formidable Competitive Weapon* (New York: John Wiley, 1985).

24. D. A. Garvin, "What Does 'Product Quality' Really Mean?" *Sloan Management Review,* Fall 1984, pp. 25–43.

25. For an excellent discussion of technology and the value chain, see M. E. Porter (1985).

26. M. A. Maidique, "Entrepreneurs, Champions, and Technological Innovation," *Sloan Management Review,* Winter 1980, pp. 59–76.

27. A further look into the critical roles needed for the successful development of the technology-based innovation process is provided by E. B. Roberts and A. F. Fusfeld, "Staffing the Innovative Technology-Based Organization," *Sloan Management Review,* Spring 1981, pp. 19–34.

28. F. W. McFarlan, "Information Technology Changes the Way You Compete," *Harvard Business Review,* May–June 1984, pp. 98–103.

29. J. F. Rockart and M. S. Scott Morton, "Implications of Changes in Information Technology for Corporate Strategy," *Interfaces,* January–February 1984.

30. On interorganizational systems, see J. I. Cash, Jr., and B. R. Konsynski, "IS Redraws Competitive Boundaries," *Harvard Business Review,* March–April 1985, pp. 134–142.

31. M. E. Porter (1980). For an alternative application of Porter's industry and competitive analysis framework to the information-technology issue, see M. E. Porter and V. E. Millar, "How Information Gives You Competitive Advantage," *Harvard Business Review,* July–August 1985, pp. 149–160.

32. G. L. Parsons, "Information Technology: A New Competitive Weapon," *Sloan Management Review,* Fall 1983, pp. 3–14.

33. T. Levitt, "The Globalization of Markets," *Harvard Business Review,* May–June 1983, pp. 92–102.

34. M. E. Porter, "Competition in Global Industries: A Conceptual Framework," Harvard Business School, 75th Anniversary Colloquium, 1984.

35. Y. L. Doz, "Strategic Management in Multinational Companies," *Sloan Management Review,* Winter 1980, pp. 27–46.

36. C. K. Prahalad and Y. L. Doz, "An Approach to Strategic Control in MNCs," *Sloan Management Review,* Summer 1981, pp. 5–13.

Chapter 1

1. H. E. Wrapp, "A Plague of Professional Managers," *New York Times,* April 8, 1979.

2. J. B. Quinn, "Strategic Goals: Process and Politics," *Sloan Management Review,* Fall 1977, pp. 21–37; and J. B. Quinn, "Strategic Change: 'Logical Incrementalism'," *Sloan Management Review,* Fall 1978, pp. 7–21. The study, which deals only with strategic changes in ten major corporations, will be published as a book entitled *Strategies for Change: Logical Incrementalism* (Homewood, IL: Dow Jones-Irwin, 1980).

3. R. M. Cyert and J. G. March, *A Behavioral Theory of the Firm* (Englewood Cliffs, NJ: Prentice-Hall, 1963), p. 123, call this learning-feedback-adaptiveness of goals and feasible alternatives over time "organizational learning."

4. See H. E. Wrapp, "Good Managers Don't Make Policy Decisions," *Harvard Business Review,* September–October 1967, pp. 91–99; R. Normann, *Management for Growth,* trans. N. Adler (New York: John Wiley, 1977); D. Braybrooke and C. E. Lindblom, *A Strategy of Decision: Policy Evaluation as a Social Process* (New York: Free Press, 1963); C. E. Lindblom, *The Policy-Making Process* (Englewood Cliffs, NJ: Prentice-Hall, 1968); and W. G. Bennis, *Changing Organizations: Essays on the Development and Evolution of Human Organizations* (New York: McGraw-Hill, 1966).

5. Quinn (Fall 1977); and Quinn (Fall 1978).

6. J. B. Quinn, *Xerox Corporation (B),* (copyrighted case, Amos Tuck School of Business Administration, Dartmouth College, Hanover, NH, 1979).

7. O. G. Brim, D. Glass et al., *Personality and Decision Processes: Studies in the Social Psychology of Thinking* (Palo Alto, CA: Stanford University Press, 1962).

8. Crises did occur at some stage in almost all the strategies investigated. However, the study was concerned with the attempt to manage strategic change in an ordinary way. While executives had to deal with precipitating events in this process, crisis management was not—and should not be—the focus of effective strategic management.

9. For some formal approaches and philosophies for environmental scanning, see W. D. Guth, "Formulating Organizational Objectives and Strategy: A Systematic Approach," *Journal of Business Policy,* Autumn 1971, pp. 24–31; and F. J. Aguilar, *Scanning the Business Environment* (New York: Macmillan, 1967).

   For confirmation of the early vagueness and ambiguity in problem form and identification, see H. Mintzberg, D. Raisinghani, and A. Théorêt, "The Structure of 'Unstructured' Decision Processes," *Administrative Science Quarterly,* June 1976, pp. 246–275.

10. For a discussion of various types of "misfits" between the organization and its environment as a basis for problem identification, see Normann (1977), p. 19.

11. For suggestions on why organizations engage in "problem search" patterns, see R. M. Cyert, H. A. Simon, and D. B. Trow, "Observation of a Business Decision," *The Journal of Business,* October 1956, pp. 237–248; and for a discussion of the problems of timing in transitions, see L. R. Sayles, *Managerial Behavior: Administration in Complex Organizations* (New York: McGraw-Hill, 1964).

12. A classic view of how these screens operate is described in C. Argyris, "Double Loop Learning in Organizations," *Harvard Business Review,* September–October 1977, pp. 115–125.

13. Quinn (copyrighted case, 1979).

14. Cyert and March (1963) suggested that executives choose from a number of satisfactory solutions: later observers have suggested they choose the first truly satisfactory solution discovered.

15. F. F. Gilmore, "Overcoming the Perils of Advocacy in Corporate Planning," *California Management Review,* Spring 1973, pp. 127–137.

16. J. B. Quinn, *General Motors Corporation: The Downsizing Decision* (copyrighted case, Amos Tuck School of Business Administration, Dartmouth College, Hanover, NH, 1978).

17. E. Rhenman, *Organization Theory for Long-Range Planning* (New York: John Wiley, 1973), p.63, notes a similar phenomenon.

18. Quinn (copyrighted case, 1978).

19. R. M. Cyert, W. R. Dill, and J. G. March, "The Role of Expectations in Business Decision Making," *Administrative Science Quarterly,* December 1958, pp. 307–340, point out that existing polities may unconsciously bias information to support views top management is known to value.

20. J. H. Dessauer, *My Years with Xerox: The Billions Nobody Wanted* (Garden City, NY: Doubleday, 1971).

21. See H. Mintzberg, *The Nature of Managerial Work* (New York: Harper & Row, 1973). Note that this "vision" is not necessarily the beginning point of the process. Instead it emerges as new data and viewpoints interact. Normann (1977).

22. Mintzberg, Raisinghani, and Théorêt (June 1976) liken the process to a decision tree where decisions at each node become more narrow, with failure at any node allowing recycling back to the broader tree trunk.

23. Wrapp (September-October 1967) notes that a conditioning process that may stretch over months or years is necessary in order to prepare the organization for radical departures from what it is already striving to attain.

24. See J. G. March, J. P. Olsen, S. Christensen et al., *Ambiguity and Choice in Organizations* (Bergen, Norway: Universitetsforlaget, 1976).

25. T. A. Wise, "I.B.M.'s $5,000,000,000 Gamble," *Fortune,* September 1966, pp. 118–124; T. A. Wise, "The Rocky Road to the Marketplace (Part II: I.B.M.'s $5,000,000,000 Gamble)," *Fortune,* October 1966, pp. 138–152.

26. For an excellent overview of the processes of co-optation and neutralization, see Sayles (1964); for perhaps the first reference to the concept of the "zone of indifference," see C. I. Barnard, *The Functions of the Executive* (Cambridge, MA: Harvard University Press, 1938); the following two sources note the need of executives for coalition behavior to reduce the organizational conflict resulting from differing interests and goal preferences in large organizations: Cyert and March (1963); and J. G. March, "Business Decision Making," in *Readings in Managerial Psychology,* H. J. Leavitt and L. R. Pondy, eds. (Chicago: University of Chicago Press, 1964).

27. Cyert and March (1963) also note that not only do organizations seek alternatives but that "alternatives seek organizations" (as when finders, scientists, bankers, etc., bring in new solutions).

28. March, Olsen, Christensen et al. (1976).

29. Much of the rationale for this approach is contained in J. B. Quinn, "Technological Innovation, Entrepreneurship, and Strategy," *Sloan Management Review,* Spring 1979, pp. 19–30.

30. C. Argyris, "Interpersonal Barriers to Decision Making," *Harvard Business Review,* March-April 1966, pp. 84–97. The author notes that when the president introduced major decisions from the top, discussion was "less than open" and commitment was "less than complete," although executives might assure the president to the contrary.

31. March (1964).

32. The process tends to be one of eliminating the less feasible rather than of determining a target or objectives. The process typically reduces the number of alternatives through successive limited comparisons to a point where understood analytical techniques can apply and the organization structure can function to make a choice. See Cyert and March (1963).

33. For more detailed relationships between authority and power, see H. C. Metcalf and L. Urwick, eds., *Dynamic Administration: The Collected Papers of Mary Parker Follett* (New York: Harper & Brothers, 1941); and A. Zaleznik, "Power and Politics in Organizational Life," *Harvard Business Review,* May-June 1970, pp. 47–60.

34. J. D. Thompson, "The Control of Complex Organizations," in *Organizations in Action* (New York: McGraw-Hill, 1967).

35. G. T. Allison, *Essence of Decision: Explaining the Cuban Missile Crisis* (Boston: Little, Brown, 1971).

36. C. E. Lindblom, "The Science of 'Muddling Through'," *Public Administration Review* (Spring 1959): 79–88. The author notes that the relative weights individuals give to values and the intensity of their feelings will vary sequentially from decision to decision, hence the dominant coalition itself varies with each decision somewhat.

37. Zaleznik (May-June 1970) notes that confusing compliance with commitment is one of the most common and difficult problems of strategic implementation. He notes that often organizational commitment may override personal interest if the former is developed carefully.

38. A. D. Chandler, *Strategy and Structure: Chapters in the History of the Industrial Enterprise* (Cambridge, MA: MIT Press, 1962).

39. K. J. Cohen and R. M. Cyert, "Strategy: Formulation, Implementation, and Monitoring," *The Journal of Business* (July 1973): 349–367.

40. March (1964) notes that major decisions are "processes of gradual commitment."

41. Sayles (1964) notes that such decisions are a "flow process" with no one person ever really making the decisions.

42. J. M. Pfiffner, "Administrative Rationality," *Public Administration Review* (Summer 1960): 125–132.

43. R. James, "Corporate Strategy and Change—The Management of People" (monograph, The University of Chicago, 1978). The author does an excellent job of pulling together the threads of coalition management at top organizational levels.

44. Cyert and March (1963), p. 115.

45. Lindblom (Spring 1959) notes that every interest has a "watchdog" and that purposely allowing these watchdogs to participate in and influence decisions creates consensus decisions that all can live with. Similar conscious access to the top for different interests can now be found in corporate structures.

46. Zaleznik (May-June 1970).

47. For an excellent view of the bargaining processes involved in coalition management, see Sayles (1964), pp. 207–217.

48. For suggestions on why the central power figure in decentralized organizations must be the person who manages its dominant coalition, the size of which will depend on the issues involved, and the number of areas in which the organizations must rely on judgmental decisions, see Thompson (1967).

49. Wrapp (September-October 1967) notes the futility of a top manager trying to push a full package of goals.

Chapter 2

1. J.-J. Servan-Schreiber, *The American Challenge* (New York: Atheneum, 1968).
2. S. Ramo, *America's Technology Slip* (New York: John Wiley, 1980).
3. R. Pascale and A. Athos, *The Art of Japanese Management* (New York: Simon & Schuster, 1981).
4. T. J. Peters and R. H. Waterman, Jr., *In Search of Excellence* (New York: Harper & Row, 1982). For purposes of this article, the high-technology industries are defined as those that spend more than 3 percent of sales on R&D. These industries, though otherwise quite different, are all characterized by a rapid rate of change in their products and technologies. Only five U.S. industries meet this criterion: chemicals and pharmaceuticals; machinery (especially computers and office machines); electrical equipment and communications; professional and scientific instruments; and aircraft and missiles. See National Science Foundation, *Science Resources Studies Highlights,* NSF81–331, December 31, 1981, p. 2.
5. W. Ouchi, *Theory Z: How American Management Can Meet the Japanese Challenge* (New York: John Wiley, 1980).
6. C. E. Makin, "Ranking Corporate Reputations," *Fortune,* January 10, 1983, pp. 34–44. Corporate reputation was subdivided into eight attributes: quality of management, quality of products and services, innovativeness, long-term investment value, financial soundness, ability to develop and help talented people, community and environmental responsibility, and use of corporate assets.
7. M. A. Maidique and B. J. Zirger, "Stanford Innovation Project: A Study of Successful and Unsuccessful Product Innovation in High-Technology Firms," *IEEE Transactions on Engineering Management,* in press. See also M. A. Maidique, "The Stanford Innovation Project: A Comparative Study of Success and Failure in High-Technology Product Innovation," *Management of Technological Innovation Conference Proceedings* (Worcester Polytechnic Institute, 1983).
8. A similar conclusion was reached by Romanelli and Tushman in their study of leadership in the minicomputer industry, which found that successful companies alternated long periods of continuity and inertia with rapid reorientations. See E. Romanelli and M. Tushman, "Executive Leadership and Organizational Outcomes: An Evolutionary Perspective," *Management of Technological Innovation Conference Proceedings* (Worcester Polytechnic Institute, 1983).
9. One of the authors in this article has employed this framework as a diagnostic tool in audits of high-technology firms. The firm is evaluated along these six dimensions on a 0–10 scale by members of corporate and divisional management, working individually. The results are then used as inputs for conducting a strategic review of the firm.
10. General Electric evidently has also recognized the value of such concentration. In 1979, Reginald Jones, then GE's CEO, broke up the firm into six independent sectors led by "sector executives." See R. Vancil and P. C. Browne, "General Electric Consumer Products and Services Sector" (Boston, MA: Harvard Business School Case Services 2–179–070).
11. Personal communication with David Packard, Stanford University, March 4, 1982.
12. After only eighteen months as Geneen's successor as president, Lyman Hamilton was summarily dismissed by Geneen for reversing Geneen's way of doing business. See G. Colvin, "The Re-Geneening of ITT," *Fortune,* January 11, 1982, pp. 34–39.
13. "RCA: Still Another Master," *Business Week,* August 17, 1981, pp. 80–86.
14. "R&D Scoreboard," *Business Week,* July 6, 1981, pp. 60–75.
15. R. Stata, Analog Devices *Quarterly Report,* 1st Quarter, 1981.
16. "Why They Are Jumping Ship at Intel," *Business Week,* February 14, 1983, p. 107; and M. Chase, "Problem-Plagued Intel Bets on New Products, IBM's Financial Help," *Wall Street Journal,* February 4, 1983.

17. These SAPPHO findings are generally consistent with the results of the Stanford Innovation Project, a major comparative study of U.S. high-technology innovation. See M. A. Maidique, "The Stanford Innovation Project: A Comparative Study of Success and Failure in High Technology Product Innovation," *Management of Technology Conference Proceedings* (Worcester Polytechnic Institute, 1983).

18. Maidique and Zirger (in press); Several other authors have reached similar conclusions. See, for example, Peters and Waterman (1982).

19. Personal communication with Tom Jones, chairman of the board, Northrop Corporation, May 1982.

20. W. R. Thurston, "The Revitalization of GenRad," *Sloan Management Review,* Summer 1981, pp. 53–57.

21. T. Wise, "I.B.M.'s $5,000,000,000 Gamble," *Fortune,* September 1966; and "A Rocky Road to the Marketplace," *Fortune,* October 1966.

22. A. P. Sloan, *My Years with General Motors* (New York: Anchor Books, 1972), p. 401.

23. Personal communication with Ken Fisher, 1980. Mr. Fisher was president and CEO of Prime Computer from 1975 to 1981.

24. At Genentech, Cetus, Biogen, and Collaborative Research, four of the leading biotechnology firms, a top scientist is also a member of the board of directors.

25. See, for example, J. A. Morton, *Organizing for Innovation* (New York: McGraw-Hill, 1971).

26. Jimmy Treybig, president of Tandem Computer, Stanford Executive Institute Presentation, August 1982.

27. See D. A. Schon, *Technology and Change* (New York: Dell, 1967), and Peters and Waterman (1982).

28. S. Myers and E. F. Sweezy, "Why Innovations Fail," *Technology Review,* March–April 1978, pp. 40–46.

29. *Texas Instruments* (A), 9–476–122, Harvard Business School case; *Texas Instruments Shows U.S. Business How to Survive in the 1980's,* 3–579–092, Harvard Business School case; *Texas Instruments "Speak and Spell Product,"* 9–679–089, revised 7/79, Harvard Business School case.

30. Arthur K. Watson, Address to the Eighth International Congress of Accountants, New York City, September 24, 1962, as quoted by D. A. Schon, "Champions for Radical New Inventions," *Harvard Business Review,* March–April 1963, p. 85.

31. Personal communication with Tom Jones, chairman of the board, Northrop Corporation, May 1982.

32. Personal communication with Bob Hungate, general manager, Medical Supplies Division, Hewlett-Packard, 1980.

33. Personal communication with Richard Frankel, president, Kevex Corporation, April 1983.

34. Personal communication with Herb Dwight, president and CEO, Spectra-Physics, 1982.

35. Personal communication with Alexander d'Arbeloff, cofounder and president of Teradyne, 1983.

36. Personal communication with Ray Stata, president and CEO, Analog Devices, 1980.

37. Personal communication with Bernie Gordon, president and CEO, Analogic, 1982.

38. Personal communication with Paul Rizzo, 1980.

39. Personal communication with Tom McAvoy, president of Corning Glass, 1979.

40. Personal communication with Milt Greenberg, president of GCA, 1980.

41. Wise (September 1966).

42. L. R. Sayles and M. K. Chandler, *Managing Large Systems: Organizations for the Future* (New York: Harper & Row, 1971).

43. R. A. Burgelman, "A Model of the Interaction of Strategic Behavior, Corporate Context and the Concept of Corporate Strategy," *Academy of Management Review* (1983); pp. 61–70.

44. S. Zipper, "TI Unscrambling Matrix Management to Cope with Gridlock in Major Profit Centers," *Electronic News,* April 26, 1982, p. 1.
45. M. Barnfather, "Can 3M Find Happiness in the 1980's?" *Forbes,* March 11, 1982, pp. 113–116.
46. R. Hill, "Does a 'Hands Off' Company Now Need a 'Hands On' Style?" *International Management,* July 1983, p. 35.
47. Barnfather (March 11, 1982).
48. *Quotations from Chairman Mao Tse Tung,* ed. S. R. Schram (Bantam Books, 1967), p. 174.
49. D. G. Marquis, "Ways of Organizing Projects," *Innovation,* August 1969, pp. 26–33; and T. Levitt, *Marketing for Business Growth* (New York: McGraw-Hill, 1974), in particular, ch. 7.
50. Charles Ames, former CEO of Reliance Electric, as quoted in "Exxon's $600-million Mistake," *Fortune,* October 19, 1981.
51. See, for example, W. J. Abernathy and J. M. Utterback, "Patterns of Industrial Innovation," *Technology Review,* June–July 1978, pp. 40–47.
52. T. Kuhn, *The Structure of Scientific Revolutions,* 2d ed. (Chicago, IL: University of Chicago Press, 1967).
53. After reviewing an early draft of this article, Ray Stata wrote, "The articulation of dynamic balance, of yin and yang . . . served as a reminder to me that there isn't one way forever, but a constant adaption to the needs and circumstances of the moment." Ray Stata, president, Analog Devices, letter of November 29, 1982.
54. Quoted in "Some Contributions of James E. Webb to the Theory and Practice of Management," a presentation by Elmer B. Staats before the annual meeting of the Academy of Management on August 11, 1978.
55. Romanelli and Tushman (1983).

Chapter 3

1. J. M. Burns, *Leadership* (New York: Harper & Row, 1978).
2. N. M. Tichy, *Managing Strategic Change: Technical, Political and Cultural Dynamics* (New York: John Wiley, 1983).
3. *Ibid.*
4. K. H. Blanchard and S. Johnson, *The One Minute Manager* (New York: Berkeley Books, 1982).
5. T. J. Peters and R. J. Waterman, Jr., *In Search of Excellence* (New York: Harper & Row, 1982).
6. M. Maccoby, *The Leader* (New York: Ballantine Books, 1981).
7. W. Bridges, *Making Sense of Life's Transitions* (Reading, MA: Addison-Wesley, 1980).
8. *Ibid.*
9. T. E. Deal and A. A. Kennedy, *Corporate Cultures* (Reading, MA: Addison-Wesley, 1982); "Corporate Culture: The Hard-to-Change Values That Spell Success or Failure," *Business Week,* October 27, 1980, pp. 148–160; and W. Ulrich, "HRM and Culture: History, Rituals, and Myths," *Human Resource Management,* Summer 1984.

Chapter 4

1. See P. Slater, *The Pursuit of Loneliness* (Boston, MA: Beacon, 1970).
1a. W. Ouchi, *Theory Z: How American Business Can Meet the Japanese Challenge* (Reading, MA: Addison-Wesley, 1981); and R. T. Pascale and A. G. Athos, *The Art of*

Japanese Management: Applications for American Executives (New York: Simon & Schuster, 1981).

2. E. H. Schein, "Management Development as a Process of Influence," *Industrial Management Review* (now *Sloan Management Review*), May 1961, pp. 59–77; and E. H. Schein, *Coercive Persuasion* (New York: Norton, 1961).

3. W. H. Whyte, Jr., *The Organization Man* (New York: Simon & Schuster, 1956).

4. C. Argyris, *Integrating the Individual and the Organization* (New York: John Wiley, 1964); A. H. Maslow, *Motivation and Personality* (New York: Harper & Row, 1954); and D. M. McGregor, *The Human Side of Enterprise* (New York: McGraw-Hill, 1960).

5. S. Silverzweig and R. F. Allen, "Changing the Corporate Culture," *Sloan Management Review,* Spring 1976, pp. 33–49; A. M. Pettigrew, "On Studying Organizational Cultures," *Administrative Science Quarterly,* 1979, pp. 570–581; and H. Schwartz and S. M. Davis, "Matching Corporate Culture and Business Strategy," *Organizational Dynamics,* Summer 1981, pp. 30–48.

6. E. H. Schein, "The Individual, the Organization, and the Career: A Conceptual Scheme," *Journal of Applied Behavioral Science,* 1971, pp. 401–426; and E. H. Schein, *Career Dynamics: Matching Individual and Organizational Needs* (Reading, MA: Addison-Wesley, 1978).

7. J. Van Maanen and E. H. Schein, "Toward a Theory of Organizational Socialization," in *Research in Organizational Behavior* (Vol. 1) B. Staw, ed. (Greenwich, CT: JAI Press, 1979).

8. See, for example, F. Harbison and C. A. Myers, *Management in the Industrial World* (New York: McGraw-Hill, 1959).

9. W. J. Dickson and F. J. Roethlisberger, *Counseling in an Organization: A Sequel to the Hawthorne Researches* (Boston: Division of Research, Harvard Business School, 1966); and H. W. Johnson, "The Hawthorne Studies: The Legend and the Legacy," in *Man and Work in Society,* E. L. Cass and F. G. Zimmer, eds. (New York: Van Nostrand Reinhold, 1975).

10. E. H. Schein and W. G. Bennis, *Personal and Organizational Change through Group Methods* (New York: John Wiley, 1965).

11. McGregor (1960); and Argyris (1964).

12. R. Likert, *The Human Organization* (New York: McGraw-Hill, 1967); and A. H. Maslow, *The Farthest Reaches of Human Nature* (New York: Viking, 1971).

13. A. Etzioni, *Complex Organizations* (New York: Holt, Rinehart, & Winston, 1961).

14. Pascale and Athos, (1981), p. 102.

15. *Ibid.,* p. 106.

16. *Ibid.,* p. 105.

17. E. H. Schein, *Process Consultation* (Reading, MA: Addison-Wesley, 1969).

18. Schein and Bennis (1965).

19. A. S. Waterman, "Individualism and Interdependence," *American Psychologist,* 1981, pp. 762–773.

20. J. McLendon, *Rethinking Japanese Groupism: Individual Strategies in a Corporate Context,* unpublished paper, Harvard University, 1980.

21. E. H. Schein, *Organizational Psychology,* 3d ed. (Englewood Cliffs, NJ: Prentice-Hall, 1980).

22. J. Galbraith, *Designing Complex Organizations* (Reading, MA: Addison-Wesley, 1973).

23. W. M. Fruin, "The Japanese Company Controversy," *Journal of Japanese Studies,* 1978, pp. 267–300; and B. S. Lawrence, *Historical Perspective: Seeing through Halos in Social Research,* unpublished paper, MIT, 1981.

24. G. Hofstede, *Culture's Consequences: International Differences in Work-Related Values* (Beverly Hills, CA: Sage Publications, 1980); and G. W. England, *The Manager and His Values* (Cambridge, MA: Ballinger, 1975).

25. Some excellent efforts in this direction can be found in W. H. Newman, "Cultural Assumptions Underlying U.S. Management Concepts," in *Management in an International Context,* J. L. Massie and Luytjes, eds. (New York: Harper & Row, 1972); and in J. J. O'Toole, "Corporate Managerial Cultures," in *Behavioral Problems in Organizations,* C. L. Cooper, ed. (Englewood Cliffs, NJ: Prentice-Hall, 1979).
26. F. R. Kluckhohn and F. L. Stodtbeck, *Variations in Value Orientations* (Evanston, IL: Row, Peterson, 1961).
27. J. M. Evans, *America: The View from Europe* (Stanford, CA: The Portable Stanford, 1976).

Chapter 5

The authors express their deep appreciation to an anonymous reviewer who assisted in clarifying a number of aspects of this article.

1. E.B. Roberts, "New Ventures for Corporate Growth," *Harvard Business Review,* July–August 1980, pp. 134–142.
2. R.P. Rumelt, *Strategy, Structure and Economic Performance* (Harvard Business School, Division of Research, 1974).
3. R.P. Rumelt, "Diversification Strategy and Profitability," *Strategic Management Journal* 3, 1982, pp. 359–369.
4. H.R. Christensen and C.A. Montgomery, "Corporate Economic Performance: Diversification Strategy versus Market Structure," *Strategic Management Journal* 2, 1981, pp. 327–344.
5. R. A. Bettis and W.K. Hall, "Risks and Industry Effects in Large Diversified Firms," *Academy of Management Proceedings '81,* pp. 17–20.
6. O.J. Holzmann, R.M. Copeland, and J. Hayya, "Income Measures of Conglomerate Performance," *Quarterly Review of Economics and Business* 15, 1975, pp. 67–77.
7. T. Peters, "Putting Excellence into Management," *Business Week,* July 21, 1980, pp. 196–205.
8. T.J. Peters and R.H. Waterman, *In Search of Excellence* (New York: Harper & Row, 1982).
9. M.H. Meyer and E.B. Roberts, "New Product Strategy in Small High Technology Firms: A Pilot Study" (MIT Sloan School of Management Working Paper #1428-1-84, May 1984).
10. H.R. Biggadike, "The Risky Business of Diversification," *Harvard Business Review,* May–June 1979, pp. 103–111.
11. L.A. Weiss, "Start-Up Businesses: A Comparison of Performances," *Sloan Management Review,* Fall 1981, pp. 37–53.
12. S. S. Miller, *The Management Problems of Diversification* (New York: John Wiley, 1963).
13. J.S. Gilmore and D.C. Coddington, "Diversification Guides for Defense Firms," *Harvard Business Review,* May–June 1966, pp. 133–159.
14. M.S. Salter and W.A. Weinhold, "Diversification via Acquisition: Creating Value," *Harvard Business Review,* July–August 1978, pp. 166–176.
15. Miller (1963).
16. J. P. Killing, "Diversification through Licensing," *R&D Management,* June 1978, pp. 159–163.
17. Roberts (1980).
18. R.A. Burgelman, "Managing the Internal Corporate Venturing Process," *Sloan Management Review,* Winter 1984, pp. 33–48.
19. A.D. Chandler, *Strategy and Structure* (Cambridge, MA: MIT Press, 1962).

20. J.D.W. Morecroft, "The Feedback Viewpoint in Business Strategy for the 1980s" (MIT, Sloan School of Management, Systems Dynamics Memorandum D–3560, April 1984).

21. J. P. Killing, "How to Make a Global Joint Venture Work," *Harvard Business Review,* May–June 1982, pp. 120–127.

22. J.D. Hlavacek, B.H. Dovey, and J.J. Biondo, "Tie Small Business Technology to Marketing Power," *Harvard Business Review,* January–February 1977; and Roberts (1980).

23. "Acquiring the Expertise but Not the Company," *Business Week,* June 25, 1984, pp. 142B–142F; and "The Age of Alliances," *Inc.,* February 1984, pp. 68–69.

24. Roberts (1980).

25. R.P. Greenthal and J.A. Larson, "Venturing into Venture Capital," *Business Horizons,* September–October 1982, pp. 18–23.

26. G.F. Hardymon, M.J. Denvino, and M.S. Salter, "When Corporate Venture Capital Doesn't Work," *Harvard Business Review,* May–June 1983, pp. 114–120.

27. K.W. Rind, "The Role of Venture Capital in Corporate Development," *Strategic Management Journal* 2, 1981, pp. 169–180.

28. N.D. Fast, "Pitfalls of Corporate Venturing," *Research Management,* March 1981, pp. 21–24.

29. Procter & Gamble Company, *1983 Annual Report* (Cincinnati, OH: 1984), p. 5.

30. Miller (1963).

31. Gilmore and Coddington (1966).

32. W.L. Shanklin, "Strategic Business Planning: Yesterday, Today and Tomorrow," *Business Horizons,* October 1979, pp. 7–14.

33. *Business Week* (June 25, 1984); Hlavacek, Dovey, and Biondo (1977); and *Inc.* (February 1984).

34. C.A. Berry, "New Business Development in a Diversified Technological Corporation" (MIT Sloan School of Management/Engineering School Master of Science Thesis, 1983).

35. Salter and Weinhold (July–August 1978).

Chapter 6

1. A. Chandler, *Strategy and Structure: Chapters in the History of American Industrial Enterprise* (Cambridge, MA: MIT Press, 1962).

2. *Ibid.*

3. J. Galbraith and D. Nathanson, *Strategy Implementation: The Role of Structure and Process* (St. Paul, MN: West Publishing, 1978).

4. R. Anthony, *Planning and Control Systems: A Framework for Analysis* (Boston, MA: Division of Research, Graduate School of Business Administration, Harvard University, 1965).

5. *Business Week,* 25 February 1980, p. 173.

6. *Ibid.,* p. 166.

7. *Ibid.,* p. 166.

8. *Ibid.,* p. 168.

9. *Ibid.,* p. 168.

10. *Ibid.,* p. 168.

11. *New York Times,* 24 April 1980.

12. *Business Week,* 18 September 1978, p. 68.

13. *New York Times,* 4 September 1980.

14. J. Lorsch and S. Allen, *Managing Diversity and Interdependence* (Boston, MA: Division of Research, Harvard Business School, 1973).

15. M. Haire, "A New Look at Human Resources," *Industrial Management Review* (now *Sloan Management Review*), Winter 1970, pp. 17–23.

Additional Readings

M.A. Devanna, C. Fombrun, and N. Tichy, "Human Resource Management: A Strategic Approach," *Organizational Dynamics,* Winter 1981.

J. Galbraith and D. Nathanson, *Strategy Implementation: The Role of Structure and Process* (St. Paul, MN: West Publishing, 1978), p. 118.

B. Henderson, *Henderson on Corporate Strategy* (Cambridge, MA: Abt Books, 1979).

C. Hofer and D. Schendel, *Strategy Formulation: Analytical Concepts* (St. Paul, MN: West Publishing, 1978), p. 42.

T. Peters, "Putting Excellence into Management," *Business Week,* 21 July 1980.

Chapter 7

Notes

Much of the research on which this article is based was done under the sponsorship of the Group Psychology branch of the Office of Naval Research. Their generous support has made continuing work in this area possible. I would also like to thank my colleagues Lotte Bailyn and John Van Maanen for many of the ideas expressed in this article.

1. See Pigors and Myers [24], and Burack [10].
2. See Hackman and Suttle [13], and Meltzer and Wickert [21].
3. See McGregor [20], Bennis [6], Pigors and Myers [24], Schein [29], Van Maanen [36], Bailyn and Schein [4], and Katz [18].
4. See Beckhard [5], Bennis [6], Schein [28], Galbraith [12], Lesieur [19], and Alfred [1].
5. Schein [31].
6. Schein [32].
7. Bailyn and Schein [4], Myers [22], Van Maanen, Bailyn, and Schein [38], and Roeber [25].
8. Van Maanen and Schein [39], Bailyn [3] and [2], and Kanter [17].
9. Sheehy [33], Troll [35], Kalish [16], and Pearse and Pelzer [23].
10. Burack [10], pp. 402–403.
11. Schein [29].
12. See Dalton and Thompson [11], Super and Bohn [34], Hall [14], and Schein [32].
13. See Schein [32].
14. See Schein [32].
15. Schein [26] and [32].
16. Schein [27], and Van Maanen [36].
17. Schein [26].
18. Schein [30] and [32].
19. Schein [26], Bray, Campbell, and Grant [9], Berlew and Hall [8], and Hall [14].
20. Dalton and Thompson [11], and Katz [18].
21. Heidke [15].
22. See Bailyn [2].
23. Katz [18].
24. Bailyn [2].

References

[1] Alfred, T., "Checkers or Choice in Manpower Management," *Harvard Business Review,* January–February 1967, pp. 157–169.
[2] Bailyn, L., "Involvement and Accommodation in Technical Careers," in *Organizational Careers: Some New Perspectives,* J. Van Maanen, ed. (New York: John Wiley, 1977).

[3] Bailyn, L., "Career and Family Orientations of Husbands and Wives in Relation to Marital Happiness," *Human Relations,* 1970, pp. 97–113.

[4] Bailyn, L., and Schein, E. H., "Life/Career Considerations as Indicators of Quality of Employment," in *Measuring Work Quality for Social Reporting,* A. D. Biderman and T. F. Drury, eds. (New York: Sage Publications, 1976).

[5] Beckhard, R. D., *Organization Development: Strategies and Models* (Reading, MA: Addison-Wesley, 1969).

[6] Bennis, W. G., *Changing Organizations* (New York: McGraw-Hill, 1966).

[7] Bennis, W. G., *Organization Development: Its Nature, Origins, and Prospects* (Reading, MA: Addison-Wesley, 1969).

[8] Berlew, D., and Hall, D. T., "The Socialization of Managers," *Administrative Science Quarterly* 11, 1966, pp. 207–223.

[9] Bray, D. W., Campbell, R. J., and Grant, D. E., *Formative Years in Business* (New York: John Wiley, 1974).

[10] Burack, E., *Organization Analysis* (Hinsdale, IL: Dryden, 1975).

[11] Dalton, G. W., and Thompson, P. H., "Are R&D Organizations Obsolete?" *Harvard Business Review,* November–December 1976, pp. 105–116.

[12] Galbraith, J., *Designing Complex Organizations* (Reading, MA: Addison-Wesley, 1973).

[13] Hackman, J. R., and Suttle, J. L., *Improving Life at Work* (Los Angeles: Goodyear, 1977).

[14] Hall, D. T., *Careers in Organizations* (Los Angeles: Goodyear, 1976).

[15] Heidke, R., *Career Pro-Activity of Middle Managers,* Master's Thesis, Massachusetts Institute of Technology, 1977.

[16] Kalish, R. A., *Late Adulthood: Perspectives on Aging* (Monterey, CA: Brooks-Cole, 1975).

[17] Kanter, R. M., *Work and Family in the United States* (New York: Russell Sage, 1977).

[18] Katz, R., "Job Enrichment: Some Career Considerations," in *Organizational Careers: Some New Perspectives,* J. Van Maanen, ed. (New York: John Wiley, 1977).

[19] Lesieur, F. G., *The Scanlon Plan* (New York: John Wiley, 1958).

[20] McGregor, D., *The Human Side of Enterprise* (New York: McGraw-Hill, 1960).

[21] Meltzer, H., and Wickert, F. R., *Humanizing Organizational Behavior* (Springfield, IL: Charles C. Thomas, 1976).

[22] Myers, C. A., "Management and the Employee," in *Social Responsibility and the Business Predicament,* J. W. McKie, ed. (Washington, D.C.: Brookings, 1974).

[23] Pearse, R. F., and Pelzer, B. P., *Self-directed Change for the Mid-Career Manager* (New York: AMACOM, 1975).

[24] Pigors, P., and Myers, C. A., *Personnel Administration,* 8th ed. (New York: McGraw-Hill, 1977).

[25] Roeber, R. J. C., *The Organization in a Changing Environment* (Reading, MA: Addison-Wesley, 1973).

[26] Schein, E. H., "How to Break in the College Graduate," *Harvard Business Review,* 1964, pp. 68–76.

[27] Schein, E. H., "Organizational Socialization and the Profession of Management," *Industrial Management Review,* Winter 1968, pp. 1–16.

[28] Schein, E. H., *Process Consultation: Its Role in Organization Development* (Reading, MA: Addison-Wesley, 1969).

[29] Schein, E. H., *Organizational Psychology* (Englewood Cliffs, NJ: Prentice-Hall, 1970).

[30] Schein, E. H., "The Individual, the Organization, and the Career: A Conceptual Scheme," *Journal of Applied Behavioral Science* 7, 1971, pp. 401–426.

[31] Schein, E. H., "How 'Career Anchors' Hold Executives to Their Career Paths," *Personnel* 52, no. 3 (1975), pp. 11–24.

[32] Schein, E. H., *The Individual, the Organization and the Career: Toward Greater Human Effectiveness* (Reading, MA: Addison-Wesley, forthcoming).

[33] Sheehy, G., "Catch 30 and Other Predictable Crises of Growing Up Adult," *New York Magazine,* February 1974, pp. 30–44.

[34] Super, D. E., and Bohn, M. J., *Occupational Psychology* (Belmont, CA: Wadsworth, 1970).

[35] Troll, L. E., *Early and Middle Adulthood* (Monterey, CA: Brooks-Cole, 1975).

[36] Van Maanen, J., "Breaking In: Socialization to Work," in *Handbook of Work, Organization, and Society,* R. Dubin, ed. (Chicago: Rand McNally, 1976).

[37] Van Maanen, J., ed., *Organizational Careers: Some New Perspectives* (New York: John Wiley, 1977).

[38] Van Maanen, J., Bailyn, L., and Schein, E. H., "The Shape of Things to Come: A New Look at Organizational Careers," in *Perspectives on Behavior in Organizations,* J. R. Hackman, E. E. Lawler, and L. W. Porter, eds. (New York: McGraw-Hill, 1977).

[39] Van Maanen, J., and Schein, E. H., "Improving the Quality of Work Life: Career Development," in *Improving Life at Work,* J. R. Hackman and J. L. Suttle, eds. (Los Angeles: Goodyear, 1977).

Chapter 8

I would like to thank Ken Goodpaster, Ted Levitt, John Quelch, members of the Production and Operations Management area at the Harvard Business School, and an anonymous referee for their helpful comments on an earlier draft of this paper. I would also like to thank the Division of Research at the Harvard Business School for its financial support.

1. W.J. Abernathy, K.B. Clark, and A.M. Kantrow, *Industrial Renaissance* (New York: Basic Books, 1983); D.A. Garvin, "Quality on the Line," *Harvard Business Review,* September–October 1983, pp. 64–75; D.A. Garvin, "Japanese Quality Management," *Columbia Journal of World Business,* in press; J.M. Juran, "Japanese and Western Quality: A Contrast," *Quality Progress,* December 1978, pp. 10–18; and A. L. Robinson, "Perilous Times for U.S. Microcircuit Makers," *Science,* May 9, 1980, pp. 582–586.

2. Barksdale et al., "A Cross-National Survey of Consumer Attitudes Towards Marketing Practices, Consumerism, and Government Relations," *Columbia Journal of World Business,* Summer 1982, pp. 71–86; Center for Policy Alternatives, *Consumer Durables: Warranties, Service Contracts, and Alternatives* (Cambridge, MA: Massachusetts Institute of Technology, 1978), pp. 3–127; and "Rising Concern on Consumer Issues is Found in Harris Poll," *New York Times,* February 17, 1983.

3. J.G. Miller, *The 1983 Manufacturing Futures Project: Summary of North American Survey Responses & Preliminary Report* (Boston, MA: School of Management, Boston University, 1983), p. 14.

4. R. M. Pirsig, *Zen and the Art of Motorcycle Maintenance* (New York: Bantam Books, 1974); and B. W. Tuchman, "The Decline of Quality," *New York Times Magazine,* November 2, 1980.

5. S. Buchanen, ed., *The Portable Plato* (New York: Viking, 1948); and G. Dickie, *Aesthetics: An Introduction* (New York: Bobbs-Merrill, 1971), p. 5.

6. L. Abbott, *Quality and Competition* (New York: Columbia University Press, 1955); Z. Griliches, ed., *Price Indexes and Quality Change* (Cambridge, MA: Harvard University Press, 1971); K. Lancaster, *Consumer Demand: A New Approach* (New York: Columbia University Press, 1971), p. 122; and K. B. Leffler, "Ambiguous Changes in Product Quality," *American Economic Review,* December 1982, pp. 956–967.

7. Abbott (1955), p. 129; and K. Lancaster, *Variety, Equity, and Efficiency* (New York: Columbia University Press, 1979), p. 28.

8. D. Levhari and T. N. Srinivasan, "Durability of Consumption Goods: Competition versus Monopoly," *American Economic Review,* March 1969, pp. 102–107; R. L. Schmalensee,

"Regulation and the Durability of Goods," *Bell Journal of Economics and Management Science,* Spring 1970, pp. 54–64; P. L. Swan, "Durability of Consumption Goods," *American Economic Review,* December 1970, pp. 884–894; P. L. Swan, "The Durability of Goods and the Regulation of Monopoly," *Bell Journal of Economics and Management Science,* Autumn 1971, pp. 347–357; and T. R. Saving, "Market Organization and Product Quality," *Southern Economic Journal,* April 1982, p. 856.

9. C. D. Edwards, "The Meaning of Quality," *Quality Progress,* October 1968, pp. 36–39; A. A. Kuehn and R. L. Day, "Strategy of Product Quality," *Harvard Business Review,* November–December 1962, pp. 100–110.

10. Kuehn and Day (November-December 1962); R. M. Johnson, "Market Segmentation: A Strategic Management Tool," *Journal of Marketing Research,* February 1971, pp. 13–18; P. Kotler, *Marketing Decision Making: A Model Building Approach* (New York: Holt, Rinehart & Winston, 1971), pp. 491–497; and B. T. Ratchford, "The New Economic Theory of Consumer Behavior: An Interpretive Essay," *Journal of Consumer Research,* September 1975, pp. 65–75.

11. E. H. Chamberlin, "The Product as an Economic Variable," *Quarterly Journal of Economics,* February 1953, pp. 1–29; R. Dorfman and P. O. Steiner, "Optimal Advertising and Optimal Quality," *American Economic Review,* December 1954, pp. 822–836; L. J. White, "Quality Variation When Prices Are Regulated," *Bell Journal of Economics and Management Science,* Autumn 1972, pp. 425–436.

12. J. M. Juran, ed., *Quality Control Handbook,* 3d ed. (New York: McGraw-Hill, 1974), p. 2; and H. L. Gilmore, "Product Conformance Cost," *Quality Progress,* June 1974, pp. 16–19.

13. Edwards (October 1968), pp. 36–39; Lancaster (1979), p. 28; and H. Theil, *Principles of Econometrics* (New York: John Wiley, 1971), pp. 556–573.

14. E. Sheshinski, "Price, Quality, and Quantity Regulation in a Monopoly Situation," *Economica,* May 1976, pp. 127–137; and White (Autumn 1972).

15. R. B. Yepsen, Jr., ed., *The Durability Factor* (Emmaus, PA: Rodale Press, 1982), pp. 12–15.

16. P. B. Crosby, *Quality Is Free* (New York: McGraw-Hill, 1979); and Gilmore (June 1974).

17. G. Boehm, " 'Reliability' Engineering," *Fortune,* April 1963, pp. 124–127, 181–182, 184, 186; A. V. Feigenbaum, *Total Quality Control* (New York: McGraw-Hill, 1961), ch. 14; and Juran (1974).

18. Feigenbaum (1961), chs. 10–13; and J. M. Juran and F. M. Gryna, Jr., *Quality Planning and Analysis* (New York: McGraw-Hill, 1980).

19. J. Campanella and F. J. Corcoran, "Principles of Quality Costs," *Quality Progress,* April 1983, p. 21; and Crosby (1979).

20. R. A. Broh, *Managing Quality for Higher Profits* (New York: McGraw-Hill, 1982), ch. 1; and Juran (1974), ch. 5.

21. Broh (1982); and Feigenbaum (1961).

22. The Consumer Network, Inc., *Brand Quality Perceptions* (Philadelphia, PA: The Consumer Network, Inc., August 1983).

23. K. Ishikawa, "Quality and Standardization: Program for Economic Success," *Quality Progress,* January 1984, p. 18.

24. Juran (1974).

25. E. S. Maynes, "The Concept and Measurement of Product Quality," in *Household Production and Consumption,* N. E. Terleckyj, ed. (New York: National Bureau of Economic Research, 1976), pp. 550–554.

26. K. Lancaster, "A New Approach to Consumer Theory," *Journal of Political Economy,* April 1966, pp. 132–157; Lancaster (1971); and Lancaster (1979).

27. Lancaster (1971), p. 7.

28. Juran (1974), pp. 8–12.

29. C. J. Bliss, *Capital Theory and the Distribution of Income* (Amsterdam: North-Holland, 1975), ch. 6.

30. "Retiring Autos at 14," *New York Times,* April 3, 1983, sec. 3, p. 1.

31. S. W. Burch, "The Aging U.S. Auto Stock: Implications for Demand," *Business Economics,* May 1983, pp. 22–26.

32. J. A. Quelch and S. B. Ash, "Consumer Satisfaction with Professional Services," in *Marketing of Services,* J. H. Donnelly and W. R. George, eds. (Chicago, IL: American Marketing Association, 1981).

33. Kuehn and Day (November-December 1962); and Johnson (February 1971).

34. D. F. Cox, ed., *Risk Taking and Information Handling in Consumer Behavior* (Boston, MA: Division of Research, Harvard University, Graduate School of Business Administration, 1967), ch. 11; and D. R. Lambert, "Price as a Quality Signal: The Tip of the Iceberg," *Economy Inquiry,* January 1980, pp. 144–150.

35. W. O. Hagstrom, "Inputs, Outputs, and the Prestige of American University Science Departments," *Sociology of Education,* Fall 1971, pp. 384–385; and D. D. Knudsen and T. R. Vaughan, "Quality in Graduate Education: A Reevaluation of the Rankings of Sociology Departments in the Cartter Report," *American Sociologist,* February 1969, p. 18.

36. *Steinway & Sons* (Boston, MA: Harvard Business School, HBS Case Services #9-682-625, 1981), p. 5.

37. P. C. Riesz, "Price-Quality Correlations for Packaged Food Products," *Journal of Consumer Affairs,* Winter 1979, p. 234.

38. Lambert (January 1980).

39. Riesz (1979), p. 244.

40. H. J. Leavitt, "A Note on Some Experimental Findings about the Meanings of Price," *Journal of Business,* July 1954, pp. 205–210; A. Gabor and C. W. J. Granger, "Price as an Indicator of Quality: Report on an Enquiry," *Economica,* February 1966, pp. 43–70; and J. D. McConnell, "An Experimental Examination of the Price-Quality Relationship," *Journal of Business,* October 1968, pp. 439–444.

41. Riesz (1979), p. 236.

42. R. A. Westbrook, J. W. Newman, and J. R. Taylor, "Satisfaction/Dissatisfaction in the Purchase Decision Process," *Journal of Marketing,* October 1978, pp. 54–60.

43. "The Buying Consumer: Room Air Conditioners," a report by *Appliance Manufacturer* (Chicago, IL: Cahners Publishing, 1979).

44. Lambert (January 1980).

45. P. Nelson, "Information and Consumer Behavior," *Journal of Political Economy,* March–April 1970; pp. 311–329; and P. Nelson, "Advertising as Information," *Journal of Political Economy,* July–August 1974, pp. 729–754.

46. R. L. Schmalensee, "A Model of Advertising and Product Quality," *Journal of Political Economy,* June 1978, pp. 485–504.

47. *Ibid.,* pp. 485–486.

48. H. J. Rotfeld and K. B. Rotzoll, "Advertising and Product Quality: Are Heavily Advertised Products Better?" *Journal of Consumer Affairs,* September 1976, p. 46.

49. C. T. Gilligan and D. E. A. Holmes, "Advertising Expenditure and Product Quality," *Management Decision,* Vol. 17, No. 5, p. 392.

50. Barksdale et al. (Summer 1982), p. 78.

51. R. D. Buzzell and F. D. Wiersema, "Modeling Changes in Market Share: A Cross-Sectional Analysis," *Strategic Management Journal,* 1981, pp. 27–42; R. D. Buzzell and F. D. Wiersema, "Successful Share-Building Strategies," *Harvard Business Review,* January-February 1981, pp. 135–144; C. S. Craig and S. P. Douglas, "Strategic Factors Associated with Market and Financial Performance," *Quarterly Review of Economics and Business,* Summer 1982, pp. 101–111; B. T. Gale and B. S. Branch, "Concentration versus Market Share: Which Determines Performance and Why Does It Matter?" *The Antitrust Bulletin,* Spring 1982, pp.

83–105; L. W. Phillips, D. Chang, and R. D. Buzzell, "Product Quality, Cost Position, and Business Performance: A Test of Some Key Hypotheses," *Journal of Marketing,* Spring 1983, pp. 26–43; and S. Schoeffler, R. D. Buzzell, and D. F. Heany, "Impact of Strategic Planning on Profit Performance," *Harvard Business Review,* March–April 1974, pp. 137–145.

52. Buzzell and Wiersema (January–February 1981), p. 140.

53. Schoeffler, Buzzell, and Heany, March–April 1974, p. 141; and Gale and Branch, Spring 1982, pp. 93–95.

54. Buzzell and Wiersema (1981); Craig and Douglas (Summer 1982); and Phillips, Chang, and Buzzell (Spring 1983).

55. R. E. Cole, "Improving Product Quality through Continuous Feedback," *Management Review,* October 1983, pp. 8–12; and Garvin (in press).

56. Campanella and Corcoran (April 1983), p. 17.

57. Campanella and Corcoran (April 1983); Crosby (1979); Gilmore (June 1974); H. L. Gilmore, "Consumer Product Quality Cost Revisited," *Quality Progress,* April 1983, pp. 28–33.

58. R. S. Kaplan, "Measuring Manufacturing Performance: A New Challenge for Managerial Accounting Research," *The Accounting Review,* October 1983, pp. 686–705; and S. C. Wheelwright, "Japan—Where Operations Really Are Strategic," *Harvard Business Review,* July–August 1981, pp. 70–71.

59. Phillips, Chang, and Buzzell (Spring 1983), p. 27.

60. Garvin (September–October 1983).

61. Crosby (1979).

62. "Quality Cost Survey," *Quality,* June 1977, pp. 20–22.

63. Gilmore (June 1974); and Gilmore (April 1983).

64. Gale and Branch (Spring 1982), pp. 96–97.

65. Phillips, Chang, and Buzzell (Spring 1983), pp. 38–39.

66. *Ibid.,* p. 37.

67. M. E. Bader, *Practical Quality Management in the Chemical Process Industry* (New York: Marcel Dekker, 1983), ch. 1.

68. Chamberlin (February 1953); and Dorfman and Steiner (December 1954).

69. Craig and Douglas (Summer 1982); Phillips, Chang, and Buzzell (Spring 1983); and Schoeffler, Buzzell, and Heany (March–April 1974).

70. Schoeffler, Buzzell, and Heany (March–April 1974), p. 141.

71. Buzzell and Wiersema (January–February 1981); and Phillips, Chang, and Buzzell (Spring 1983).

72. A. R. Andreasen, "A Taxonomy of Consumer Satisfaction/Dissatisfaction Measures," *Journal of Consumer Affairs,* Winter 1977, pp. 11–24.

73. H. Takeuchi and J. A. Quelch, "Quality Is More Than Making a Good Product," *Harvard Business Review,* July–August 1983, pp. 139–145.

74. W. Skinner, "Manufacturing—Missing Link in Corporate Strategy," *Harvard Business Review,* May–June 1969, pp. 136–145; W. Skinner, "The Focused Factory," *Harvard Business Review,* May–June 1974, pp. 113–121; and S. C. Wheelwright, "Reflecting Corporate Strategy in Manufacturing Decisions," *Business Horizons,* February 1978, pp. 57–66.

75. Wheelwright (July–August 1981).

Chapter 9

1. K. J. Arrow in *The Rational Direction of Inventive Activity: Economic and Social Factors,* R. Nelson, ed. (Princeton: Princeton University Press, 1962), p. 624.

2. E. B. Roberts, "Entrepreneurship and Technology," in *The Factors in the Transfer of*

Technology, W. H. Gruber and D. G. Marquis, eds. (Cambridge, MA: MIT Press, 1969), p. 259.

3. I am indebted to Anil Gupta for first suggesting the use of the word *network* to describe this system of communication and political links.

4. The stages of corporate development used in this article follow the work of B. R. Scott. See, for instance, B. R. Scott, "The New Industrial State, Old Myths and New Realities," *Harvard Business Review,* March–April 1973, pp. 133–148; and B. R. Scott, "Stages of Corporate Development 1, 2" (Case Clearing House, Harvard Business School, the President and Fellows of Harvard College, 1971).

5. For a definition, see Table 9.3.

6. These terms are defined later in this article.

7. J. A. Schumpeter, *History of Economic Analysis* (England: Oxford University Press, 1954), p. 554.

8. J. A. Schumpeter, *Capitalism, Socialism, and Democracy* (New York: Harper & Row, 1975), p. 132.

9. D. A. Schon, "Champions for Radical New Inventions," *Harvard Business Review,* March–April 1963, p. 84.

10. One of the first to suggest means of managing this resistance to change was P. R. Lawrence, "How to Deal with Resistance to Change," *Harvard Business Review,* January–February 1954. However, in 1969 in a disarmingly candid retrospective commentary on his *Harvard Business Review* classic, Professor Lawrence wrote, "There is . . . an implication in the article that the social and human costs of change can be largely avoided by thoughtful management effort. Today I am less sanguine about this."

11. R. Rothwell, C. Freeman, A. Horlsey, V. T. P. Jervis, A. B. Robertson, and J. Townsend, "SAPPHO Updated—Project SAPPHO Phase II," *Research Policy* 3 (1974), pp. 258–291.

12. E. B. Roberts and A. B. Frohman, "Internal Entrepreneurship: Strategy for Growth," *The Business Quarterly,* Spring 1972, pp. 71–78.

13. E. B. Roberts, "Generating Effective Corporate Innovation," *Technology Review,* October–November 1977, pp. 27–33.

14. L. Grossman, *The Change Agent* (New York: AMACOM, 1974).

15. J. A. Morton, *Organizing for Innovation* (New York: McGraw-Hill, 1971), p. 95.

16. I. Kusiatin, "The Process and Capacity for Diversification through Internal Development" (DBA diss., Harvard Graduate School of Business Administration, April 1976).

17. O. Collins, and D. G. Moore, *The Organization Makers* (New York: Appleton-Century-Croft, 1970).

18. *Ibid.*

19. O. F. Collins, D. G. Moore, and D. B. Umwalla, *The Enterprising Man* (Board of Trustees, Michigan State University, 1964).

20. T. D. Duchesneau and J. B. Lafond, "Characteristics of Users and Nonusers of an Innovation: The Role of Economical Organizational Factors" (Paper presented at the Annual Convention of the Eastern Economic Association, Hartford, Connecticut, April 1977). In addition, private correspondence of November 30, 1977, provided expanded details on research data.

21. R. P. Olsen, "Equipment Supplier—Producer Relationships and Process Innovation in the Textile Industry" (Harvard University Graduate School of Business Administration, November 17, 1975).

22. *Ibid.* Olsen's champions generally were each identified with a *series* of innovations.

23. Rothwell, Freeman, Horlsey, Jervis, Robertson, and Townsend (1974).

24. *Ibid.*

25. The five key areas identified by the SAPPHO group are all interdisciplinary in character. The first is at the boundary of research and development and organizational behavior; the fourth and fifth are at the boundary of research and development and administrative

systems; the second and the third are at the interface between marketing and R&D. Two of these areas have been studied by MIT investigators, Allen (communications) and von Hippel (user needs), who have broadly confirmed and significantly extended the SAPPHO results. A substantial literature also exists in the area of marketing management and project management and related techniques for maximizing the efficiency of R&D. Managerial characteristics, particularly those of the technological entrepreneur, have been studied extensively by another MIT scholar, Roberts, whose conclusions regarding entrepreneurship are also broadly consistent with the SAPPHO group. See Roberts and Frohman (Spring 1972); Roberts (October–November 1977); T. A. Allen, *Managing the Flow of Technology: Technology Transfer and the Dissemination of Technological Information within the R&D Organization* (Cambridge, MA: MIT Press, 1977); R. S. Rosenbloom and F. W. Wolek, *Technology and Information Transfer* (Boston: Division of Research, Graduate School of Business Administration, Harvard University, 1977); and E. von Hippel, "The Dominant Role of Users in the Scientific Instrument Innovation Process," *Research Policy* 5 (1976), pp. 212–239.

26. J. L. Bower, *Managing the Resource Allocation Process* (Homewood, IL: Richard Irwin, 1972).

27. In this article, the terms *sponsorship* and *business definition* will be used in preference to *impetus* and *context*. Bower's context also includes the administrative system, while business definition, as it is used here, is a narrower term that includes only the strategic part of the context.

28. Roberts (October-November 1977); "What Do We Really Know about Managing R&D" (A talk with Ed Roberts), *Research Management, TK,* November 1978; and R. Rhoades, E. B. Roberts, and A. R. Fusfeld, "A Correlation of R&D Laboratory Performance with Critical Function Analysis," *Research Management* 9, October 1978, pp. 13–17.

29. J. K. Galbraith, *The New Industrial State* (Boston: Houghton Mifflin, 1967).

30. A. D. Chandler, *Strategy and Structure* (Cambridge, MA: MIT Press, 1962); B. R. Scott, *An Open Model of the Firm* (DBA diss., Graduate School of Business Administration, Harvard University, 1962); J. H. McArthur and B. R. Scott, *Industrial Planning in France* (Boston: Division of Research, Harvard Business School, 1969); M. Salter, *Stages of Corporate Development: Implications for Management Control* (Mimeo, 1967); and L. Wrigley, *Diversification and Divisional Autonomy* (DBA diss., Graduate School of Business Administration, Harvard University, 1970).

31. Chandler (1962).

32. Scott (1971).

33. Wrigley (1970).

34. A single business is defined here as one that manufactures a single product, a line of products with variations in size and style, or a closely related set of products linked by technology or market structure.

35. W. J. Abernathy and J. Utterback, "A Dynamic Model of Process and Product Innovation," *Omega* 3 (1975), pp. 639–656.

36. W. J. Abernathy and P. L. Townsend, "Technology, Productivity, and Process Change," in *Technological Forecasting and Social Change* 7 (New York: American Elsevier Publishing, 1975), pp. 379–396.

37. S. Myers and D. G. Marquis, *Successful Technological Innovations* (Washington, DC: National Science Foundation, NSF 69–17).

38. Dr. James Utterback, personal communication.

39. T. Burns and G. M. Stalker, *The Management of Innovation* (London: Tavistock Publications, 1966).

40. Rimbruster Office Automation, Inc. (Intercollegiate Case Clearing House, 4–674–009, Rev. 10.76), p. 9. An updated case of this firm reveals that Rimbruster was a disguised

name for Redactron (see Redactron Corporation, Intercollegiate Case Clearing House, 1–276–163) and Redactron's president, Evelyn Berezin.

41. *Ibid.,* p. 3.
42. *Ibid.,* p. 8.
43. For background information on Henry Kloss, see "Advent Corporation (C)" (Intercollegiate Case Clearing House, 9–674–027). The quotation is from "Advent Corporation (D)" (Intercollegiate Case Clearing House, 9–676–053), p. 3.
44. Sci-Tex (Intercollegiate Case Clearing House, 1–678–009), p. 10.
45. J. K. Galbraith, *The New Industrial State* (Boston: Houghton Mifflin, 1967), pp. 88–89.
46. G. Bylinsky, *The Innovation Millionaires* (New York: Charles Scribner's Sons, 1976), p. 161.
47. R. Adams, "Do You Sincerely Want to Be a Millionaire?" *Boston Magazine,* November 1972, p. 45.
48. J. S. Schwartz, "The Decision to Innovate" (DBA diss., Harvard University Graduate School of Business Administration, 1973), p. 107.
49. Interview with Digital Equipment Corporation executive.
50. Schwartz (1973); and J. W. Lorsch and P. J. Lawrence, "Organizing for Product Innovation," *Harvard Business Review,* January–February 1965.
51. Schwartz (1973), p. 111.
52. "Pilkington Float Glass (A)" (International Case Clearing House, Harvard Business School, 9–670–069).
53. Alistair Pilkington is now chairman of Pilkington Brothers, the first person outside the direct lineage of the founder to hold that position. See J. B. Quinn, "Technological Innovation, Entrepreneurship, and Strategy," *Sloan Management Review,* Spring 1979, pp. 19–30.
54. L. Wrigley, "Divisional Autonomy and Diversification" (DBA diss., Harvard Business School, 1970).
55. Bob Evans, as quoted by T. A. Wise, "I.B.M.'s $5,000,000,000 Gamble," *Fortune,* September 1966.
56. Interview with IBM executive.
57. Wise (September 1966); and T. A. Wise, "The Rocky Road to the Marketplace," *Fortune,* October 1966.
58. M. A. Maidique and J. Ince, " 'The Grumman Corporation' and 'Grumman Energy Systems' " (Intercollegiate Case Clearing House, 1979).
59. *Business Week,* June 27, 1977.
60. Shortly after his appointment as general manager, Peterson was promoted to president of Grumman Energy Systems, Inc., a wholly owned subsidiary of the Grumman Corporation.
61. Roberts (October–November 1977).
62. W. J. Abernathy and J. M. Utterback, "Innovation and the Evolving Structure of the Firm" (Harvard University Graduate School of Business Administration, Working Paper 75018, June 1975).
63. J. M. Utterback, "Management of Technology" (Center for Policy Alternatives, MIT, February 28, 1978).
64. W. J. Abernathy and J. M. Utterback, "Patterns of Industrial Innovation," *Technology Review,* June–July 1978.
65. A. C. Cooper and D. Schendel, "Strategic Responses to Technological Threats," *Business Horizons,* February 1976.
66. B. Uttal, "Gene Amdahl Takes Aim at IBM," *Fortune,* September 1977. For a case study of a data-processing center (Hughes) that saw performance/price ratio in favor of the Amdahl 470 over the IBM 370, see J. B. Woods, "Converting from 370 to 470," *Datamation,* July 1977. The sales rate information is from Amdahl 1978 quarterly reports.
67. Frank Cary, as quoted by Uttal (September 1977).
68. T. Levitt, *Marketing for Business Growth* (New York: McGraw-Hill, 1974), p. 148.

Chapter 10

1. S. C. Blumenthal, *MIS—A Framework for Planning and Development* (Englewood Cliffs, NJ: Prentice-Hall, 1969); C. H. Kriebel, "The Strategic Dimension of Computer Systems Planning," *Long Range Planning,* September 1968; F. W. McFarlan, "Problems in Planning the Information System," *Harvard Business Review,* May–June 1971; and F. W. McFarlan, J. L. McKenney and P. Pyburn, "Information Archipelago—Charting the Course," *Harvard Business Review,* January–February 1983.
2. E. R. McLean and J. V. Soden, *Strategic Planning for MIS* (New York: John Wiley, 1977).
3. A. D. Chandler, Jr., *Strategy and Structure* (Cambridge, MA: MIT Press, 1962); and B. Tregel and J. W. Zimmerman, *Top Management Strategy* (New York: Simon and Schuster, 1980).
4. M. E. Porter, *Competitive Strategy* (New York: The Free Press, 1980).
5. W. J. Abernathy, K. B. Clark, and A. M. Kantrow, *Industrial Renaissance* (New York: Basic Books, 1983).
6. G. Davis, *Managing the DP Function* (New York: McGraw-Hill, 1967).
7. Porter (1980), p. 35.

Chapter 11

The author is indebted to the Associates and the Division of Research of the Harvard Business School for providing support for the research on which this article is based. The author is also most grateful to Joseph L. Bower and C. K. Prahalad for their encouragement, insights, and suggestions. The ideas presented in this article are drawn from a book, *Multinational Strategic Management: Economic and Political Imperatives.*

1. See, for instance, L. G. Franko, *The European Multinationals* (Stamford, CT: Greylock, Inc., 1976).
2. See, for instance, J. Dunning and M. Gilman, "Alternative Policy Prescriptions," in *The Multinational Enterprise in a Hostile World,* Curzon and Curzon eds. (London: Macmillan, 1977); R. Vernon, *Storm over the Multinationals* (Cambridge, MA: Harvard University Press, 1977); and R. Vernon, *Sovereignty at Bay* (New York: Basic Books, 1971).
3. See, for instance, C. Stoffaes, *La Grande Menace Industrielle* (Paris: Calmann-Levy, 1977).
4. Some authors have opposed worldwide and regional management within MNCs. See J. M. Stopford and L. T. Wells, Jr., *Managing the Multinational Enterprise* (New York: Basic Books, 1972). The evidence in the companies studied suggests that in either case a business strategy responding to the economic imperative underlies regional or worldwide management. Which strategy is preferred in a particular company depends upon cost analysis based primarily on differences in factor costs, freight rates, and barriers to trade between various countries and regions of the world. In terms of responsiveness to individual country policies, there is little difference between regional and worldwide management. See L. G. Franko, *Joint Venture Survival in Multinational Corporations* (New York: Praeger, 1972).
5. Y. Doz, "Managing Manufacturing Rationalization within Multinational Companies," *Columbia Journal of World Business,* Fall 1978.
6. R. Vernon, "The Location of Economic Activity," in *Economic Analysis and the Multinational Corporation,* Dunning, ed. (London: Allen and Unwin, 1974).
7. Ford's costs are estimated by the author from various industry interviews. For many product families, experience-curve models suggested unit-cost levels in smaller European firms equal to several times the costs in such firms as Texas Instruments for integrated circuits or Motorola for discrete semiconductors. Exact figures are not public, but their significance can be deduced from the Boston Consulting Group and Macintosh publications. Large

losses among European national semiconductor companies and private communications about losses in Philips' or Siemens's semiconductor businesses support the same point. See P. Gadonneix, "Le Plan Calcul" (DBA diss., Harvard Business School, 1974).

8. D. G. Bradley, "Managing against Expropriation," *Harvard Business Review*, July–August 1977, pp. 75–83; and B. D. Wilson, "The Disinvestment of Foreign Subsidiaries by U. S. Multinational Companies" (DBA diss., Harvard Business School, 1979).

9. For political strategies, see J. Zysman, *Political Strategies for Industrial Order* (Berkeley, CA: University of California Press, 1976); and Y. Doz, *Government Control and Multinational Strategic Management* (New York: Praeger, 1979). For economic strategies, see U. Wiechmann, "Integrating Multinational Marketing Activities," *Columbia Journal of World Business*, Winter 1974. Wiechmann studied intensively the food and beverage industries.

10. For a comprehensive treatment of strategy as an optimal fit between environmental opportunities and threats and the organizational strengths and weaknesses (consistent with the personal values of top management and the social responsibilities of the corporation), see K. R. Andrews, *The Concept of Corporate Strategy* (Homewood, IL: Dow Jones Irwin, 1971); and D. Braybrooke and C. E. Lindblom, *A Strategy of Decision* (New York: The Free Press, 1963).

11. On strategic planning, see, for example, G. A. Steiner, *Top Management Planning* (New York: Macmillan, 1966); H. I. Ansoff, *Corporate Strategy* (New York: McGraw-Hill, 1965); and P. Lorange and R. F. Vancil, eds., *Strategic Planning Systems* (Englewood Cliffs, NJ: Prentice-Hall, 1977). On "muddling through," see Braybrooke and Lindblom (1963); R. Cyert and J. March, *A Behavioral Theory of the Firm* (Englewood Cliffs, NJ: Prentice-Hall, 1963); and J. D. Steinbruner, *The Cybernetic Theory of Decision* (Princeton: Princeton University Press, 1974).

12. For instance, see S. M. Davis and P. R. Lawrence, *Matrix* (Reading, MA: Addison-Wesley, 1977).

13. N. Jéquier, *Les Télécommunications et l'Europe* (Geneva: Centre d'Etudes Industrielles, 1976); and J. Surrey, *World Market for Electric Power Equipment* (Brighton, England: SPRI, University of Sussex, 1972).

14. O. Williamson, *Markets and Hierarchies: Analysis and Antitrust Implications* (New York: The Free Press, 1975).

15. Y. S. Hu, *The Impact of U.S. Investment in Europe* (New York: Praeger, 1973); and N. Jéquier, "Computers," in *Big Business and the State*, R. Vernon, ed. (Cambridge, MA: Harvard University Press, 1974).

16. There is ample evidence of this phenomenon in the computer and microelectronics industries. See E. Sciberras, *Multinational Electronic Companies and National Economic Policies* (Greenwich, CT: JAI Press, 1977); and "International Business Machines: Can the Europeans ever Compete?" *Multinational Business*, 1973, pp. 37–46.

17. For a discussion of strategic decision making and environmental uncertainty, see E. Rhenman, *Organization Theory for Long-Range Planning* (New York: John Wiley, 1973).

18. F. T. Knickerbocker, *Oligopolistic Reaction and Multinational Enterprise* (Boston: Harvard Business School Division of Research, 1973).

19. For a discussion of strategic differentiation and competition in a domestic oligopoly, see R. Caves and M. Porter, "From Barrier to Entry to Barrier to Mobility," *Quarterly Journal of Economics*, May 1977.

20. For instance, see Vernon (1977), ch. 3. The evolution of industries such as nuclear power or aerospace is revealing. As the technology for a given product (e.g., light-water nuclear reactors or bypass turbofan jet engines) becomes more widespread, the bargaining power of MNCs is eroded. See H. R. Nau, *National Politics and International Technology* (Baltimore, MD: Johns Hopkins University Press, 1974). For lesser developed countries, see N. Fagre and L. T. Wells, "Bargaining Power of Multinationals and Host Governments" (Mimeo, July 14, 1978). On increasing economies of scale, for instance, see M. S. Hoch-

muth, "Aerospace," in *Big Business and the State,* R. Vernon, ed. (Cambridge, MA: Harvard University Press, 1974).

21. Innovations in mature products are an occasional exception. They are sometimes introduced in the most competitive market. For instance, Sony introduced several innovations in the U.S. before introducing them in Japan. Yet many other Sony innovations were first introduced in Japan. For a summary, see Vernon (1977), ch. 3.

22. Doz (1979). For recent evidence, see "ITT Fights U.K. Bid for Plessey Control of STC," *Electronic News,* October 23, 1978, p. 4. On electrical power, see B. Epstein, *The Politics of Trade in Power Plants* (London: The Atlantic Trade Center, 1972); Central Policy Review Staff, *The Future of the United Kingdom Power Plant Manufacturing Industry* (London: Her Majesty's Stationery Office, 1976); and Commission des Communautés Européenes, *Situation et Perspective des Industries des Gros Equipements Electroméca-niques et Nucléaires liés à la Production d'Energie de la Communauté* (Brussels: CEE, 1976). For related data on the U.S., see I. Bupp, Jr., and J. C. Derian, *Light Water: How the Nuclear Dream Dissolved* (New York: Basic Books, 1978).

23. J. Behrman and H. Wallender, *Transfers of Manufacturing Technology within Multinational Enterprises* (Cambridge, MA: Ballinger, 1976).

24. For a detailed analysis of GTE and LM Ericsson's administrative mechanisms, see Doz (1979).

25. Used here in the sense given by Steinbruner (1974), as the simplifying logic used by a particular function to reduce complexity in its environment by focusing on a few key parameters and taking cybernetic decisions based on them.

26. Davis and Lawrence (1977); C. K. Prahalad, "The Strategic Process in a Multinational Company" (DBA diss., Harvard Business School, 1975).

27. C. K. Prahalad and Y. Doz, "Strategic Change in the Multidimensional Organization" (Harvard Business School-University of Michigan Working Paper, October 1979).

28. M. Crozier, *The Bureaucratic Phenomenon* (Chicago: University of Chicago Press, 1964); and D. J. Hickson et al., "A Strategic Contingencies' Theory of Intraorganizational Power," *Administrative Science Quarterly* 2 (1971), pp. 216–229.

29. This section draws upon Y. Doz and C. K. Prahalad, "Strategic Management in Diversified Multinationals," in *Functioning of the Multinational Corporation in the Global Context,* A. Negandhi, ed. (New York: Pergamon Press, forthcoming).

30. Taken here in the sense of Barnard's "strategic factors" or Selznick's "critical factor." See C. L. Barnard, *The Functions of the Executive* (Cambridge, MA: Harvard University Press, 1938); and P. Selznick, *Leadership in Administration* (New York: Harper & Row, 1957).

31. A. Katz, "Planning in the IBM Corporation" (Paper submitted to the TIMS-ORSA Strategic Planning Conference, New Orleans, February 16–17, 1977).

32. S. M. Davis, "Trends in the Organization of Multinational Corporations," *Columbia Journal of World Business,* Summer 1976, pp. 59–71. Information on Dow Chemical came from the 1976 *Annual Report* and the author's interviews.

Chapter 12

1. P. Abell, "Parent Companies' Control of Subsidiaries: Evidence from the U.K.," *Multinational Business,* 1974.

2. Several studies have demonstrated the extent of globalization of the competitive structure of industries. For example, see The Boston Consulting Group's study of *Strategy Alternatives for the British Motorcycle Industry,* HMSO, 1975. On the steel industry, see American Iron & Steel Institute, *Steel at the Crossroads: The American Steel Industry in the 1980's,* January 1980; American Iron & Steel Institute, *The Economic Implications of Foreign Steel Pricing Practices in the U.S. Market,* August 1978; and American Iron & Steel Institute, *Economics of International Steel Trade: Policy Implications for the U.S.,* May 1977.

On the watch industries in Switzerland, Japan, and the U.S., see ICCH #9-373-090, Rev. 9/76; "Japanese Heat on the Watch Industry," *Business Week,* May 5, 1980; and "Digital Watches: Bringing Watchmaking Back to the U.S.," *Business Week,* October 27, 1975.

See also Volkswagen A.G., ICCH #9-376-108; Ford in Spain (A), #4-380–091; Ford in Spain (B), #380–092; Ford Bobcat (A), #4-380–093; Ford Bobcat (B), #9-380–100; Ford Bobcat (C), #4-380–101; and Ford Bobcat (D), #4-380–102.

Finally, see The U.S. TV Set Market, Prewar to 1970, #1–380–180; The U.S. TV Set Market, 1970–1979, #1–380–181; and The Television Set Industry in 1979: Japan and Europe, #1–380–191.

3. Y. L. Doz and C. K. Prahalad, "How MNCs Cope with Host Government Intervention," *Harvard Business Review,* March–April 1980.

4. L. G. Franko, *Joint Venture Survival in International Business* (New York: Praeger, 1971); Also see, "Disinvestment-Corporate Strategy or Admission of Failure," *Multinational Business,* 1975.

5. See the following case studies: Brown Boveri & Cie, ICCH #9–378–115; and Corning Glass Works International (A), ICCH #9–379–051.

6. J. Stopford and L. T. Wells, Jr., *Managing the Multinational Enterprise* (New York: Basic Books, 1972); and L. G. Franko, *The European Multinationals* (Stanford, CT: Greylock, 1977).

7. Y. L. Doz, C. A. Bartlett, and C. K. Prahalad, "Global Competitive Pressure vs. Host Country Demands: Managing Tensions in MNCs," *California Management Review,* Winter 1981.

8. For example, see E. P. Neufeld, *A Global Corporation: A History of the International Development of Massey Ferguson Ltd.* (Toronto, Canada: University of Toronto Press, 1969).

9. R. Ronstadt, "R and D Abroad: The Creation and Evolution of Foreign Research and Development Activities of U.S. Based Multinational Enterprise" (Boston, MA: DBA diss., Harvard Business School, 1975).

10. Some tentative evidence on divestment patterns from a sample of MNC operations in Europe suggests that divestments occur more often in these situations. See N. Hood and S. Young, *European Development Strategies of US Owned Manufacturing Companies* (Edinburgh: HMSO, 1980).

11. LM Ericsson's approach is described in Y. L. Doz, *Government Control and Multinational Strategic Management* (New York: Praeger, 1979).

12. A. Katz, "Planning in the IBM Corporation" (paper submitted to the TIMS-ORSA Strategic Planning Conference, New Orleans, February 1977).

Index